Anne Spencer
between Worlds

Anne Spencer
between Worlds

Noelle Morrissette

The University of
Georgia Press
ATHENS

A Sarah Mills Hodge Fund Publication
This publication is made possible, in part, through a grant from the
Hodge Foundation in memory of its founder, Sarah Mills Hodge, who devoted
her life to the relief and education of African Americans in Savannah, Georgia.
Grateful acknowledgment is made to the College of Arts and Sciences,
the University of North Carolina Greensboro, for its generous support of this book.

Set in 10/13 Kepler Std Regular by Kaelin Chappell Broaddus

Most University of Georgia Press titles are
available from popular e-book vendors.

Printed digitally

Library of Congress Cataloging-in-Publication Data

Names: Morrissette, Noelle, author.
Title: Anne Spencer between worlds / Noelle Morrissette.
Description: Athens : The University of Georgia Press, [2023] | Series: The new
    southern studies | Includes bibliographical references and index.
Identifiers: LCCN 2022033683 | ISBN 9780820362953 (hardback) |
    ISBN 9780820362939 (paperback) | ISBN 9780820362946 (ebook)
Subjects: LCSH: Spencer, Anne, 1882–1975—Criticism and interpretation. |
    LCGFT: Literary criticism.
Classification: LCC PS3537.P444 Z75 2023 | DDC 811/.52—dc23/eng/20220930
LC record available at https://lccn.loc.gov/2022033683

for Shaun Spencer-Hester

J. Lee Greene

John Mark Hall

In loving memory

Pray you for unceasing springs,
Swelling deep in pardon;
That into twin lives may grow
Time's unfading garden—

He's faith turning into you straight
That your faith in him keep growing
Time's unfading garden.

—ANNE SPENCER

CONTENTS

ILLUSTRATIONS

In this book I have attempted to emulate the communal processes that formed the intellectual milieu of 1313 Pierce Street, Spencer's home and a hub of intellectual exchange and social justice activism for over one hundred years now. Spencer's many collaborations with a diverse community of friends informs my work. I have drawn on the firsthand knowledge of Shaun Spencer-Hester, Anne's granddaughter and curator of the Anne Spencer House and Garden Museum; on the local gardening and civic knowledge of Jane Baber White; on the burial records of Old City Cemetery; on the archival expertise of Molly Shwartzburg, curator of Albert and Shirley Small Special Collections at the University of Virginia's Harrison Institute; and on the guidance of Nancy Kuhl, curator of Poetry, Yale Collection of American Literature, Beinecke Rare Book and Manuscript Library. This book would have been impossible to write without these guides and their knowledge and insight into the archival stories informing Spencer's. Sara Lee Barnes, development and stewardship coordinator of the University of Virginia Library, put me in touch with those closest to the Spencer story. Shaun and Sara Lee's support and advocacy of this book was crucial in sustaining me through the many years of its development. The welcoming and supportive staff of the service desk at the University of Virginia's Special Collections provided an ideal setting for conducting this intensive archival research, and I'd like to especially thank Regina Rush, Petrina Jackson, and Ed Gaynor. Conversation with Molly Shwartzburg sparked new lines of inquiry, producing a more comprehensive research narrative. I am grateful to Sharon Defibaugh, processing archivist at the University of Virginia's Special Collections, who organized the Anne Spencer manuscript collection and produced an unusually detailed and useful finding aid to a collection that was profoundly challenging to catalogue.

Research for this project was supported by a Lillian Gary Taylor fellowship in the Albert and Shirley Small Special Collections at the Harrison Institute, a H. D. Fellowship in English or American Literature at the Beinecke Rare Book and Manuscript Library, a Marc C. Friedlaender Faculty Excellene Award from the English Department at the University of North Carolina Greensboro, from which I also received a research assignment to complete the writing of this book, and by a Linda Arnold Carlisle Faculty Research Grant from the Women's, Gender, and Sexuality Studies Program and a travel grant from the African American and African Diaspora Studies Program at the University of North Carolina Greensboro. I am grateful to Dean John Z. Kiss and the College of Arts and Sciences at the University of North Carolina Greensboro and to Lisa Bayer, Patrick Allen, and the University of Georgia Press for their support of this book. Grateful acknowledgment is made to MJ Delvaney and Jon Davies for their editorial vision for this book.

Along the way in the writing of this manuscript, I presented portions of my research findings at the American Literature Association, the Society for the Study of American Women Writers, the South Atlantic Modern Language Association, and the Modern Language Association. I'm especially grateful for collaborative conversations at various stages in the project with Evie Shockley, Sheila Smith McKoy, Michael Nowlin, and Shana Russell. Special thanks go to the University of Virginia Special Collections for sponsoring my lecture that was part of the opening event marking the first-ever exhibition of Anne Spencer's manuscripts in 2016 and its support and hosting of my webinar lecture in 2021, "Anne Spencer, Her Book: Reading the Author's Library."

It is through the kind of interactive and collaborative intellectual and creative community that Spencer fostered and on which I continue to draw through Shaun Spencer-Hester and many others that the strongest human bonds are created. My study reflects this wide-ranging community of knowledge through the guidance, encouragement, and rigorous questions I received from my mentors, colleagues, and friends, including Robert Stepto, Karen Kilcup, Mary Ellis Gibson, Maria Carla Sanchez, Karen Weyler, Scott Romine, Alison Booth, Sara Lee Barnes, Andrea Douglas, Jenny Dale of UNC Greensboro libraries, and Valerie Kelco, my graduate research assistant, who was enthusiastic, supportive, and resourceful. I am indebted to all of these individuals and many more.

J. Lee Greene and John Mark Hall, two passionate advocates of Anne Spencer who have passed away, are acknowledged here for their devotion to Spencer's story. Their works on Spencer and her home live in the "unfading garden" of memory.

Grateful acknowledgment is made to Shaun Spencer-Hester and the Anne Spencer Memorial Foundation for permission to quote from the Anne Spencer Papers at the University of Virginia Special Collections and the Anne Spencer House and Garden Museum. Grateful acknowledgment is made also to Jill Jones, literary executor of the James Weldon Johnson literary estate, for permission to quote from the James Weldon Johnson and Grace Nail Johnson Papers in the James Weldon Johnson Memorial Collection, Beinecke Rare Book and Manuscript Library. I'm grateful to Mr. Art Blakeslee, the Moorland-Spingarn Research Center, Howard University, and Williams College, for permission to quote from the Sterling Brown Papers and to Arnold Rampersad for permission to quote from the Langston Hughes Papers in the James Weldon Johnson Memorial Collection at the Beinecke Rare Book and Manuscript Library. Thanks also go to Nancy Marion of the Design Group for permission to use Jimmie Ray's circa 1948 photo of Anne Spencer and to the New York Times/ Redux for permission to use Neil Boenzi's photograph of Amiri Baraka (then LeRoi Jones) and family.

I have dedicated this book to Shaun Spencer-Hester, who will understand perfectly, I think, this quotation from Emerson that her grandmother liked so much she copied it out in her own hand: "A true friend is somebody who can make us do what we can"

Anne Spencer
between Worlds

Anne Spencer between Worlds

> Women are least convincing when they attempt the truth.
>
> —ANNE SPENCER, notebook

On a Saturday in late February 1977, dignitaries, artists, family, neighbors, and city residents gathered at 1313 Pierce Street, Lynchburg, the home of Anne Spencer, for an auspicious occasion: the dedication ceremony of it as a Virginia landmark.[1] The ceremony featured Pulitzer Prize–winning author Gwendolyn Brooks, who read "an original poem" and also Spencer's "A Letter to My Sister." A handful of individuals offered the invocation, blessing, song of praise, and a reading of Sterling Brown's "To a Certain Lady in Her Garden," a poem about Spencer featured in his 1932 *Southern Road*, which he dedicated to his mother and Spencer (Brown himself was unable to attend, although he was invited. He sent a statement, which was read at the event).[2]

Brooks, at that time poet laureate of Illinois, was a fitting guest speaker for the inaugural event. She was familiar with Spencer's poetry, having discovered at the age of fifteen "a little book called *Caroling Dusk*," which features no less than eleven original poems by Spencer.[3] Fifty years after that anthology's publication, Brooks read "A Letter to My Sister" to the group of dignitaries, family members, and friends. The dedication program also reprinted selected poems by Spencer that she especially valued: "Creed," "Dunbar," and "For Jim." The program outlined the purpose of the Friends of Anne Spencer Memorial Foundation, Inc., which had been formed by Spencer's son, Chauncey: it would preserve the memory of Spencer and "assist in locating, cataloging, preserving, and maintaining the literary documents, photographs, letters, and other memorabilia associated" with her. "Her literary star is still ascending," declared the program, offering the prospect that not just the landmark site but also Spencer's letters would achieve greater recognition.[4]

Yet Spencer did not facilitate this recognition in her lifetime. This deserved memorial event, an acknowledgment of her legacy, emphasized the contradiction of Spencer's refusals and her seemingly incongruous public ambition and private desire. Her biographer J. Lee Greene recalled the poet's defiant privacy even though she had consented to collaborate on his project of telling her life story. Wishing to know more of the nature of her friendship with James Weldon Johnson, who played a pivotal role in bringing Spencer's poetry to public attention during the New Negro Renaissance and who became a dear friend, Greene asked the poet to share her recollections, correspondence, and notes. While affirming Johnson's—"Gem's"—deep meaning to her personal evolution as a writer, Spencer refused to share those words and thoughts:

> During our conversations she mentioned several times in passing that she had recorded comments about Johnson in her Notebooks. But of the materials she would show to me on occasion, she was careful not to show her notes about Johnson. To her these were among her most private and sacred thoughts, written only for herself, as were notes and poems which she wrote about her husband, her immediate family, and the Dixies. A few times when we were sifting through some materials I noticed Mrs. Spencer would come across a letter or a note about Johnson (and at times about her husband and family) which she would quietly and carefully retrieve from the material and tuck away, as if by mistake these very private writings had been placed among her more general papers.[5]

By the time Greene began conducting his interviews in 1971, he had already read the lively letters between Spencer and Johnson in the James Weldon Johnson Memorial Collection at Yale University to which Spencer had donated her correspondence with Johnson in 1943, five years after his untimely death.[6] Imagine the frustration, even the horror of the biographer simultaneously learning of the existence of and being denied access to such personal reflections.

Reserving some thoughts for herself only, in the "sacred space" of her manuscripts and journals, Spencer, like fellow writer Ann Petry, "took control, in part at least, of what she wanted to leave behind as a usable resource."[7] It is significant that both women authors exerted this control in the decades following the establishment of definitive archives of African American literature such as the Johnson Memorial Collection, indicating that they did not believe such institutions would adequately value and respect their papers, indeed their thoughts. The Black literary archive, Jean-Christophe Cloutier writes, is "fraught with absences, removals, and delayed restorations," disruptions that are of special concern in reading Black women's archives. Yet "by disrupting textual stability, special collections further encourage 'a willingness to recognize the unfinished' as a condition of the literary."[8] If we acknowledge the instability of archives, Black women's writings and collections may become more visible. Such a recognition is especially important as we consider Spencer's manuscripts, where the unfinished and the missing and repurposed portions of drafts and published poems occupy the same space.

Greene's characterization of Spencer's adamant privacy—"tucking away" her writing—encapsulates her elusive and defiant life, indeed her reputation beyond death. The effect of her concealments has been a diminished awareness and incomplete understanding, of her writing and aesthetics in their proper contexts. Spencer denied her biographer not just personal reflections.

She refused to share entire manuscripts that she was actively working on. She published twenty-one poems from 1920 to 1934, during the New Negro Renaissance, and continued writing poetry until her death in 1975. After taking a few years to recover from the loss of Johnson, she produced even more writing. From 1940 to 1975 Spencer's poetics expanded from her early embrace of the lyric in her published works to epic, ballad, and other public forms, demonstrating her ambition to tell a national story and be recognized as an American author. And yet her poems remained virtually unknown. Not only did the manuscripts go unpublished but even as she was being encouraged to complete them by her committed biographer, she refused to share them. In fact, it was because of her interviews with Greene in the early to mid-1970s that she was inspired to return to and revise some of her published poems, such as "A Letter to My Sister." Despite her emphatic privacy and outright defiance of her biographer, she was still ambitious enough to complete a poetic trajectory. The public awareness of her accomplishment that has developed in the years since her death has ensured her poems will survive for posterity.

Through this book, I hope to offer a fuller account of Spencer's poetry and life than was possible for Greene by examining her archives, focusing in particular on her manuscripts between 1940 and 1975. Directed to the task of understanding Spencer's archive, we discover what Cloutier describes as "the multifaceted literary means by which authors redeploy their records, whether through revision, insertion, falsification, translation, redaction, remediation, or even fictionalization, sometimes across vast expanses of time."[9] The revisions, recontextualizations, and citations of lines from her published poems in her manuscripts generate an imperative: that we reassess her known works by taking her unknown oeuvre into account.

I address Spencer's published poems from 1920 to 1938 by providing close readings of a selection of them in this later context of her manuscript writings. This expanded interpretive framework reveals that these poems are continuous with her later writing, a fact that was obscured from public view until 2011, when her papers at the University of Virginia became available to researchers. Archives require interpreters; it is through them that different kinds of evidence are made available By drawing on these archives, I hope to invite further interpretation of Spencer's full body of works. For while archives may expand our understanding of authors' lives and works and document their artistic production and imaginative development, they are not the final word. We must understand Spencer's poetry as a "living artifact" of life—of both hers and ours.[10]

Both the manuscripts written from 1940 until 1975 and the continual revisions of the poems she published from 1920 to 1934 sustained Spencer over the course of her lifetime. Through them she grew and developed a wider perspective on the material world in which she lived. And through the living memorial archive of personal experience she created in and through these manuscripts we are able to attend to the contours of her world.[11] I hope that the readings of Spencer's work that I offer in this book not only stimulate further critical responses to her published poems and further attention to her archival writings but also encourage further research on other understudied or as yet undiscovered African American women authors and artists. Scholarly work that makes a place for Black women in intellectual history continues to be imperative.[12] Spencer's life and writings are part of this history. Together with other women artists and professionals, including children's author and poet Effie Lee Newsome and architect and artist Amaza Lee Meredith, she formed a network of creatives, and they sought inspiration and encouragement from each other in their various mediums.[13]

Interpreting Spencer's "Sybil Warns Her Sister" / "Letter to Her Sister"

Spencer's "Sybil Warns Her Sister," originally published in *Opportunity* magazine's *Ebony and Topaz: A Collectanea* in 1927 (and republished in a revised form in 1947 under the title "Letter to My Sister"), functions as a poetic principle as well as a physical object, evoking correspondence as a transformative relation of parts in a poetics of relation and emphasizing the forging of a female-to-female bond through the transmission of wisdom from an older prophet figure to a "sister" addressed as "you."[14] Highlighting the unique plight of women, the speaker warns from experience that "it is dangerous for a woman to defy the gods" and evaluates potential (futile) responses to their forces, even providing advice that is not meant to be followed.[15]

> It is dangerous for a woman to defy the gods;
>   To taunt them with the tongue's thin tip,
>   Or strut in the weakness of mere humanity,
>   Or draw a line daring them to cross;
> The gods who own the searing lightning,
> The drowning waters, the tormenting fears,
> The anger of red sins . . .
> Oh, but worse still if you mince along timidly—
> Dodge this way or that, or kneel, or pray,
> Or be kind, or sweat agony drops,
> Or lay your quick body over your feeble young,
> If you have beauty or plainness, if celibate,
> Or vowed—the gods are Juggernaut,
> Passing over each of us . . .
>   Or this you may do:
>   Lock your heart, then, quietly,

And, lest they peer within,
Light no lamp when dark comes down
Raise no shade for sun,
Breathless must your breath come thru,
If you'd die and dare deny
The gods their god-like fun!

The admonishment is organized into fourteen lines describing the challenge to a woman's individual survival and is followed by an octet in which the speaker provides advice. Voice and power are brought together in lines replete with action words such as "defy," "taunt," "strut," and "draw." The gods themselves are actively demonstrating their power, "searing," "drowning," "tormenting." Yet it is worse to "mince," "dodge," "kneel," "pray," "sweat"—to cower from the active and unpredictable forces of the gods—than the confront them. To live without breath? With a locked heart? With no lamp or imagination? This state of being is a deprivation of life. Why not live defiantly in the knowledge that "the gods are Juggernaut"—mercilessly destructive and unstoppable—and will have their fun?

Both the original and 1947 revised poem link the lyric and the political, describing a female imagination that can be defiantly unleashed in dark times.[16] The "sister's" body itself—its "thin-tipped" tongue and "strut," its "agony drops" and "quick body"—is a channel to a self that needs to experience revelation in order to be authentic. Such revelation is contingent on active living, however; not defying, mincing, or dying but living through breath, heart, and self-revelation.

Sybil imparts the value of a mortal life to the young woman she addresses. The youthful and silent woman who receives her message holds the power to live right and to live well, knowing her life will end. Her heart, breath, and the light of day are engaged in defiance of the gods. The unstoppable force is life itself. But for Sybil, "the tongue's thin tip," which may direct taunts at the gods, is all she has. Reduced to possession of only her voice, Sybil is heard but so diminished of body, Apollo having fated her to wither away until all that remained was her voice, that she is consigned to seeing others' future fates rather than living her own life. Yet by seeing the future, she may claim another, different possession: a bond with "her sister," "my sister" in its revised title. It is a warning, then, to other women, in a claimed sisterly bond that acknowledges the "dangerous" nature of an *embodied* female imagination.[17]

Presented as a riddle to be solved in order to crack the code of authentic living, this personal advice suggests that mortal woman takes her best revenge against the gods by living a full, expressive, and enlightened life. As a form of communal advice, invoked through the words "her" and "sister" in the original title, this message directs itself to African American female existence in a national discourse that all too often represented African American citizenship as a matter of male rights. In 1927, when this poem was published, the speaker's coded advice that living freely and bravely by searching for truth, the light of day, and the illumination of spiritual understanding is the only way to fight the gods suggests a means for women to achieve personal and expressive liberation in the context of the broader African American quest for citizenship and equal rights.

Spencer devised her poem as an extension of a pivotal conversation about women and art that appears in Elizabeth Barrett Browning's *Aurora Leigh*, the epic poem of the female poet. In Barrett Browning's crucial passage, the female speaker states that a woman can't simply present her perfect art but must "prove what she can do . . . / prate of woman's rights, / . . . woman's mission, woman's function," diminishing the work of art with talk that confirms man's limiting judgment of it.[18] Aurora's male suitor challenges her claim, asking "And you, / An artist, judge so?" (8.823–24), to which Aurora answers:

> I, an artist,—yes:
> Because, precisely, I'm an artist, sir,
> And woman, if another sate in sight,
> I'd whisper,—Soft, my sister! not a word!
> By speaking we prove only we can speak,
> Which he, the man here, never doubted. What
> He doubts is, whether we can *do* the thing
> With decent grace we've not yet done at all.
> Now, do it: bring your statue,—you have room!
> He'll see it even by the starlight here;
> And if 'tis e'er so little like the god
> Who looks out from the marble silently
> Along the track of his own shining dart
> Through the dusk of ages, there's no need to speak;
> The universe shall henceforth speak for you,
> And witness, "She who did this thing, was born
> To do it,—claims her license in her work." (8.825–41)

In this passage, the female artist suffers from an enforced silence: to speak, to explain, is to draw attention away from the art object. In the secrecy of silence, a woman artist may produce a work of art that the "universe" may "witness," preempting male judgement. Both Spencer and Barrett Browning's poems underscore the female struggle for recognition of her work of art without mediation, diminution, or commodification.[19]

And yet both poems assert the powerful potential of connection and mediation that their works of art can provide as living forms of expression that reside between the extremes of female oracular power and gendered humility. In "Sybil Warns Her Sister" / "A Letter to My Sister," "light," "lamp," and "breath" represent the female artist's suppressed inclinations and her living potential. In both poems, female imagination creates an embodied state and a physical place for the artist herself, allowing the poet to express the immediacy of experience and language.[20] For Spencer, poetry as a living form affirmed an idea of female artistry beyond commodity (a saleable book) or context (the "talk" in *Aurora Leigh*), which diminished the work of art. By living through language, the female poet engages poetry as a practice of living "beyond the book" (*Aurora Leigh* [8.278])—beyond the work of art. Even as Spencer strove to write works of ambitious scale, she also strove to live beyond the book, regardless of whether or not it was completed.

"Sybil Warns Her Sister" is an assertion of female personhood that is also crucial to understanding her manuscript poems written after 1940.[21] The poem emphasizes not only individual imaginative existence but also a collective lyrical awareness of life shaped by overpowering and uncontrollable forces, whether "gods" or more worldly authorities. The immediacy of experience itself, both feminist and racial, resides *in between* the work of art and its context.[22] Poetry is made living practice, subject to change and development from one lived moment to the next as language reveals the speaker's mediation of refusal and relation. The letter of Spencer's poem provides the link between experience and its formal expression.

Spencer revised "Sybil Warns Her Sister" for a third time in 1970; this newly conceived version, titled "Sybil Speaks," is one of several reworked poems that exemplify her approach to her poetry as a living, immediate form that is subject to change. The unpublished poem consists of a single, four-line stanza:

"Young man, all you *touch* is what you lose
That you *keep* by *faith* you choose;
Lift your soul with wings on high,
Starve your body—even let it die!"[23]

The quotation marks indicate the speaking voice of Sybil, and perhaps what is most powerful about this poem is its emphasis on voice, the voice of a female spiritual guide addressing a young man and offering him advice. Earthly temptation, greed and acquisition are countered by the boundlessness of faith and the soul it preserves. One "keeps" by "faith," not "touch," by "soul," not "body." "Sybil Speaks" makes clear that survival refers not to physical existence but to the survival of the imagination, the imaginative soul. Spencer's notebook containing the complete manuscript version of the poem confirms imagination's survival, even as she writes below it that "women are least convincing when they attempt the truth."[24]

The Sybil poems emphasize the speaker, a female prophet whose words may or may not be heeded. Their female speaker draws attention to female authority and its articulation, bringing together distinct experiences of age and youth, women and men, defiance and temerity. Her voice initiates affiliation or, better yet, challenges its listener to connect, to hear, and to heed. The lyric individual is not yet fully revealed in these poems: just as even if prophecy knows the future it still requires a life to transmit it, so too the individual's life and course of action remains undetermined. The young woman addressed in 1927 must renew her imagination through female embodiment, life; the young man addressed in 1970 must strive for the metaphysical through faith. In both poems poetic imagination serves as the antidote to the corrupt physical world, which is figured as the world of man.

These poems are representative of two significant phases of Anne Spencer's poetics, one from the period prior to the death of her cherished friend and mentor James Weldon Johnson, the other after a period of mourning, when she resumed writing. Written in this latter period, the manuscript works were lengthy and urgent projects spanning a lifetime of letters from her youth, which was when she became literate and began reading serious literary works, to her twilight years, during which the author wrote blind as a result of cataracts and with her tongue partially removed owing to cancer.[25] Like Sybil, Spencer occupies a space between worlds. From the threshold year of 1940, Spencer took up the pen again, writing about new subjects in incomplete and unpublished manuscripts that drew on expansive, public forms like the epic, the author and her works defiantly occupying an in-between state. The manuscripts function both as public proclamation and personal, sustaining inquiry—offering, through the defiant life lived by the author, an interpretation of America to itself.

These manuscripts undertake an aesthetic inquiry into poetics in relation to ecological existence. As I show, they assert proximity to and not isolation from her world of readers and writers. Earth itself becomes a negotiating space for Spencer's imagination, providing a setting for the continuous and transitory movement of place and time. Her works insist on extension and modification through the garden. Here, the author devises an expansive location in which she explores her relation to the world, establishing a transformative ecology.

In her manuscripts, Spencer uses spatial maps, stark visuals, and charismatic personae such as John Brown and Amiri Baraka (formerly Leroi Jones) to connect to the reader through space and time—whether that space is celestial, as in the case of her John Brown manuscript, or earthly, as in her poem "Leroi Meets Lincoln." A series of key visual representations of human agents of change—from Thomas Hovenden's *The Last Moments of John Brown* to Gutzon Borglum's *Seated Lincoln*, to a photograph of Amiri Baraka (then Leroi Jones) and his wife descending the courthouse steps in Newark—inform these later works. They are paired by Spencer with accounts of Black female experiences, creating a balance among human beings who share in a world. She presents Black life in ecological terms, using physical space informed by the natural world and experienced by natural and human agents to forge relation between lyric and epic, poetic forms that are usually kept separate. She is therefore able to present both deeply personal experience and elements of shared memory in her poems.

In referring to Spencer's ecology of relation as it pertains to a poetics of Black experience, I build on what Sonya Posmentier refers to as "lyric time"—the way in which poetry mediates between text and experience, providing an ecological understanding of lyric: "Poems sometimes mimic or approximate organic forms and processes . . . that can exceed their own boundaries," Posmentier argues, and "that may in turn yield new models for social and ecological relation."[26] Spencer's writing creates physical, palpable encounters with public and natural spaces that are cultivated and defined by humans. Addressing human and nonhuman experiences of the world, Spencer's manuscripts generate spaces of transformative possibility, moving beyond the limitations imposed by Jim Crow segregation. Using human agents such as John Brown and Leroi Jones, Spencer calls attention to the potential ethical transformation of human beings as they attend to their natural environment and to each other.[27]

The physical presence of Black environmental experience in Spencer's later writing lends special meaning to Spencer's *archive* that is distinct from that of the individual poems she published early in her career. Spencer's manuscripts *as manuscripts* function as an aesthetic archive of this experience and reflect the physical experience of writing. The manuscripts are tactile, and the act of reading them calls attention to the author in her works, insisting that we join her experiences with ours.

At the center of this study stands the small garden that for Spencer embodied creativity, autonomy, and relation. It came into maturity in the 1930s, the years of her vigorous correspondence with other writers and her developing national reputation. Ideas circulated in her and her husband Edward's home at 1313 Pierce Street among the well-to-do residents of her street and also circulated beyond in the wider neighborhood and city as a whole and among writers of the New Negro Renaissance who lived in the Northeast and Midwest. Her garden, reached either through the house or by a pathway adjacent to it, was at once physical and metaphysical.[28] It was not a subsistence garden. Its fruits were grown for birds, some of whom were named after the literary personae of Spencer's world.

Spencer's manuscripts offer a material history of her life, and a physical encounter with her writings is necessary to understanding that history.[29] The spatial and creative contexts of her unpublished poems—their physical and imaginative placement on the page or wall or in the book or box—demonstrate her desire to put her writing and its subjects in motion. Her post-1940 manuscripts feature multiple, coexisting versions of works, and in this period she also altered many of her previously published works, sometimes multiple times, we have seen in her "Sybil" poems. Yet her manuscripts defied the printed form; they were not intended to be published. As expressive manuscripts, they demonstrate the author's need to experiment, to produce multiple versions and to take into account a multiplicity of temporalities in the changing contexts of life, landscape, and nation.[30] Approaching her writing as both physical and abstract yields a textured understanding of the manuscripts she produced over several decades of reading, writing, and living.

She scavenged paper, writing on the backs of bills and receipts, stationery left by others, envelopes, on boxes and box tops, and day journals from other authors and prior years, in between the lines of mimeographed depositions, and on the walls of her home. Writing possessed urgency for Spencer. It was an act of devotion to humanity and a means of sudden revelation of truths in the garden of humankind. Those truths were sometimes grasped line by line. Her manuscripts often begin in a single line, which is then repeated, altered, and extended over time, giving rise to far-reaching works. Spencer's lines in these manuscript works are sometimes ordinary placeholders, yet as she returns to them to revise them over the decades of her life, they take on an imaginative and experiential weight and expansiveness.

Spencer's words in these manuscripts move quickly, vigorously, as if to keep pace with the author's thought process and wit. Parataxis enables this quick movement. Often one idea will leap to another association without the orientation of preposition or punctuation, producing wonderful synaesthetic experiences or unexpectedly linked ideas. It is a fast-paced, experimental style that produces an interrogation of the relation of words and images. Often a thought's presumed end joins a new idea that is not explicitly or fully expressed but is considered by the author. With rare exception, I have left Spencer's lines and spellings as they were written to preserve their dynamic vitality.

Spencer preferred to write by hand in pencil, usually graphite and on occasion blue or red—whatever was at hand. She always had a little pencil in the pocket of her dresses and, later, her vests. As her eyesight worsened from cataracts, she began to use ink pens, blue only. She favored legal pads and Blue Horse composition notebooks, possibly because unlike loose-leaf paper, the pages were bound together, lending a physical coherence to her medium when the visual order provided by lined paper eluded her. When her sight failed her and she was blind, she continued to write. Words in the lines of her verse in these later years are frequently illegible, and on many occasions one line overwrites another, the lines trailing off the page. Even with these challenges of sight and medium, particularly the disorientation of not being able to see the page on which she was writing or her own words—words that had surrounded her in her visual and tactile experiences of her physical world—Spencer continued composing until her death.

In this book, I offer a look into the manuscripts, the literary conversations and social relationships, the travels of the road and of the mind, and the accomplishments and incompletions of this lively, magnetic personality and those who were drawn to her. Her correspondence with other figures from the New Negro Renaissance period of the 1920s and beyond such as Sterling Brown, Georgia Douglas Johnson, Langston Hughes, and James Weldon Johnson provide a record of Spencer, while her archives convey the aspiring author's self-concept, vigorous interpretation of literature, and moments of outrage, discouragement, and despair.

I have largely preserved Spencer's spellings, spacing, and word inventions. These manuscripts demand that we endeavor to understand the spatial relationship between the words she wrote, the visual and rhythmic patterns and varying paces of time her words create. Although I have transcribed her manuscripts here, something is lost in that transcription. They are not so much Emersonian "confessions of a poetic age" as they are experimentations with an age as yet to be determined: one envisioned but not arrived at. The archive she left behind is defined by her refusal to publish and her assurances—to herself, to others—that she would.[31]

The Chapters

Anne Spencer between Worlds maps the intellectual and geographic routes of the New Negro Renaissance into and out of Lynchburg, Spencer's writing out of and into an originary Virginia, and her engagement with Black Arts Movement poetry. For African Americans, literary circles provided a way of organizing people, ideas, and life, the literature itself serving as a means to creativity and existence in the world.[32] The first chapter, "Anne Spencer's Creed: Reading the Author's Library" introduces the author through her extensive library, through which she formed her literary circles and that became the basis of her lifetime of writing. The second chapter, "Routes of the Renaissance: Anne Spencer's Lynchburg Circle," places Spencer at the center of the New Negro Renaissance in Lynchburg, Virginia, showing how the Spencer family's home developed into a hub for intellectual engagement out of the deprivations of segregation, creating a space for generative thought and action, and how prominent poets James Weldon Johnson, Sterling Brown, Langston Hughes, and Georgia Douglas Johnson drew from Spencer's southern surroundings, including Lynchburg's southern folk culture, in their poetry. The geographic and intellectual encounters of these writers there provided the opportunity for thinking about both the folk and the "New Negro" modern in relation to regions, gardens, and time.

Moving to her unfinished works, each subsequent chapter addresses one of the major poems from the second phase of her writing. Although it is customary in poetry criticism to supply a chronology of a poet's unknown works, it is impossible to do this in the case of Spencer. One of the most intriguing and challenging aspects of Spencer's manuscripts is their layered and simultaneous quality over a span of decades. While her ongoing experiences and observations led her to revise these manuscripts repeatedly, they also demonstrate her sustained commitment to certain personae that represented her ideals. "Virginia as Narcissus," in which Spencer engages mainstream modernism, confronts the legacy of the Southern Agrarians and the midcentury's reckoning with segregation in the context of the codeveloping fields of poetry and criticism. "John Brown: An Epic of Democracy" shows Spencer's engagement with the tradition of American epic writing through a long poem that asserts its distinction from mid-twentieth century published forms. "'Leroi Meets Lincoln' / 'Bastion at Newark'" discusses Spencer's multidecade layering of poems about liberty, through which she ultimately relayed her view of Black Arts and Black Power in the northern, urban setting of this work. The afterword, "Till: Soil and Civil Rights in Anne Spencer's Poetry," explores Spencer's response to Emmett Till's murder through the ballad form, using a fragment from "Leroi Meets Lincoln" to make the case for further scholarly attention to her archives, specifically further study of her poetry in relation to the more familiar, published works of her contemporaries such as Gwendolyn Brooks.

Reading Anne Spencer's manuscripts from the period of 1940 to 1975, I aim to interpret her letter to us, made physically available through her scraps and manuscripts as a result of the Friends of Anne Spencer Memorial Foundation's commitment to assisting "in locating, cataloging, preserving, and maintaining the literary documents, photographs, letters, and other memorabilia associated with Anne Spencer."[33] This process is important, and it requires more than the recovery of documents. We must make space for African American women's writing in the American intellectual tradition of letters, libraries, and literature. "We know the meaning of our seeming valuelessness, of being 'forgotten but not gone,'" writes Daphne Brooks, "and yet our masterful rejoinder has always been to build our own monuments."[34] Spencer's material legacy demonstrates that she, like other Black women artists, "engaged in active projects to archive their own creative practices, to document the intellectual and creative practices tied to their [art form]," resulting in "a Black feminist intellectual history" that puts the *practice* of memory rather than the possession of it front and center.[35] Such "fugitive thinkers," as Brooks calls these Black women artists, effectively interact with the archive's meaningful presence. At the same time that Spencer worked to create a memorial archive for James Weldon Johnson, wishing to advance his legacy through institutional acknowledgment, she drew into her manuscripts, creating a parallel archive devoted to the large-scale works that developed her transformative poetics and the idea of practicing memory itself.

CHAPTER ONE

Anne Spencer's Creed
Reading the Author's Library

> Sire, your creed is also mine.
> —FRIEDRICH SCHILLER, *Don Carlos*

In her copy of Sarah E. H. Lockwood and Mary Alice Henderson's *Composition and Rhetoric for Higher Schools* (1901), a newly married, eighteen-year-old "Annie B. Spencer" wrote: "Friends *are* bought. Do we not go to the shops for our books."[1] At the beginning of this friendship is the young Annie Bethel Scales, who, at five years old, could not read or write, but possessed an "urgent desire to read with ease."[2] Her first exposure to reading materials, in her West Virginia girlhood, came in the form of dime novels, pulp fiction, and newspapers; although she could not read, this exposure gave rise to a kind of improvised literacy: relying on the illustrations and the look of words on the page, she and a childhood friend would act out what they presumed the stories were about.[3] The first poems she read were from McGuffey's Reader, the bestselling primer of the nineteenth and early twentieth century.[4] Her subsequent education at the prestigious Virginia Seminary in Lynchburg, Virginia, gave her access to books and facilitated the creation of her broad-based personal library.[5]

Distinctions between popular and elite literature within the category of literacy shaped the educational tracks at Virginia Seminary, where courses of study were divided into "normal" and "academic" trajectories. When she arrived in 1893 at the age of eleven, Spencer was placed into the lowest level of the normal track "because she could barely read and write."[6] She advanced quickly to the top level of the normal track. While only the highest academic track "studied the classics as a major part of its curriculum," Spencer received "three years of good basic Latin, one year of French, and one year of German."[7] Evidently her Latin was good enough for her to help her future husband, Edward, translate Caesar.[8]

Relation operates in Spencer's poetics as a form of understanding, not just of human relations but of Earth's relation to itself, ecological patterns of nature distinct from humans. Her poetry describes scenes of encounter: social encounters as well as encounters with flora and fauna that carry the speakers and subjects of her poems into corresponding relations in a shared world of feeling and existence. The act of reading for Spencer was a communal practice, bringing her together with her fellow writers from different regions and linking their locations in an ecology of readers and writers. Their patterns of geographic movement, experimentation with formal expression, and in many instances, cultivation of gardens convey "environmental relation rooted in . . . particularities."[9] Spencer's library, like her garden, while bearing her human signature, articulates its relation to communal practices in the larger environment of city and nation, creating the promise of new models for writing and relation beyond its space.[10] Her personal library was a worldmaking endeavor tied to physical and metaphysical concerns; her books demonstrate a living practice of engagement with the world. Her library is a site that speaks to her choices: her fostering of gatherings and community, the pleasure she took in books, and her engagement in instruction and broader activism.

Spencer's couplet-driven poem "Creed," published in Countee Cullen's 1927 volume *Caroling Dusk*, best expresses this logic, underscoring the author's lifelong pursuit of the balance between physical and metaphysical relation.[11]

> If my garden oak spares one bare ledge
> For a boughed mistletoe to grow and wedge;
> And all the wild birds this year should know
> I cherish their freedom to come and go;
> If a battered worthless dog, masterless, alone,
> Slinks to my heels, sure of bed and bone;
> And the boy just moved in, deigns a glance-assay,
> Turns his pockets inside out, calls, "Come and play!"
> If I should surprise in the eyes of my friend
> That the deed was *my* favor he'd let me lend;
> Or hear it repeated from a foe I despise,
> That I whom he hated was chary of lies;
> If a pilgrim stranger, fainting and poor,
> Followed an urge and stopped at my door,
> And my husband loves me till death puts apart,
> Less as flesh unto flesh, more as heart unto heart:
> I may challenge God when we meet That Day,
> And He dare not be silent or send me away.[12]

The occasion for the poem "Creed" was the Spencers' visit to Harpers Ferry, West Virginia, where Spencer saw a mistletoe bough sprouting from an oak.[13] The image of nature's voluntary, unforced grafting is a powerful one. "Creed," the title of which derives from the line from Schiller's play *Don Carlos* that serves as the epigraph to this chapter, is a poem about space and relation, about the mutuality of natural and human circumstances, about taking pleasure in offering generous assistance that surpasses what was requested, sharing hearth and home with a seemingly worthless creature, learning from an enemy's wariness of lies and worthiness of character, and understanding marital love fully through the separation caused by the death of a spouse.[14] These earthly relationships in which faith supplants judgment emphasize the power of nature. Its power is the source of all earthly woes and yet also makes possible the improbable relations of human and nonhuman in mind, heart, and spirit. Nature provides the space for seemingly disparate parts to form a relation or even unite, from two distinct trees to one that is cleft, from friend and enemy to shared values. The extremes of loneliness and the desire for connection ("Come and play!") contribute to the balanced structure of the poem, which is also formally rendered in rhymed couplets of largely iambic pentameter: ledge, wedge, know, go, alone, bone, assay, play, friend, lend, despise, lies, poor, door, apart, heart, day, away. By the poem's close, the speaker boldly declares her union with God, a profound kinship formed through the powerful relation of opposites. These moments demonstrate the possibility of connection, of choosing to define oneself through relation rather than through separation. The poem is a series of actions describing cleaving *to* rather than cleaving from.

Returning to the subject of reading approximately sixty years after her initial remark about books as friends, Spencer observed under the title "Why Read Books?" that "a library in the making has the two paramount factors. People, and then books":

1. We read for companionship. Man from the beginning has been a lonely creature. In a book he finds another lonely creature who confirms himself— who can *express* himself; who being interpreted says to him—you and I do this or that. We belong together.

2. We read for entertainment. And this is not an unimportant reason for reading. It is actively twofold in result. A stimulation of wit and humor and maybe an outlet safe innocent and inexpensive.

3. We read for wealth. When we read a book or eat an egg we are sharing our meals with kings. No finer food can be bought.

4. Reading gives us a rational religion. And religion is the outstanding mark of humanity.[15]

Spencer's seasoned observations underscore her profound journey to literacy. Books are for pleasure and sustenance. They provide a pathway through their companionship, their stimulation of the reader's wit and humor, and their provision of intellectual wealth to reason *as* religion, which Spencer describes here as humankind's best belief system, or "creed."[16]

Lynchburg's Literary Circles

Spencer's library opens up multiple pathways for approaching a century of African American literacy and literature in which literary circles played a key role, operating in communal and national contexts. Her books demonstrate the acquisition and dissemination of knowledge not just for Spencer, but for other readers as well. As Elizabeth McHenry has shown, "Self-learning has been, and continues to be, a significant set of practices for African American communities."[17] Such practices of self-learning were responses to broad-ranging denial of access to public spaces, and educational institutions. Of necessity African American communities created their own practices of literacy acquisition and sharing. Spencer's library demonstrates how she and her reading community participated in rather than retreated from this segregated world. The communal reading that Spencer took part in in her childhood was continuous with the literary circles she participated in at her home and in those of fellow authors and with her occupation as librarian of Lynchburg's Dunbar branch, a one-room library that served the city's all-Black Dunbar High School and the city's African American community.

Among the more familiar literary salons of the 1920s, such as Georgia Douglas Johnson's Washington, D.C., home on S Street, Spencer's in Lynchburg was unique in being a southern locale for the Black intelligentsia.[18] Certainly, the aspiring young authors who found their way to Spencer's house were drawn by her magnetism. But they were also in search of relation: to the South, to folk culture and more specifically to southern Black culture. The conversations they had at Spencer's home provided more immediate access to such folk relations. For example, Sterling Brown's Big Boy Davis, one of the folk personae that established the author as an accomplished poet of the people, was a Lynchburg native whom Spencer knew.

Virginia was a gateway to the South, and Lynchburg was not at a remove from either transportation or culture: it was proximate to Washington, D.C.— about four hours by car—and was on the railroad line, about an hour from Danville, a major industrial rail stop. Lynchburg was, moreover, a unique city because of its coeducational institution for Blacks, the Virginia Seminary, whose leadership was Black and which had secured a curricular and instructional independence from the Baptist institution that had founded it after Reconstruction by the time Spencer arrived.[19]

Between 1906 and 1916, a series of events catalyzed the small African American community of Lynchburg, events that made explicit the necessity of Black networks of literacy and of collective action as a defense against racial exploitation and means of asserting citizenship.[20] Ota Benga, a Congolese man of the Mbuti ethnic group then commonly referred to as "pygmy" who had been kidnapped from his home by the explorer Samuel Phillips Verner, found himself first at the St. Louis World's Fair in 1906 and then at the Bronx Zoo's "human exhibit," where he was imprisoned and subjected to pursuit by violent mobs. These exhibits asserted "white supremacy and civilization's ascendancy through the 'White Man's Burden.'"[21] Benga was presented as "the missing link" in this civilization by more than one newspaper.

The exhibition of Benga at the Bronx Zoo provoked vocal protests from African American religious and community leaders.[22] After a lengthy tug-of-war, Benga was sent to the Howard Colored Orphans Asylum in Brooklyn, where African American religious educators aimed to improve the quality of his life by introducing him to Christian virtues and biblical teachings. But Benga, who had been pursued by "public interest"—mobs—in the Bronx, found himself similarly besieged in Brooklyn, where the press and city-going spectators found him.[23] By the time of his release to the Colored Orphans Asylum, Benga had been exhibited in a cage for twenty days. Pamela Newkirk notes that "the exhibition had contributed to a doubling of park attendance compared with the preceding year. Some 220,800 people had visited the park in September, and nearly all, if not all of them, had seen Benga."[24] Through the religious network of the National Baptist Ministers' Convention, Rev. James Gordon arranged in late 1906 for Benga to be sent to live with Rev. Gregory Hayes, who was then president of Virginia Seminary, and his wife, Mary, and their two children. But Hayes died suddenly that year, and Benga was sent back to the orphanage, this time to its Long Island farm. Mary Hayes again took Benga in after she had completed a stint as interim president of the seminary in the wake of her husband's death. Mary, by this time a good friend of Anne Spencer's, probably coordinated the tutoring of Benga in English that Spencer ended up undertaking. "Benga found a kindred spirit in one of his instructors," writes Newkirk. "Annie Bethel Spencer was not quite twenty-six when Benga arrived at Virginia Seminary."[25] Spencer's son, Chauncey, born in 1906, recalled playing with Benga as a child, not recognizing that despite his small stature he was a man in his thirties.

No one was able to get Benga's name right, and so in Lynchburg, where he worked in tobacco, he was known as Otto Bingo. He took his life on March 20, 1916, still in Lynchburg at the time, shooting himself through the heart in a hayloft with a shotgun he stole from a neighbor, as he saw no prospect for returning to his original homeland in Africa's rainforest, where in any event his wife and children had already been murdered. It was a profoundly upsetting event in the small Lynchburg community that had set about trying to make a life for him away from the pseudoscientific and mass cultural spectacle that had set the terms of his identity on American soil.[26] His suicide , just two houses from Spencer's home, was felt as a personal tragedy and a communal loss, one that coincided in 1916 with almost twenty years of state legislation in Virginia aimed at regulating Black people's movements, opportunities, and overall prosperity. Such legislation continued to be enacted into the next decade; the Racial Integrity Act, passed on March 20, 1924, just eight years after Ota Benga's death to the day, enforced the Black-white divide from birth by dictating that birth and marriage certificates indicate whether the person was white or "colored" and eradicated official recognition of Native Americans by forcing them to identify as Black.[27]

There are no records in Spencer's papers of Ota Benga's life and the impact of his death on the Lynchburg African American community in which he last lived. But it was shortly after his death that James Weldon Johnson arrived in Lynchburg as field secretary of the NAACP and met with interested citizens who wished to start a local chapter. Benga's story is, I believe, the event that catalyzed the civic interest in forming a chapter and that inspired Spencer to assume a more active role in politics on a national scale, which in turn led, by way of her friendship with Johnson, to the formation of her Lynchburg literary circle.

Johnson arrived in Lynchburg in April 1918, less than two years after Benga's death and just following the barbaric double lynching of Mary Turner and her unborn baby in Valdosta, Georgia. Spencer recalled to Greene that Johnson "told a terrible tale" after he arrived and that during a small party the Spencers held later that evening for him, she "tried to get Johnson to repeat the tale to the group gathered there, but evidently he did not."[28] When Johnson arrived, Virginia's deeply restrictive segregationist legislation was more than a decade old. As field secretary, a new position the NAACP created for him in 1916, Johnson traveled extensively throughout the South as part of a newly defined effort by the institution to increase membership through the establishment of local branches. By the time the young Walter White succeeded Johnson in the position, institutional membership had increased by over sixty thousand, and over two hundred new branches had been established, many of the new members coming from the South. Lynchburg was one of the last chapters Johnson helped to organize, passing the baton to White in 1920 as he stepped into a role in the executive branch of the NAACP. But he didn't stop visiting Lynchburg. He fit yearly visits to Lynchburg into his schedule, stopping off after visiting D.C., Richmond, and Durham on official business, and from 1930 onward, he would combine a visit to the Spencers with his annual return trek from Nashville, where he was a chaired professor of English at Fisk, to Great Barrington, Massachusetts, where he and his wife had their summer home, Five Acres. Johnson was guest speaker at the Virginia Seminary finals, and he also appeared on local broadcasts.[29]

It was a fast friendship, and it mutually shaped their lives. "From the first, Jim and I were Jim and Anne to each other," Spencer told Greene, although this is not exactly so: at the start of their correspondence, she was "My dear Mrs. Spencer," but by November 1920 she was "my dear, dear friend."[30] Spencer's dynamic and sustained correspondence with James Weldon Johnson over almost two decades evinces both wit and modesty, a critical acuity, an au courant awareness of the literary journals and newspapers of the day, and a passionate engagement with the writing life. Spencer and Johnson's correspondence exudes a personal warmth that shaped their lives as well as their literary expression, an intimacy kindled by reverence for the printed word, especially poetry, and most of all for the nation that both writers loved and critiqued in their writing. When they met in 1918, Johnson had newly emerged as a public persona of national caliber—field secretary of the NAACP *and* a published poet (his *Fifty Years and Other Poems* had just been published in 1917).

Johnson's visit in April 1918 "was the beginning of what became a delightful tradition with the Spencers of entertaining as house guests many noted persons whom they met as a result of knowing Johnson," Greene reports.[31] Johnson and Spencer's efforts to provide creative and social outlets for African Americans were fueled by an optimism about imminent social and political change but also by the deep outrage they shared over Turner's savage lynching while eight months pregnant. That atrocity underscored what was at stake and informed their writing from that period: the preservation of their livelihood and that of all African American citizens regardless of class or gender necessitated the pursuit of justice and equal treatment before the law.

Johnson and Spencer met through these political circumstances, and they also shared their poetry with each other on their first visit. Edward was ill with the flu, no light matter in 1918, but encouraged his wife to continue on with the plan to host the stranger. The chance series of events created the opportunity for Spencer to show Johnson some of her poems. The rest is fairly well known but is related in a one-sided way. Johnson, male and nationally recognized, is usually credited with having shaped Spencer as a poet. Johnson suggested that she adopt the pen name Anne in place of the more familiar Annie, and he debuted and promoted her poems in his 1922 anthology *The Book of American Negro Poetry*. But their friendship was mutually defining, as their correspondence reveals, and Spencer helped shape Johnson's work on the sermonic poems that became *God's Trombones*. He consulted her on the subject of the final title of this work, indicating her involvement in prior conversations about the collection. And although he did not choose the title she proposed—"Gabriel's Trumpet"—he held her advice in high regard.[32]

Greene speculated that Spencer and Johnson had an affair, but even if this were true, it was not the only kind of intimacy they shared. As Spencer frequently reflected in her manuscript writings, books themselves created an intimacy with individuals and brought together readers in a shared experience. The "friend" of her poems, including "I Have a Friend" (1927) and "Translation" (1930), affirms the human spirit *becoming* as it generates understanding in relation: the spirit of friendship, whether between a human and a nonhuman environment or between humans, is conveyed in a setting in which words themselves are secondary to an understanding of the soul.

Bibliophiles make lists, and, as McHenry has shown, they tend to "think

... bibliographically." To think with and through books is to engage in list making, a favorite activity of Spencer's that is exhibited throughout her manuscripts. McHenry notes that "lists ... appear to be authoritative and certain, but they are in fact forms that compel us into discussion, enticing readers to intervene by questioning a list's very existence or calling attention to its excesses and gaps."[33] Spencer's library, volumes from which were lent to readers and placed in spatial relation, evokes the incompletions in and interventions of her manuscripts: "Lists become meaningful in part because of their disrupted, unfinished quality."[34]

Spencer's library of over ten thousand volumes, now housed in the University of Virginia's Albert and Shirley Small Special Collections, is a physical manifestation of her extensive imaginative geography. It is Spencer's unique channel of knowledge that connects diverse individuals, nations, and their writings. Her library demonstrates both her deeply personal engagement with and wide navigation of humankind's intellectual and creative history. On her bookshelf, room is made for British and American authors representing the history of literature in English from medieval, Renaissance, romantic, Victorian, American colonial, gothic, transcendental, and realist perspectives. Poetry occupies a central place; the library contains works by Spenser, Milton, Pope, Swinburne, Longfellow, Tennyson, Keats, Shelley, Nathaniel Hawthorne, Robert Browning, Elizabeth Barrett Browning, Walt Whitman, Emily Dickinson, Paul Laurence Dunbar, and James Weldon Johnson. Intellectual histories also predominate, represented through biographies of major figures, philosophical treatises and histories of philosophy, religious history, revolutionary histories of the Enlightenment (French, American and Haitian), and Greek and Roman classics. An abundance of prose short stories and novels occupy her library shelves, too: those of US authors James Fenimore Cooper, Rebecca Harding Davis, O. Henry, Frank Norris, Upton Sinclair, and Anita Loos are joined by those of British authors William Makepeace Thackeray, Charles Dickens, George Eliot, the Brontes, Thomas Hardy, and Joseph Conrad. Skeptics and satirists form their own category in her prose collection: Jonathan Swift, Thomas Carlyle, H. L. Mencken, Sinclair Lewis. Dramatists fill the space as well, with Euripides, Shakespeare, and Alice Childress representing the range of her interests. Among her collection of African American authors are works by her intellectual circle of friends and acquaintants: besides Johnson's *God's Trombones* are titles by W. E. B. Du Bois, Georgia Douglas Johnson, Alain Locke, Zora Neale Hurston, Rayford W. Logan, Langston Hughes, and Ann Petry. Then, too, there are Spencer's several books on design, including Edith Wharton's *The Decoration of Houses*, as well as cookbooks, seed catalogues, bird guides, and gardening manuals. Classics in translation also appear: Pope's translation of the Iliad, and translations of the works of Victor Hugo, Leo Tolstoy, and Marcel Proust. The juvenilia of Sir Walter Scott, Edgar Allen Poe, Emily Dickinson, Robert Louis Stevenson, and Rudyard Kipling, much of it bearing endearing inscriptions from and to her immediate family, stands on shelves with guides and manuals on teaching and education.

This extensive library was not for display, nor did she amass it as means of posturing. It was for use, was meant to be read, and there is abundant evidence that Spencer *talked to* her books emphatically, treated them not as revered objects but instead handled them, making them well-thumbed and companionable friends—physical manifestations of the intellectual inquiry and imaginative engagement of an author and a reader. She wrote in the majority of her books, whether underlining, annotating, or jotting down unrelated remarks (including her own poetry), and in the mid-twentieth century, she also began tipping in reviews or related newspaper pieces. Some books were gifted for special occasions and so convey the history of the Spencer family, and many of the books contain Spencer's signature autograph hand: "Anne Spencer—her book."

The persistent segregationist practices of public libraries throughout the South partly explains why Spencer's personal library was so large. As Karla Holloway notes, "Public libraries were not available to all publics, either before or for many years after the school integration case." As late as 1960, the nearby Danville, Virginia, public library "created a 'stand-up pick-up-your-books-and-go' policy for blacks. The library went so far as to remove tables and chairs so that there would be no place for black patrons to sit." Such restrictions recalled "pre–civil war days, when laws prohibiting the teaching of reading and writing to blacks were one way of maintaining the privileges and distinctions of class."[35] In Lynchburg, the Jones Memorial Library, a privately owned institution, remained segregated until 1966. It was only twelve years after the Supreme Court ruling in *Brown v. Board of Education* that Black and other nonwhite patrons were finally permitted to access branches other than the Dunbar branch that had been designated for African Americans. Black leaders had filed a lawsuit in the early 1960s to obligate the city to recognize the federal decree.

Using a freshly minted copy of *The Book of American Negro Poetry*, James Weldon Johnson's anthology, which featured three of her poems, Spencer made the case to a Jones Memorial Library hiring committee that she was qualified for the position of librarian. In this act, we find young Annie, transformed into Anne Spencer, asserting her literacy and her literariness at the same time.[36] In her new position she attempted to create a future of readers. She used her poem "Dunbar," which had been published in November 1920 in *Crisis Magazine*, to teach her students at Dunbar Library about meter, rhyme, and how to write verse.[37]

Ah, how poets sing and die!
Make one song and Heaven takes it;

Have one heart and Beauty breaks it;
Chatterton, Shelley, Keats and I—
Ah, how poets sing and die!

Read as an instruction to children about how to write poetry, "Dunbar" takes on new meaning. It presents the writing of verse not as the solitary endeavor of a poet but rather as a space-making and space-sharing one: Paul Laurence Dunbar occupies space with Chatterton, Shelley, and Keats. Spencer occupies space with Dunbar and his companions. The students of Dunbar High School occupy space, indeed a library, with Spencer and the surrounding poets. As an exercise in teaching the writing of verse to African American children, we see the author Spencer's recognition of the way poetry opens up worlds and of the power to be gained from writing in the company of other poets of renown.

The one-room Dunbar branch of the Jones Memorial Library opened its doors in 1923 with Dunbar High School, constructed by the city to fulfill the request of local Black leaders for a high school for Black students. Until 1923, when Spencer was hired at the Dunbar branch, there had not been an African American librarian in the city of Lynchburg, and there was no other library for its Black citizens. Spencer would prove pivotal in her role as librarian, serving as an intermediary between books and African American readers until she resigned in 1946. Spencer told Greene that in her twenty-three years of service, she had never received a raise. Dunbar Library received the discarded, threadbare volumes of the Jones branch, and Spencer brought many of the books from her personal collection in to compensate. A 1931–32 annual report of the Dunbar Library, completed and signed by Spencer, shows that there were five tables and thirty chairs to serve over five hundred students and that there were 22,224 circulating volumes for the year. In 1946, Dunbar High School raised funds for its own school library, and the Dunbar branch books were returned to Jones branch.

Reading and annotating provided Spencer with opportunities for encounter. Her annotations offer evidence of the spirit with which she participated in reading circles with others, both students and peers. In her 1900 copy of John Ruskin's *The Crown of Wild Olive*, Spencer notes that "once, happily you've been born into the 19th century and living under far into the 20th, you find yourself repeatedly drawing back into the Victorian matrix."[38] Spencer repeatedly remarked on her longevity as a reader and writer straddling two centuries. She lived among the romantics, the Victorians, the modernists and later, Black Arts practitioners, and regarded these volumes as expansive and fertile ground for her imagination.

She had a fondness for puns and riddles and did not turn her nose up at popular framings of literature and of knowledge more generally; she had titles like *The World's Greatest Books* (1910, 10 vols.) and *The World's Best-Loved Poems*

(1927) and John Bartlett's *Collection of Familiar Quotations* (1890) in her collection. Indeed, Spencer's library reflects her pursuit of an encyclopedic knowledge of the intellectual and cultural history of humankind. One of her favorite passages from Alexander Pope's "An Essay on Man" was from the oft-quoted second epistle: "Know then thyself, presume not God to scan, / the proper study of mankind is man." She was drawn to Emerson among the transcendentalists, to the philosophical critiques and skepticism of Thomas Carlyle and Ruskin, to the emotional depth of Percy Bysshe Shelley and Alfred Tennyson, and to the popular serial novelists Dickens and Thackeray.[39]

Spencer also owned a few books by her white modernist contemporaries—works by Dorothy Parker, Edith Wharton, Katherine Anne Porter, T. S. Eliot, Margaret Sanger, and H. L. Mencken—and she cherished her books signed by those prominent in the Harlem Renaissance, such as Georgia Douglas Johnson, W. E. B. Du Bois, Alain Locke, Langston Hughes, Zora Neale Hurston, Rayford Logan, Victor Daly and Ann Petry.

Many of Spencer's books were thoughtful gifts from others that affirmed the order she observed of "people, and then books" in creating a library.[40] Such gifts could mean many things. For example, James Weldon Johnson lovingly inscribed *God's Trombones* to Spencer with the words "For my very dear friend Anne Spencer, herself a fellow artist. James Weldon Johnson." He also sent Spencer a copy of Anita Loos's *Gentlemen Prefer Blondes* to mark what was evidently a memorable visit to the Spencer household. The inscription reads "To my dear friend Anne Spencer, with memories of the fourth visit, March 20–23, 1920. James Weldon Johnson." Spencer's library speaks to the self-invention of a modern who, like Johnson, aspired to the "high" aesthetics of modernism while also desiring to write popular, best-selling works.

A writer's library represents the regions of the imagination explored by the writer over a lifetime of circulating books and ideas. Yet it is also a physical space. While the built-in bookshelves in the parlor of 1313 Pierce Street contained many of the books that made up Spencer's library, the house also contained writing on its walls—a poem painted in the kitchen, lines of poetry in the parlor, writing next to the Spencers' bed, and phone numbers in the telephone "booth." In approaching the physicality of Spencer's words and her library, we observe her simultaneously deliberate and spontaneous creation of the space in which she brought her writing to life.[41] The physical and metaphysical dimensions of Spencer's library call on readers both to consider their imaginative relation to her world and take into account her embodied existence.[42]

Spencer's life has often been reduced to a rather precious narrative about her closeness to nature and how she took refuge in her garden. It is an account advanced both by her detractors and her supporters. Critics from the New Negro era such as Alain Locke to that of the Black Arts eras, such as David Levering Lewis dismiss her poetry as apolitical and ladylike; more recent gardening and design magazine features present her as an American exceptionalist, emphasizing her class and taste over her abiding commitment to racial awareness and civil rights advocacy. It makes for a simpler story, more appealing because it is politically neutralized, but Spencer was more outspoken than many of the attempts to describe her through her home and garden indicate.[43] Further, Spencer's centering of her writing as a means a politicized engagement is often overlooked in such features that focus on her house and garden.[44] As Shockley insists, "We must never lose sight of Spencer's garden as a material place, if we hope to take an accurate measure of its role in the black feminist aesthetics underwriting her poetry."[45]

Developing in tandem with her poetry, Spencer's garden was a physical manifestation of her imagination, an embodied reality that infiltrates her published poems and unpublished manuscripts. Her garden is not simply a metaphor for a domestic, private, apolitical, or feminine space, as it often has been suggested.[46] It is a physical, material space, not symbolic, and, as Shockley suggests, it simultaneously serves as "a retreat from *and* a model of the social world."[47] The garden and Spencer's poetry reflect the poet's will to enact a living practice of memory and environmental existence and to acknowledge human care, loss, and mortality in relation to Earth itself.

"A lot of people are good at standing on their heads in private who fall down at once in public," Spencer observes. "When I come before an audience there are 3 quest's [questions] uppermost at once: what in heaven am I doing here? 2. What on earth am I doing here? + 3. What in hell am *I* doing here! And I feel like [going] off whateve[r] it is I'm doing in public . . . !"[48] Her refusals were a conscious choice, a way of interrogating relation and assuming an empathetic position vis-à-vis the public from which she was excluded.[49] Building on Shockley's innovative way of reading Black aesthetics as fluid rather than as falling into defined forms such as "protest poetry," which allows us to "understand black aesthetics to refer to types of engagement rather than specific styles," I show how in resisting static repositories of knowledge, including the archive, Spencer offers us dynamic and transforming encounters with her words and with memory itself.[50]

In 1930, Johnson requested new material from Spencer for his revised edition of *The Book of American Negro Poetry* (1931). This request for new work became a common refrain among Spencer's admirers, anthologizers, and would-be editors. And Spencer's reply also became a refrain: "I have nothing new finished. But there are twenty-seven bits stuck in as many different places that promise something if I ever get at them."[51] As compelling as it is to think of Spencer reserving her writing for a better forum, a better publishing world, she was never finished. Despite receiving a steady stream of solicitations for new work and several proposals from editors to publish a book of her poems, Spencer turned them all down. Even her biographer was limited by the poet's own restrictions of what she would share.[52] Even as she undertook a monumental design for works begun in 1940 that she worked on over the next three decades, she wrote less than people believed or expected in a refusal that represented a potential beginning, not an ending. Her major manuscript works were not bounded by time or place, and they were unfinished because their truths were contingent and still unfolding. Her dislike of endings—which was so intense that she began her poems on the second page only to "conclude" them on the first—affirm *betweenness* as an aesthetics of relation and potential transformation.[53] "My inner life is mine," her dear friend Johnson had asserted in *Negro Americans, What Now?*, his 1935 polemic. Spencer's refusal to publish after her friend's death allowed her to maintain the integrity of her inner life—whether she wrote or not.

Anthologizing Spencer

Some of the very anthologies that debuted Spencer's work—notably James Weldon Johnson's *The Book of American Negro Poetry*, Robert T. Kerlin's *Negro Poets and Their Poems* (1923), Countee Cullen's *Caroling Dusk* (1927), and Robert Hayden's *Kaleidoscope: Poems by American Negro Poets* (1967)—have contributed to Spencer's "minor" status. She is not alone in this treatment. The critical account of women authors overall in these anthologies that their editors offer shows their marginal status. Johnson's evaluation of Spencer's verse in his 1922 anthology set the terms followed by other editors:

> She is the first woman to show so high a degree of maturity in what she wrote. There is an absence of juvenility in her work. She is less obvious and less subjective than any of her predecessors and most of her contemporaries. Economy of phrase and compression of thought are, perhaps, more characteristic of her than of any other Negro poet. At times her lines are so compact that they become almost cryptic, and have to be read more than once before they will yield their meaning and beauty. Mrs. Spencer is unique in another respect; practically none of her poetry has been motivated by race. . . . She lives in Lynchburg, and takes great pride and pleasure in the cultivation of her beautiful garden.[54]

These evaluative terms demarcate mature and juvenile, compression and (one presumes) looseness, cryptic and straightforward, and racial and race-less verse. Although any of these distinctions might give a reader pause, this last designation in particular is problematic, and it unfortunately shaped Spencer's reputation through decades of twentieth-century anthologies of African American literature, even in those edited by her contemporaries and friends.[55]

From 1922 on, Spencer is described by her editors as having "no compulsion to comment on the race issue" and as seldom "even remotely concerned with this subject." Her poetry, it is suggested, is "mildly feminist if not particularly animated."[56] Observations about her presumed disengagement from race-based themes spilled over into assessments of her form. The descriptors "cryptic" and "compressed" in the anthologies' editorial headings often suggest that her writing possesses a difficulty that is not expected and is not entirely welcome, implying that to be cryptic is not to be overtly racialist and thus political.[57] *Cavalcade: Negro American Writing from 1760 to the Present* (1971), edited by Arthur P. Davis and J. Saunders Redding, describes Spencer as "a very private person" and adds that "some of her poems are very private poems."[58] The charge that her poems are private obscures where and how protest and poetry appear in her works.[59]

Louis Untermeyer evaluates Spencer's verse in *American Poetry since 1900* (1923), contrasting her poetry to Claude McKay's in a section labeled "The Aframerican" (James Weldon Johnson and H. L. Mencken's preferred contemporary term): "Anne Spencer's work sounds the other extreme of the gamut. Her verse is remarkably restrained, closely woven, intellectually complex. 'The Wife-Woman' and 'Translation' are steeped in a philosophy that has metaphysical overtones. But there is racial opulence, an almost barbaric heat in the color of her lines."[60] Yet he did not deem these poems good enough to include them; they only are mentioned. As for the hyperbolic assessment of "barbaric heat," in his *Negro Poets and Their Poems*, editor Robert Kerlin, a white southerner, characterizes this perceived passion as representative of "the heart of Negro womanhood," "the keen sensibilities of a specially sensitive people" whose poetry would "open another avenue to the secret chambers of the Negro woman's heart."[61] Although read as a racial poet by Untermeyer and Kerlin, their readings demonstrate a narrow regard for what they perceived as Spencer's gendered contributions.

Spencer was featured in her own named section in her friend Sterling Brown's 1937 handbook *Negro Poetry and Drama*, who describes her as "the most original of all Negro women poets. Her devotion to Browning, attested by one of her best poems, 'Life-Long, Poor Browning', results in a closely-woven style that is at times cryptic, but even more often richly rewarding. She makes use of poetic tradition without being conventional, and of new styles with a regard for form; her vision and expression are those of a wise, ironic but gentle woman of her times. She is sensitive to natural beauty, praising her home-state Virginia."[62]

Countee Cullen's *Caroling Dusk*, the anthology that debuted the greatest number of new Spencer poems at one time, states bluntly that "although Anne Spencer lives in Lynchburg, Virginia, and in her biographical note recognizes the Negro as the great American taboo, I have seen but two poems by her which are even remotely concerned with this subject; rather does she write with a cool precision that calls forth comparison with Amy Lowell and the influence of a rock-bound seacoast."[63] Cullen reactively likens Spencer to Lowell, a white New Englander at the forefront of imagism, rather than to the African American women with whom she explicitly associates her identity in this anthology's biographical section. Her self-authored biography states, "I proudly love being a Negro woman—its [*sic*] so involved and interesting. We are the PROBLEM—the great national game of TABOO."[64] Spencer had not referred the taboo of being "the Negro" but rather "a Negro woman," a lively declaration of self. Cullen's statement irked Spencer for years afterward.

Anthologies from the post–World War II period repeat these diminutions of Spencer's poetry, further marginalizing its significance. Robert Hayden's 1967 anthology *Kaleidoscope: Poems by American Negro Poets* finds that "Mrs. Spencer's most engaging poems show dramatic compression and sharpness of image and phrase, though sometimes her diction is rather Victorian. Her style in general tends to be cryptic, philosophical. She is no pleader of causes. She has obviously felt no compulsion to comment on the race issue in the few poems she has been willing to publish."[65] David Levering Lewis's *The Portable Harlem Renaissance Reader* assigns a midwife role to Spencer in which she delivers other poets, describing how her "house and garden in Lynchburg, Virginia, served much the same role as Georgia Johnson's salon (Du Bois and Sterling Brown were regulars)."[66] Not only is the selection of Spencer's poetry in Lewis's anthology identical to that of Alain Locke's 1925 *The New Negro* published seventy years earlier but Lewis makes little attempt to reassess the significance of the poetry or poet.

Spencer's poems and her reputation as a poet suffer as a result of what I would describe as the "anthology effect." Spencer's characterization in these collections makes it evident that it's not so much that her poetry itself is conventional as that the anthology itself, which is a bourgeois product, conventionalized it. As Jane Kuenz observes, the "net effect" of anthologies is "to homogenize the poems included or sentimentalize them for general readers."[67] Spencer is partly to blame for the repeated use of the same poems in the anthologies, since editors, including Arna Bontemps, Robert Hayden, and Arthur P. Davis between the 1940s and early 1970s, often solicited new work, even when they also requested permission to reprint the same ones, but she never offered any. The impression created by same selection of Spencer's published poems from 1920–34 being reprinted in anthologies through the 1970s was that of a narrow author limited to sentimental, "ladylike" forms. Although pathbreaking anthologies of the New Negro era attempted to present a diversity of innovative, new authors, their evaluations gave rise to the idea of a uniform tradition. The anthologies edited by Johnson, Locke, Braithwaite, and Cullen appealed to a mass readership while simultaneously fulfilling the lofty aims of learned culture. This placed these editors in the position of having to prove a history of African American literary accomplishment that they already knew to be the case.[68]Anthologies of subsequent decades replicated these older anthologies, recycling the valuations of an era constrained by mainstream America's low regard of both African American and women authors.

Johnson had written editorials about the ongoing dilemma of publishing for African American authors in 1928 and 1929.[69] Spencer's friend J. Saunders Redding, whom she had met at Hampton Institute in 1943, updated these editorials in 1945: "By and large, published books are commercial ventures, and must be saleable. It is the publisher who must gauge the reading taste of the public and respond most sensitively to it; and it is through him that the reading public exerts a powerful influence on the methods and materials of writing. . . . Through the exertion of this control, whether conscious or unconscious, the reading public has had a tremendous effect upon books by and about Negroes."[70] The reading public was the problem *and* the solution, in Redding's view. The dilemma for African American writers was that they could either "ignore a white audience and not sell, or sell to a white audience and peddle in the exotic, limiting views whites already hold of blacks."[71] To "escape from the dilemma," according to Redding, "the Negro writer of integrity, . . . must make a common audience out of white and black America. He must believe this can be done. He must write American books for American audiences." Writing from a "racial foundation," an African American author must "make his appeal to the whole American audience." This was imperative, Redding believed. "He must do this if he is to remain true to his best creative instincts; he must do this if he is to survive as an artist. And America, both the white and black portions of it, must grant him the freedom for it. It is only in freedom that the creative man can grow. It is only when this freedom has long been established that he begins to produce his best work."[72] Redding's view of artistic success through popular forms placed emphasis on the "commercial venture" of publishing, the "reading taste" of the public, and the "exertion of control" by both. This American literary future anticipated an American political future.[73]

Editors suggested that Spencer could achieve success if she published a book of poems, the hallmark of elite modernism, rather than limiting herself to an anthologized selection of her poems directed at the masses. Sterling Brown, Arna Bontemps and Langston Hughes, and other editors who included Spencer in their anthologies often referred to the fact that she had never published a book of her poems. For example, in *The Poetry of the Negro, 1746–1948*, Bontemps and Hughes note that although her poems "have appeared in magazines and anthologies for a number of years, they have not been collected in a book."[74] Paradoxically, the value of the book of poetry Spencer never published confirmed rather than countered the slight value attributed to her few published, reprinted poems, even though it was extremely rare for an African American woman poet to publish a volume of her verses.[75] Yet the limiting views of African American literary relevance that resulted in anthologies also produced, as

Kuenz observes, "a narrative of aesthetic development that moved away from lyrics associated with a degraded and feminized genteel past and toward authentically realized folk forms linked with present and future. This narrative had even profounder effects for black women poets, who, though they accounted for roughly half of the poems published in the periodical press, disappeared under the weight of an emergent literary culture that broadly characterized their work ... as bourgeois, racially empty, and feminine."[76]

Spencer's published poetry was undercut by the emergent New Negro narrative of folk authenticity and its political relevance, which was linked with a Black working class even as it sought to appeal to a middle-class readership. Sterling Brown's *Southern Road* (1932), for example, was heralded by critics like Redding for its authentic folk and original modernist verse. While women authors struggled with reductive categorizations that limited their poetic voicings, the aesthetic innovations of male authors such as Hughes and Brown in race matters were affirmed. These authors, Spencer's friends, participated in ongoing conversations about the folk and authentic representation that took place in the South with Spencer at the center.

Spencer's "taboo" counters the homogenizing conventions of the anthology, providing an alternative understanding of the function of her poetry outside of this context. She defiantly occupies both her southern region and the imaginative expanse of her poetry, drawing on physical and metaphysical realms to create her vision of authentic expression.[77] While she continued to search for an appropriately expansive poetic voice, her refusal to publish after Johnson's death in 1938 represents her private evaluation of art in a world of her own making.

CHAPTER TWO

Routes of the Renaissance

Anne Spencer's Lynchburg Literary Circle

> The letter that you cherish becomes
> somehow a little less if answered.
>
> —ANNE SPENCER, letter to Harold Jackman, 1942

From 1918 through 1938, Spencer's home was a southern center of the Harlem Renaissance, where she regularly hosted James Weldon Johnson, the emerging poets Sterling Brown and Langston Hughes, W. E. B. Du Bois, and Georgia Douglas Johnson. Spencer was an animating force behind a modernism that drew writers to the South, shaping a mutually developing, collaborative poetics that demonstrates the shifting communal modes that created Harlem Renaissance writing. The "routes" of this chapter indicate these other sources for understanding this renaissance as well as Spencer herself. Spencer did not merely entertain at home in Lynchburg as a salon host, contrary to David Levering Lewis's characterization of her, but also traveled by car and train through the Newark, New York, and Washington, D.C., circuit and participated in African American authors' literary salons such as Georgia Douglas Johnson's Saturday Nighters in Washington, D.C., and James Weldon and Grace Nail Johnson's gatherings of literati in Harlem.[1]

Spencer's spatial, geographic, and imaginative correspondence with Johnson, Brown, Hughes, and Georgia Douglas Johnson demonstrates their diverse creative engagements as well as their common concerns. Their correspondence, both in person in meetings of literary circles and through the exchange of letters, led to the creation, exchange, publication, and distribution of finished works from this period, placing Spencer at the center of a group of writers who were deeply interested in understanding authentic southern folk culture. Through Spencer, they engaged in the creation of social networks that encouraged their mutual development as readers and authors in the decades of the New Negro Renaissance's literary formation and climax. Spencer's network facilitated physical travel as well as imaginative expansion, from providing a safe space for writers as they traveled to the South to providing a forum for their ideas. Their interactions led to sustaining relationships with one another and the cultivation of their works. While some attention has been paid to Georgia Douglas Johnson's Washington, D.C., literary circle, the Saturday Nighters, Spencer's Lynchburg circle has received little in-depth critical consideration.[2] Yet her Lynchburg circle was crucial to Georgia Douglas Johnson herself, among others including James Weldon Johnson, Brown, and Hughes. Spencer's literary circle helped advance the idea of a vernacular *culture* if not its language—the idea of the local, material circumstances of regional African American culture—in these poets' works as they formed a national aesthetic that sought to "invent the New Negro."[3]

In the Lynchburg reading circle, friends such as Johnson, Du Bois, Walter White, Brown, Hughes, and Douglas Johnson, among others, cultivated communal virtues in and through her garden. The reading circle, an informal affair that got under way after Johnson's arrival in Lynchburg in 1918, continued over the most significant years of the Renaissance (1926–27), and stretched into the late 1930s, was often contingent on the travel plans of her out-of-town friends. Developed in tandem, Spencer's garden and reading circle were spaces in which to practice public modes of human interaction, a way for Spencer and her friends to "make [themselves] . . . at home on an earth that does not necessarily make room for [them]."[4] The garden itself was positioned by Spencer as a staging ground for human action via more public modes of expression. As Elizabeth McHenry notes, "African American literary societies were formed not only as places of refuge for the self-improvement of their members but as acts of resistance to the hostile racial climate that made the United States an uncomfortable and unequal place for all black Americans, regardless of their social or economic condition. . . . [T]he members of these literary societies sought effective avenues of public access as well as ways to voice their demands for full citizenship and equal participation in the life of the nation."[5] Spencer's reading circle was strongly linked to the polis and to the public, connected to the surrounding city of Lynchburg, the state of Virginia, and the southern United States, and it promoted the circulation of human lives and cultural materials through the southern locale of Lynchburg, emphasizing the political and engaged nature of space.[6]

The Folk: A "Return to the Earth"

When in 1939 the critic J. Saunders Redding suggested that Harlem was a "disease" that had blighted the concept of African American literature, he was faulting a distorted idea of a collective New Negro culture based in Harlem that displaced a diverse body of African Americans:

> What happened in Negro literature from the appearance of Carl Van Vechten's *Nigger Heaven* in 1926 until 1935 is obvious. First of all, Negro writers, both poets and novelists, centered their attentions so exclusively upon life in the great urban centers that the city, especially Harlem, became an obsession with them. Now Harlem life is far from typical of Negro life; indeed, life there is lived on a theatri-

cal plane that is as far from true of Negro life elsewhere as life in the Latin Quarter is from the truth of life in Picardy. The Negro writers' mistake lay in the assumption that what they saw was Negro life, when in reality it was just Harlem life. Very shortly, for literary purposes anyway, Harlem became a sort of disease in the American organism.[7]

African American literary realism was, in Redding's view, the cure for the disease. What was needed was art that emanated from true Black life and living, which in Redding's view was folksy at its core: "It is this that must happen; a spiritual and physical return to the earth. For Negroes are yet an earthly people, a people earth-proud—the very salt of the earth. Their songs and stories have arisen from a loving bondage to the earth, and to it now they must return. It is to this, for pride, for strength, for endurance, that they must go back."[8] Such a return was geographical as much as it was cultural, as fuller means of expression could be drawn from the well of folk forms and a mass cultural experience that were to be found in regions outside of Harlem. While the innovation in artistic expression from the period had aesthetic significance, the cultural and political power that could be derived from such "earthly people" was even more crucial. Curing the disease that was Harlem meant displacing the pervasive stereotypical idea of the folk that much Harlem Renaissance literature had supported. What was needed was a balanced portrayal of regional and working-class experience that generated political power for both the folk subject and the author.

Redding saw such a balanced and politically determined portrayal of "an earthly people" was found in poet Sterling Brown's 1932 *Southern Road*. Yet that book, which Brown dedicated to Spencer as well as his mother, originated *through* Spencer. Spencer had provided a young Brown with the opportunity to participate in her southern literary circle, where his folk forms came into being well after he arrived in Lynchburg in 1923 to assume a teaching post at the Virginia Seminary, fresh out of Harvard. Spencer's home in the South provided Brown, Johnson, Hughes, and others who visited individually over the years, with opportunities to develop a variety of folk personae and diverse perspectives on the representation of regional Black culture in a national culture.

In Lynchburg's literary circle, Spencer and her guests discussed history, literature, literary tradition, new books, articles, essays, editorials, short stories, poems, academic studies, and literary anthologies. Discussing older traditions dating back to classical writers such as Socrates and Cicero, these authors as readers also engaged the idea of new traditions, especially as it related citizenship, territory, and habitation in the New Negro era—not simply in connection with urban, northern locations but the nation as a whole. Based in the North, South, and the nation's capital, Johnson, Brown, Douglas Johnson, and others moved through each other's spaces and through the imaginative regions of their works. Brown's, Langston Hughes's, and James Weldon Johnson's diverse stances on African American culture and expression in literature as reflected in Brown's Big Boy, Hughes's Simple and his blues beats, and Johnson's "old time Negro preacher" of his sermonic poems were not as at odds as the polemical Redding would have it. Their works should not be viewed as showing ideological progressions of thought but rather as highlighting differences that enhanced each author's representations of vernacular culture.

As Sonya Posmentier, Daphne Lamothe, and Eve Dunbar have pointed out from distinct interpretative angles, the New Negro Renaissance invented a language of discursive divides in order to advance a uniform framework for modern Black culture, and such divides between agrarian and industrial, rural and urban, have been perpetuated in critical studies of this period. Yet Spencer's Lynchburg literary circle and her garden provided geographic, intellectual, and political routes for exploration that were not informed by such oppositions.[9] Spencer's home in Lynchburg was both an affirmation of humanity and an acknowledgment of humanity's demand for a place on Earth. Her reading circle embodied a sociality that was relevant beyond the space of her garden; it was a reminder that "the civic world is what its citizens make of it through their own acts and decisions."[10]

Spencer created a practice-based ecology through her reading circle, one through which she and her participants could begin to imagine and theorize transnational, national, and regional ways that Black culture could belong, and at the same time made the communal culture she fostered more expansive. She cultivated communal culture in the same way she cultivated her garden, a comparison that advances rather than simplifies understanding of the writing produced in and through this space. Spencer's reading circle was a place where life could be reimagined, possibilities reconceived: a place where human and social virtues that had been suppressed could grow under careful watch. "Friendship, conversation, gratitude, spiritual tranquility are not private pleasures but virtues cultivated communally," Robert Harrison writes.[11] Spencer's reading circle produced *congruent experiences*, akin to those yielded by the "rational religion" Spencer describes in "Why Read Books?," that enabled its participants to imagine their works being read and appreciated by diverse audiences.[12] Through their diverse poetic processes, Spencer and her friends created a temporality for and gave a future reach to the African American subjects they discussed. In a letter to Hughes, she writes,

> We have nine *new* birds—one named Langston—quite too proud of his black and
> gold-bronze plumage, another pair George Jean and Mencken so yclept because
> of a certain spurious bitterness,—mostly pose. These gents are licked thoroly sev-

eral times a day by a nutmeg finch, thimble-size, truculent and motley known as Le Moor. Do come and meet these feathered persons. Bring a friend if you like. Love from me, and us, Anne Spencer.[13]

Spencer named the birds who visited her garden after the Smart Set editors Mencken and George Jean and after handsome Langston, while the name Le Moor is a homonym of "l'amour," effectively combining the word "love" and the idea of Blackness. These playful and yet meaningful acts of naming brought literature and nonhuman animals together in her garden space.

Sterling Brown

The major movements of Sterling Brown's *Southern Road*—from "Road So Rocky" to "On Restless River" to "Tin Roof Blues" to, finally, "Vestiges"—trace sources and movements of Black folk experience through geographic and natural and urban settings ("road," "river," "roof"). Brown's "To a Certain Lady, in Her Garden," his poem about Spencer, appears in part 4, "Vestiges." One wonders whether by "vestiges," he is referring to the remnants of Victorianism in his early poems such as "The Fall of the Year" or to the folk residue that he discovered in Lynchburg. It is also unclear what, exactly, was vestigial about Spencer or her garden, but it seems most likely that the section's title is a reference to the remnants of a living folk culture made available to Brown through Spencer and Lynchburg, the folk that would become the foundation of his poetry and shape his distinctive poetic view.

Brown was introduced to Spencer by one his students, and she immediately became, in his words, a "teacher" to him, as his correspondence to her in the summer months of 1927, after he had left Lynchburg and move the Jefferson City, Missouri, where had taken a teaching position at Lincoln University, makes abundantly clear.[14] He greatly missed the "real cup of coffee" of 1313 Pierce Street.[15] The image of the two poets convening in her home with cups of strong coffee to discuss intellectual history, politics, their literary projects, and her garden underscores the intimate, cozy nature of her reading circle.

Affirming their shared reading and conversation, Brown writes, "I miss my *Saturday Review* of Saturdays, my *New Republic* of Mondays, and my conversations with a gardener of any days." He tells Spencer he has "been reading much good fiction, some sociology and philosophy. The sociology is furthering my rebellion; the philosophy is teaching me how little I know; the fiction is showing me how to write the books I never shall write." The fiction category includes short stories by Gorky, Swift's *Gulliver's Travels*, and Toomer's *Cane* for the second time, which, he says, "is an urge in the right direction."[16] He asks Spencer for a copy of the 1926 issue of *Palms*, a poetry magazine published in Guadalajara, Mexico, that was guest edited by Countee Cullen and featured the poetry of African Americans, and reports that he's entering the *Nation*'s poetry contest with a poem about Big Boy and sending some material to *New Masses*. He writes as an appreciator of Spencer's commentaries on readings, events, and his poetry. "One must be armed at all points against the keen strokes of your irony," he observes. "I'm weaponless. I throw myself on your mercy."

Brown reflected on the importance of his relationship with Spencer on the occasion of 1313 Pierce Street's dedication as a historic landmark in 1977:

> Over half a century ago, a student of mine at Virginia Theological Seminary and College, Anne Spencer's alma mater, brought me to this house and introduced me to Anne Spencer. I was already acquainted with her work, through reading several of her poems in James Weldon Johnson's *Book of American Negro Poetry*, published in 1922, the year of my graduation from college. My student friend and others at Seminary insisted on my meeting her, praising her individuality, her intelligence, her charm.
>
> After meeting her, I soon discovered that their high praise did not do her justice. I was a young teacher, just out of college, and an aspiring writer. With her gracious hospitality she made me feel at home; there in long conversation with her mother, her husband Edward, and her family, I learned a great deal. I was struck by her wide reading, her pithy, ironic comments on mankind, her independence. She was devoted to her family, to the life of the mind, and to things of beauty, such as her famed garden. In one of my earliest poems, "To a Certain Lady, In Her Garden," written fifty years ago, I tried to pay tribute to the kind of person that she was. Today I only add: Anne Spencer was a person of unusual gifts of heart and mind; a good friend and teacher.
>
> Twenty years ago in *Negro Poetry and Drama*, I wrote of Anne Spencer as "a wise, ironic gentle woman, sensitive to natural beauty" whose "keenly observant poems should be collected for a wider audience." I was by no means alone in estimating her quality. Louis Untermeyer praised her poetry as "remarkably restrained, closely woven, intellectually complex." James Weldon Johnson praised her "maturity, objectivity, and compression of thought." Countee Cullen praised her "cool precision." Her poems and her prose (essays, commentaries, etc) should be collected, edited, and published.
>
> As wife and mother, poet, and person Anne Spencer richly deserves the honors coming to her today.[17]

In 1927, fifty years before, Brown reports to Spencer that he has "written—finished it yesterday another of the sonnets, and three new poems have taken form—one, *Farmer Brown is Riled at His Boy*; another, *The Poet Spills His Tea at the Literary Society*."[18] While dismissive of the posturing of the literary society as an idea, Brown in practice was a grateful participant in Spencer's reading circle.

Well before the publication of Brown's debut (and only) poetry collection, *Southern Road* in 1932, Brown gathered his poems together in a private "book" for Spencer to read. He kept different colored notebooks for his writing—gray, green, and brown. In a slow-moving letter that covers a lot of ground, Brown asks Spencer not to "trouble" "about the Brown Book. I'd like you to have it awhile—I want you to edit a selection of those you want, and I'll copy them in such a book for you. Yes, I do ask a great deal. I just wanted the Brown Book to scrape together the rest of the sonnets with those in it." He promises that he will return to the "'South' shortly" and that he would "like to bring three new sonnets, and *Two Dollars*, and *Annie Dabney* finished." Brown also mentions that he is planning to try to get "To a Certain Lady in Her Garden" published in *Century* Magazine. When he writes Spencer this letter, Brown is on the cusp of his long career as a poet, author, and spokesperson for the blues and the folk, and he clearly conveys that he held Spencer in high esteem, regarding her as a wise elder and editor of his young verse.

One of his sonnets, titled "October Idyll," with a nod to Tennyson's *Idylls* but carrying the title "Fall of the Year" in manuscript form, is copied in Brown's hand into the back of Spencer's copy of fellow Lynchburg poet Murrell Edmunds's *Poems* (1924) and signed by him:

> I know now why autumnal shrubs and flowers
> Are passional tinted, why the autumn yields
> A wealth of goldenrod, and profuse dowers
> Of broom and sumach to impoverished fields.
> I know now why saffron of sycamores
> And scarlet of oaks leap forth from woodland ways
> And why in riot about cottage doors
> Dahlias glow duskily, and cannas blaze.
>
> Proud and magnificent until the end
> Autumn departs in passionate endeavor
> Against the fact of dying.... Listen, friend
> Thus learn I from belated tenderness.
> So rich it was, with a wild loveliness
> Although prophetical of winter, ever....[19]

Spencer later described Murrell Edmunds as a writer who insinuated himself into poetic circles with all of the presumption of a FFV, that is, a first family of Virginia. He was a member of the Lynchburg interracial group of poets that Johnson had been invited to address and had apparently insisted on being introduced to him.[20]

Writing Brown after he had moved to Jefferson City, Missouri, to take a teaching position at Lincoln University, Spencer states that she writes from

"Lynchburg-on-the-Pathetic." She's thrilled to hear that her suggestions for editorial revision to his poetry have paved the way for their publication in Cullen's anthology *Caroling Dusk*:

Darling Professor—I've worried a lot Because of my delinquencies toward you. Wanting to say how I preen myself over your Opportunity sweepstakes, and that I made, —and of course, Cullen accepted, the changes you suggested for my sonnet. And thank you! So afraid not writing to you would mean to you that I was suffering from the usual stricken variety of poetesses who left-handedly ask for constructive criticism, right-handedly mean "praise me some praises, please!"

July 18—So far I'd got on this effusion when your kind sweet nice coals of fire, arose this a.m., this sounds like a lady lie—but it's so truthly I shan't even protest. I've been thinking about you and bragging around about "ma'ching saints"— took the book over to Danville one Sun, to show a friend who'd appreciate its genuineness. Not the least prideful feeling was, that, sadly too, it belonged to me at Lynchburg. The last poem of our talks almost, proving the first big thing of your certain career. No. I have not been so happy, I am more and more tormented by, even limited, enslaved by my too many blessings. Too much to release, too little to hold. I sound like a fool and a woman. Yet you might see it a speech. I think the psychology, pardon, is based on my fierce hatred for this rus-urbe [punning on reserve? Or rural-urban city?] in which I find myself til death. Sure, I'm happy feel better already! . . . We, Pa and I, go to New York about August 15, I'd just love it if we could say a howdy do to you somewhere.

There are many new crops of poets since we (you and I) have gone. The instant one says, pome [*sic*] to me nowadays, I want to fight 'em. I had to read one the other day, "Jesus and Lindbergh"—now you see.

Jeems sent us a copy of *God's Trombones*. Do you like it? I think he introduced an element of farce into "Listen Lord," by use of word Turpentine. "Go Down Death["] is immensely popular. "By the Fireside," too

I envy your teaching Browning. Read the niggers, also—"I'm a Gondola" and the cycle of poems under general title, *James Lee's Wife*; *One Word More*, etc. hope to go over them together sometime.

Miss Weeden leaves for Charleston, W. Va., Y. W. conference, 10 days, one hour lecture on helpless Negro Poets, per day. A lecture a day will keep the devil away! Shall save your *phish* poem to show Al.

I was in Hampton in March—almost got to see your boy—twice.

What did you send Cullen for his Anthol? Pshaw! The reason I can't write is cause there's too much to say. Your letter helped clear my sky. Do write at once, and never think I'd take umbrage. The test was when you were here & gave me plenty tryouts + getting sulks or insults or somethin'. I am often lonely. Do write without counting letters. Your Black April review was splendid. Hope to see my part of the dedication soon. Want you to meet Zilla Warren.[21]

In a single letter, Spencer dispels the many misunderstandings that a later body of critics assigned to her. She travels to New York and to Hampton; she offers criticism to other poets, rather than simply receiving it; and she reveals that among these critical conversations, Big Boy Davis, who became Brown's distinct folk persona for his innovative new poetry of the folk, grew out of their Lynchburg talks—"ma'ching saints," "the last poem of our talks almost, proving the first big thing of your certain career," refers to the first Big Boy Davis poem, "When de Saints Go Mach'ing Home"—and a separate letter to Johnson reveals that the man himself lived in Lynchburg.[22]

Spencer was a passionate advocate of Brown's poetry. Witness this letter from Cullen, at the time assistant editor at *Opportunity*, to Brown:

> My dear Mr. Brown
>
> The unexpected pleasure of having Anne Spencer and her husband call at the office yesterday reminded me smartly that I owed you at least a note and the return of your poems. Of those poems which you said I might keep for use in OPPORTUNITY, I am holding "Thoughts of Death." "Long Gone" instead of use in the magazine is to appear in the Anthology.
>
> Mrs. Spencer was lavish in her praise and enthusiasm for your work, and I was happy to be able to join in quite sincerely with her.[23]

Cullen had originally written Brown in May to say that of the poems he had sent him for consideration for the anthology, he was going to use "Maumee Ruth," "Odyssey of Big Boy," "Salutamus," "Challenge," and "Return" and that he was "keeping for subsequent use in OPPORTUNITY, 'To Christine, Thought Dying,' 'To Certain Negresses,' 'Thoughts of Death,' and 'October Fable.'" Spencer's visit to the New York office of Opportunity during the trip she mentioned to Brown in her previous letter perhaps led him to decide to include "Long Gone" in the anthology as well. The reference to "the return of your poems" suggests he sent back "To Christine, Thought Dying," "To Certain Negresses," and "October Fable," none of which were ever published in *Opportunity* or anywhere. "October Fable" survives on the back of Spencer's copy of Murrell's collection of poems, but the other two have been lost. "Thoughts of Death" was published in *Opportunity* in 1926 as well as in *Southern Road*.[24]

Spencer's magnetic personality was such that Cullen decided he wanted to visit Lynchburg following her New York visit to the office of *Opportunity*. In a letter, he expresses admiration for her writing and hope that he might "see that garden in the flesh" and thanks her for her "gallant" "biographical notice": "I wish all the poets who are to be represented in my anthology had your note to be guided by."[25] Alice Dunbar-Nelson shared Cullen's high regard. Following the anthology's publication, Cullen shared with Spencer the "delightful tribute paid to you by Alice Dunbar Nelson in her review of Caroling Dusk." Commenting on the work that she liked best in the collection, she ends with "and best of all,

Anne Spencer. Anne Spencer of the unforgettable line, cool, aloof, dispassionate, turning Browning's immortal thought and verse into even more poignant beauty and immortalizing the diving girl at the street carnival. This last surely one of the loveliest poems I have read.'"[26]

In the summer of 1927, Brown confesses to Spencer that he has sought out her conversation so often that he doesn't "feel certain about writing you. You have had so much garrulity of mine that I might have a heart during the hot months." Finding himself in the small Virginia town of Laurel, Brown admits that he "fret[s] the folks there as I feared I would. I don't want to, but I do. I'm phoney, I guess. But even Laurel gets to me. I've a restlessness and I don't understand it."[27] He had moved on from the vivacious setting of 1313 Pierce Street and had not yet quite found his footing, which the poet Alain Locke would later describe in the editorial forward to *Negro Poetry and Drama* as "a critical talent of sane but progressive and unacademic tendencies."[28] But within five years of this reflection on the folk he had published *Southern Road*. He had discovered his folk source in Lynchburg, as Spencer notes in a letter to Johnson: "Sterling has scoured the town to find 'Big Boy Davis' and succeeded—you know, of the 'Saints go marching home' fame. He can really make complete orchestration on his 'box' of John Henry and the rest, barring an *odor* like a load of moldy hay, I found him delectable—."[29] Spencer praised the Lynchburg native's vocal range and adeptness on his primitive guitar—"box"—as exemplified in his street performance of the John Henry ballad, and she was physically close enough to him to breathe his "odor." In an interview with Greene Spencer recalls how Brown and her husband, Edward, borrowed Davis from the Lynchburg jail for the night, bringing him back to 1313 Pierce Street to perform, and "returning" him at the end of the evening.[30] John "Big Boy" Davis features prominently in Brown's blues "odyssey" named for him.

Langston Hughes

Spencer's friendship with Hughes demonstrates the extension of the 1920s reading circle's ecological virtues into the decades of the 1930s, 1940s, and 1950s. Shortly after Brown left Lynchburg and the Virginia Seminary, Hughes arrived, visiting Spencer's home in 1927.[31] Spencer's relationship with Hughes strengthened over the years despite the brevity of his stay in Lynchburg. Throughout the 1940s, Spencer expressed her support for Hughes's poetry collections and repeatedly invited him to visit her home. In 1942, shortly after the publication of Hughes's *Shakespeare in Harlem*, Spencer addresses Hughes by his full name in an affirmation of his public identity in a letter she had delivered to him through a young person whose identity is not known but who was apparently a Lynchburg native living in Harlem: "Dear Langston Hughes, I'm on tonight in the same little library, we think your Shakespeare in Harlem is grand fun good poetry and a very special evaluation. I'm so glad this young friend came to say he lives in striking distance of where you are, so's I can send this note on to you."[32] Hughes in return invited Spencer to the readings he gave at Hampton Institute, which she occasionally attended. Hughes and Bontemps were among Spencer's anthologizers of the 1940s. Hughes also was responsible for the translation of two of Spencer's poems into Spanish in the 1950s.

Hughes encouraged Spencer to write, publishing a poem titled "Anne Spencer's Table" about the unsharpened pencil that sits on a "certain lady's" desk in 1930.[33] Spencer's rejoinder to Hughes, unpublished, written within the year of solicitation, acknowledges her failure to rise to his challenge:

> [Dear Langston]
> and *that* is what my days
> have brought . . .
> and this: lamp, odorless oil
> round its long
> dried wick:
> Hope without wings
> Love itself contemned
> Where Michael broods,—
> Arc after arc, you see,
> If any where I own
> A circle it is one
> frustrate beginning—

In a 1939 letter, Spencer references her failure to write and implores him to visit. "My dear Langston—Please don't hate old ladies in general or me in particular. We are the reapers and gardeners of life's big, never failing crop of misery. Not so well since I saw you sorta lethargic, and 'just poorly, thank the Lord,' this spring. Need is, I'm sure, some alien tone, fresh view paint. So *do do* come on, as you promised. I cannot go to Hampton as I hoped and desire but you can come to the mountains."[34] Her emphasis on older women as the "reapers and gardeners" of life, which includes misery, recalls the outlook of her poem "Substitution," which, as she notes in a letter to Johnson, reflects the philosophy that "no living thing can escape suffering."[35] Spencer refrains this idea in the face of World War II and her own frailty.

Hughes's work also literally figured in the connection Spencer forged between physical and imaginative spaces. Spencer not only named birds in her garden after members of her literary circle but also pinned their correspondences to the wall of her garden house, Ed-an-kraal, constructed sometime between 1939 and 1943 in the backyard garden of 1313 Pierce Street, in another physical manifestation of the imaginative cohabitation of her circle in this space. The pergola that runs the width of the garden had been built before the cabin, and in the period of the cabin's construction, Spencer's husband, Edward, began building his signature birdhouses. In the same letter that the young friend hand delivered to Hughes, Spencer notes that she "showed him your 20 grand poem you were lovely to send last year, on the wall in our garden house" and in another letter to Carl Van Vechten, she writes, "Langston sends me an occasional card which goes on the wall in the garden house Pa built."[36]

Hughes meant so much to Spencer that she went so far as to experiment in writing a poem in the sensibility and voice of Hughes at the ripe age of seventy-six. It was the watershed year of 1958—the centenary of Lincoln's "House Divided" speech and the lead up to Black writers' reflections on John Brown's rebellion at Harpers Ferry in the push for Civil Rights. Carrying forward what in the same letter hand delivered by the young friend she refers to as her "communings" with Langston, the thoughts he would know she was having even though she left them unsaid ("those one never writes," she observes, "but thinks the other fellow should know all about 'em"), Spencer references her "telepathing": "there's that very real thing of telepathing or being psychic: I'd read a piece in Times Sun. Mag. (on Grand Canyon and all crazy began to scribble some lines I thought could be made into the execrable rock n roll or Blues by Langston."[37] In a similar vein, as her observing to Jackman that "the letter that you cherish becomes somehow a little less if answered" suggests, the letter not sent but merely thought presents a challenge to her reader: to read for the spaces between correspondence while acknowledging the material difficulties of unearthing African American women's writing in the archives. Spencer's material legacy demonstrates an author's active engagement in archiving her creative practices—including the redacted, the unfinished, and the unanswered—as part of a larger intellectual history of fugitive thought. Readers must reach beyond the physical letters to discover the gaps as well as the "tucked away" in order to comprehend her worldly and metaphysical concerns. Spencer indicates the necessity of space in which a felt response to a letter is formed, a space more profound than a perfunctory reply.

By the time Spencer was experimenting in penning a Hughes-esque poem, Hughes had been confirmed as the poetry deputy of African America to the nation through his blues orientation. As with any person who occupies a position of cultural authority, Hughes was regarded ambivalently by Black Americans, and the resentment toward him and dismissive treatment of his poetry on the grounds that it was out of step with the political project of Civil Rights grew during the last years of his life, particularly as poets like Leroi Jones/Amiri Baraka and other Black Arts Movement poets came to prominence. But Hughes remained a source of inspiration to Spencer; she viewed him as a poet with a distinct and powerful ethos, an ethos that informed her experiment with a grand-scale public history of African American liberation struggles.

Georgia Douglas Johnson

In October 1926 Gwendolyn Bennett, in the pages of her arts column for *Opportunity*, noted "little knots of literary devotees" in places outside of New York.[38] The Saturday Nighters at Georgia Douglas Johnson's house in Washington, D.C., one of the groups mentioned, was in full swing by the time of Bennett's acknowledgment, and the group's meetings continued for another decade, slowing in the late 1930s and continuing intermittently through the 1940s. Among the many attendees were Spencer, Du Bois, and James Weldon Johnson. In her later years, Spencer recalled at least one occasion where the three rode together by car, with Du Bois at the wheel, from Lynchburg to D.C.[39] Partial lists have been cobbled together of Douglas Johnson's literary circle that give a sense of the range of her visitors from among those that made up the broad network of the New Negro Renaissance.[40] Many of the poets of the up-and-coming, new literary vanguard whose works appear in Cullen's innovative *Caroling Dusk* were members of Douglas Johnson's literary circle. Spencer met new authors at these get-togethers, a number of whom later visited her at her Lynchburg home, like Effie Lee Newsome. Her home became a destination in their southern travels. Both women's literary circles demonstrate the dynamic networks of exchange propelled by place. Douglas Johnson and Spencer have been viewed as "in place," unmoving. Yet each of these women fostered the powerful movement of ideas, people, and affiliations through their literary circles, enabling the transformation of intimate conversation into public discourses such as newspapers articles, essays in literary journals, poetry, and reviews and into local and national civic engagements.

Spencer and Douglas Johnson's writing and social networks, which they established and strengthened through their literary circles, generated a vital connection between the two women. Their writing is not at all alike, but the two authors were engaged in the same political project, and they forged an alignment through radically different expressions. They were sustained by each other's attempts in their writing to address the "taboo" of "being a Negro woman," as Spencer had described it in her biographical entry for *Caroling Dusk*.

Douglas Johnson also provided Spencer with her first opportunity to experiment with a new form, the one H. L. Mencken encouraged her to take up: prose commentary.[41] Spencer's March 1929 review in the *Crisis* of Douglas Johnson's poetry collection *An Autumn Love Cycle*—one of her first and her only published prose review—marks an important threshold in both women's writing. Douglas Johnson, in her poetry, and Spencer, in her prose review, acknowledge the politicized, challenging nature of writing about and affirming Black women's perspectives, feelings, and personhood.[42] The review features Spencer's signature declarative and yet open-ended phrases in a positive evaluation of Douglas Johnson's work. The book is innovative in form and substance, Spencer finds. Spencer observes that it is challenging to write about Black women and love stripped of cliché and stereotype linked to primitivism but that Douglas Johnson's decision to do so is a powerful one. To "write of love without hypothecating atavistic jungle tones: the rumble of tom-tom, voodoo ebo, fetish of sagebrush and high spliced palm tree" is to reinvent the language of love and its speaking subject as well.

The "daring[ness]" of Douglas Johnson's work, as Spencer vigorously presents it in her review, is the elemental lyricism of an individual Black woman's subjectivity in an evolving emotional landscape whose metaphors of nature do not rely on stereotypical characterizations of Black love. The very innovation of *An Autumn Love Cycle*, according to Spencer, is that it asserts Black female personhood through nature images that appear to represent that personhood as aspecific and universal but that is in fact political. An undated manuscript reflection elaborates on her review: "Women in my day," she notes, "wrote weakly of love—because of excess pardon, expectation on the subject—'they' kept love in a state of infancy—and they stayed there with it."[43]

Spencer's review of Douglas Johnson's *An Autumn Love Cycle* underscores her high regard of her friend's poetry and the value of Black women's lyrical contributions in the Harlem Renaissance period, which have often been reduced to the condescending category of woman poet, a characterization that was common, it should be noted, during the Harlem Renaissance and that likewise appears in critical accounts of the period.[44] Spencer's review is significant because it demonstrates her unfulfilled project of creating an appropriate evaluative language in prose to discuss African American women's lives and their writing.[45] The challenge more broadly for Black authors like Brown and Hughes who regularly wrote for newspapers was to generate an evaluative language that countered racial spectacle.

Spencer, the New Negro Mencken

Spencer's manuscript reflections confirm that Mencken encouraged Spencer to write prose. "When I was young with a younger family, I was a scrap scribbler in pencil, so now there is nothing save a whetted gnawing hope of doing what H. L. Mencken advised me once: Prose pieces my mind has chewed on for a decade or so."[46] Early on in her experimentations in prose writing, Spencer styled herself as a black female Mencken. This authorial persona was exciting to Walter White and to James Weldon Johnson precisely because there was no such voice among the women authors of the period. Acknowledgment of Spencer's presence and promise in the Harlem Renaissance was predicated on this projected but largely unrealized prose writing. She would be more than a satirist, although this voice itself would be noteworthy owing to her gender. She would be an iconoclast and use her marginal position as a "Negro woman" and a "taboo" to expose the maddening contradictions and shortcomings of her nation. Such critiques would lay bare—not without controversy—the reality of a shared national *and* racial identity. This writing would reveal the pervasiveness of sexual transgression by white men in the nation, the state of Virginia, and Lynchburg itself. African Americans continued to bear the brunt of those transgressions in a highly fraught environment in which lynching was always a threat.

An unpublished self-reflection titled "Taboo" was revised by Cullen for the biographical statement that appears in *Caroling Dusk*. The original manuscript version reads as follows:

> Being a Negro Woman is the world's most exciting game of "Taboo": By hell there is nothing you can do that you want to do and by heaven you are going to do it anyhow—We do not climb into the jim crow galleries of scenario houses [theaters] we stay away and read I read garden and seed catalogs, Browning, Housman, Whitman, Saturday Evening Post detective tales, Atlantic Monthly, American Mercury, Crisis, Opportunity, Vanity Fair, Hibberts Journal, oh, anything. I can cook delicious things to eat ... we have a lovely home—one that money did not buy—it was born and evolved slowly out of our passionate, poverty-stricken agony to our own home. *Happiness*[47]

Spencer's discussion of the "taboo" of being a Negro woman was inspired, I believe, by Mencken's corrective, *In Defense of Women*, that supported women's right to vote. In this book, which he had revised and updated for a 1922 edition that is part of Spencer's library, Mencken remarks on Americans' "unprecedented dislike for novelty in the domain of the intellect."[48] Such "illicit ideas are construed as *attentats* against democracy, which, in a sense, perhaps they are. For democracy is grounded upon so childish a complex of fallacies that they must be protected by a rigid system of taboos, else even half-wits would argue it to pieces. Its first concern must thus be to penalize the free play of ideas."[49]

Spencer was particularly interested in what she saw as a link between Mencken's ironic critique of democracy and African American women's labor and creativity. There was "the growing disposition of American women to regard all routine labor, particularly in the home, as *infra dignitatem* and hence intolerable," Mencken notes.[50] Spencer underlined the following passage: "A woman's disinclination to acquire the intricate expertness that lies at the bottom of good housekeeping is due primarily to her active intelligence; it is difficult for her to concentrate her mind upon such stupid and meticulous enterprises."[51] When Spencer later remarked to her biographer Greene that she never washed one of her husband's shirts, she was making this point rather speaking the literal truth. She was referencing Mencken's description of this disposition of the modern woman and privileging the crucial importance of black women turning away from domestic labor to think and lead on behalf of

African Americans and America. For Spencer, the New Negro was a category that included women.

The Negro woman, according to Spencer, is at the heart of America's taboos, and she is able break them by revealing the truth and dispelling the crippling myths and fears that marginalize her. Utterly cast out, she can do what she is prevented from doing in the world that has cast her out. It's a paradoxical freedom, of course; but it also holds the key to a future in which Black women are less constrained in their ability to publicly express themselves and are more recognized. This view of African American women recalls Spencer's poem "Sybil Warns Her Sister" and inflects a reading of it with Spencer's race-specific "taboo."

Johnson, White, and Mencken all spoke very highly of her unpublished review of "In a Thicket," a short story by Glenway Wescott published in the *Dial* featuring African American characters, in an effort to foster what they saw as Spencer's aptitude for evaluative prose. This review was an exhibit of what Spencer was capable of. The author of the short story, she writes, "presents us with three ages of man: the girl fifteen, the Negro of middle-age, the girl's aged grandfather. Each character is a recluse, the girl by resignation, the Negro by force, the grandfather from choice."[52] Even though it was never published, Spencer emphasized it precisely because it was her attempt at writing prose in a Mencken-style voice.

By 1930 Spencer had promised Johnson and Mencken more prose. She wrote several reviews in the late 1940s but only published one of them.[53] Mencken's mere presence as an interested reader both inspired and intimidatingly influenced Spencer's literary vision, voice, and personae. His feedback was blunt and unvarnished. Johnson and White were more encouraging. By 1934, she acknowledges that she owes Johnson "one American novel & intend to pay within the year—or forever shut up." She felt "encouraged" to do it.[54] Through conversation with them she had come up with an idea: a Black *Main Street*, set in Lynchburg: "a quiet, sympathetic satire on the social life of the Negro here in Main Street."[55] Both Johnson and White were thrilled with the idea and continually encouraged her to write it.

It was a short step from Mencken's style to Sinclair Lewis's. *Main Street* (1920) made a big mark on the American literary scene, and most likely there were many African American writers who envied its literary acclaim and aspired to write their own great American novel, one that would provide insight into the American social order. Spencer's idea for a Main Street story set in Lynchburg was unique, though, and Johnson and White recognized this: it would depict and analyze southern black life in a modern vein, breaking from the typical literary conventions that attached themselves to Black southernness. Moreover, it would offer the point of view of a modern Black southern woman.

There are few novels from the New Negro Renaissance that feature African American southern women who remained in the South. As Robert Stepto, Farah Jasmine Griffin, and others have shown, the migration narrative, or narratives of ascent and descent, dominated the modern century's narrative of African Americans. African American writers matched the reality of the Great Migration with the desire to invent a new self, a "New Negro," distanced from the close history of enslavement. That self, as Houston Baker, Daphne Lamothe, and others have shown, was tied to the invention of a homogeneous black culture that, although largely fictitious, could advance the collective pursuit of equality and citizenship. What Spencer proposed had no peer. A Black woman satirist? A novel set in the South that called out racial and sexual taboos for what they were? As Spencer noted while reading Mencken's exposure of American lies, "The most mischievous liars are those who keep sliding on the verge of truth."[56] A satirist could lay bare that mischief and debunk the false ideals supporting it.

The Federal Writers Project work *The Negro in Virginia* (1940), based out of Hampton Institute and in which Spencer was featured as a poet, affirmed the necessity of exposing the appearance and reality of "living Black" in a segregated society. "'Living Negro' has its compensations, especially in the cities," its authors wrote.[57] "The lure of a crowd is strong among Negroes; every city has a 'street' that serves as the social, as well as the commercial, center of Negro life" (the study references "Fifth Street in Lynchburg"). But the chapter "City Life" acknowledges, "no matter how carefree the outward appearance of Negroes may be, behind their outward masks are poverty, disease, and suffering, inherent in the existence of a people relegated to a neglected, segregated, and economically precarious way of life."[58]

Main Street served as a satiric model that would expose such dualities, but James Weldon Johnson also suggested to Spencer that Anita Loos's popular *Gentlemen Prefer Blondes* (1925), a satire of sexual mores and of the "self-improvement" model of a blonde protagonist's knowledge pursuit that drew Edith Wharton's praise as "the great American novel" could as well.[59] To aspire to write a great American novel that was also popular was not contradictory. That her personal library contained more than ten handbooks on writing fiction and collections of contemporary short stories and essays is proof of the seriousness with which Spencer took the charge of writing prose. And she was hard on her writing: "No one could be more critical than I of my prose—," Spencer observes in her personal reflections.[60]

Johnson attempted to provoke Spencer into writing, referring to her "still-born novel": "No," he writes in 1934. "I have not forgotten that you are the author of a still-born novel; but you really must do something about that ... you ought to do it."[61] Even in her correspondence with Hughes, Spencer referred to her gestating prose work. Spencer may have begun a draft, since her sometime literary circle friend Murrell Edmunds recalled visiting Spencer at Dunbar library to hear her read the opening chapter of her novel to children. By 1935, news of her unwritten novel also reached New York. In a letter home from her daughter Alroy, who studied at Columbia University together with her sister Bethel, she describes an event she attended at the 135th Street Public Library (later renamed the Schomburg, after the collector) at which Claude McKay discussed his new book, Jessie Fauset faulted the new generation of writers "for not living up to the pace that her group of writers had set," and Walter White discussed some of the material conditions accounting for the slower pace, mentioning Spencer's "great" idea for a novel in the course of his explanation: "I spoke to Mr. White 'n he sent his love to you 'n Pop after explaining to the folks around us that my 'mother had the best idea for a novel he'd ever heard—she also had one of the few creative minds he'd *ever* met and you 'n Pop had one of the loveliest homes and gardens it had *ever* been his pleasure to visit'—in such a way that the folks listening understood at least *my* reason for existing."[62]

Johnson and White recognized that Spencer had a unique perspective on the American South, its myths, and the reality of African American life there—an African American woman's perspective and a modern take, one that dismissed useless or obfuscating conventions of gentility and gender as well as racial spectacle. Lynchburg would contribute to the Harlem Renaissance by offering a glimpse of modern Black life in the South, potentially creating a best seller along the way.

Johnson encouraged Spencer to write prose as early as 1919 and continuously encouraged her through the early 1920s.[63] "Let me say that you must," he writes in March 1919, "by all means, do the article 'Madam and Maid.' I feel sure you can get it accepted by New Republic, The Dial, or some such publication, if it is well done; and I feel especially sure that you can do it well."[64] In another letter from 1922, Johnson tells Spencer that she should send her prose to Mencken. Spencer writes in return that "my mind swears to make him accept prose from me—whenever there is time to write it."[65] Johnson tells Spencer in 1924, "Mencken is right. You ought to devote yourself to writing prose. You have a prose style that few of us possess. You had better get to work on those stories."[66]

In another undated letter, probably also from 1924, Johnson remarks that he is "glad to know you are working on your story. You are right in keeping the propaganda out, unless it is so disguised as not to be discovered, except by the most skilled eye," adding, "this is the great moment for literature on the race question. You ought to set for yourself the task of doing your story and having it ready to submit to a publisher. You know you can depend on me for all I may be able to do; and besides, you already have the great Mencken interested in your work."[67] In an undated letter of 1925, Spencer announces to Johnson that she has "an article for Mencken, and a story I want you to see. Mr. White is to read the story last—he promised."[68] Yet further along, Spencer confesses, in an undated letter from 1927, "Dreadfully sorry that 'White Man' came to nothing—I almost did too—I am writing Mr. White to please do it since he likes the idea. My muses are all dead ... quite sure the younger ones must do the 'carrying on.'"[69] And in 1937 Johnson remarks that "every time I get a letter from you—and they are consistently good—I enjoy it so much that it makes me mad. Mad because, despite the fact that you write finer, sharper, more brilliant prose than almost anybody I know, I cannot, with all of my entreating, cajoling, or browbeating get you to write the story that you could write so well."[70]

"I lack the strength of character to be an outlaw, having only the desire!," Spencer writes Johnson. "Someone suggests that there is only one Mencken, and one G. B. S. [George Bernard Shaw] to every 100,000 simpler folk because this proportion is all the world could stand of such devoted ruthlessness. I'd like to make it triumvirate by adding one of ours, tho part of his expiation shall be credited by this letter."[71] What Spencer meant was that she wanted Johnson or herself to realize the satiric projects that they had assigned to each other. By supplanting Shaw's stinging social critique with their own, they would, by taking center stage, provide him with a means for forgiveness. An African American satirist would join the ranks of Mencken and Shaw in "devoted ruthlessness"—the barb of wit and critique, whether the devotion was to ruthlessness or to a nation that needed to be subjected to ruthlessness to be restored to its ideals. An undated letter asks if Johnson saw Mencken's article on sterilization: "Did you read Mencken's Sterilization article—it was my own dictum without his clever sapience, some months before." Mencken's vigorous satire and critique was a model for both Johnson's and Spencer's projected works in a satiric-realist vein.

"Green and Wordless Patterns": Spencer's Memorial to James Weldon Johnson

Spencer *felt* connection—telepathed it, as she writes Langston Hughes—without necessarily producing tangibles such as responses to letters or literary works. Writing Van Vechten in 1943, Spencer recalled, "Jim once said to Pa, 'Ed, Anne has made an honest woman out of herself.' He never lived to find out—thank God! I'll never do the book nor the story now, but at 60-odd [years] I still have a colossal reserve of constructive indignation."[72] Reflecting on the nature of her relationship with James Weldon Johnson and the import of their correspondence, which would shortly become a matter of public record through her donation of her letters to him to the James Weldon Johnson Memorial Collection, Spencer tells Van Vechten, "I wouldn't wish my letters, if any, to go in the collection unless I edited them: I'm afraid with surety that in those days I was ingenuous enough to try to appear intellectual without being intelligent. 1917–18 when I first knew 'Mr. Johnson,' I was straining to escape Lynchburg without realizing I might just 'take over'—...!"[73] Spencer donated the letters just one month later. Acknowledging that she would not complete her prose projects, she nevertheless kept alive the possibility of publishing work that would link her local surroundings in Lynchburg with a national discourse of rights shaped by World War II and school desegregation.

The 1940s wartime efforts of Douglas Johnson and Anne Spencer marked two epochal shifts: the death of Johnson, man of letters and indefatigable race leader, and the outbreak of World War II. These two poets shared and cultivated a new network from their literary circles out of James Weldon Johnson's untimely death in 1938. Spencer was instrumental in advancing the idea of a memorial fund that would specifically collect and archive Black writings as an appropriate memorial to Johnson's legacy. She wrote White and Van Vechten to declare her support of such a memorial fund and sent ten dollars to initiate the collection.[74] Spencer was a persistent advocate of this memorial archive, frequently checking on the plan's development, even in the midst of her disabling grief. Douglas Johnson, too, set to work, drawing on her skills as a correspondent and matchmaker. She provided Van Vechten and Harold Jackman, the Harlem-based author and correspondent who significantly organized contributions to the memorial archive with "suggestions about whom to ask for documents, supplying addresses, and even personally contacting authors" in the early 1940s.[75] Drawn out of grief with the help of time as well as her good friend Douglas Johnson's endeavors to support the memorial, Spencer worked to advance the memorial collection of letters from her home in Lynchburg. In 1942 she donated the correspondence she'd received from Johnson as well as a handful of typescript poems, including "Sybil Warns Her Sister."[76] In sending the letters to Jackman, she explains,

> I'd all along been afraid that the letters would be asked for. Pa—that's Ed, my husband—is due most credit that they can be sent today with not more than a half-dozen missing. Do understand, I treasure the letters + they were safe—too safe: Because the persons I can here to help out in the confusion of what I call housekeeping are even as I "on-relief-minded" They feel greater urge to annihilate than to situate. So these go on to you & hope especially to send 2 others and the card received the morning after my friend had *rested*.[77]

Spencer and Douglas Johnson made use of the reading circle networks that had fostered the artistic vision of many writers to bring into being the James Weldon Johnson Memorial Collection of African American letters at Yale University, now a cornerstone of the Beinecke Rare Book and Manuscript Library. Yet their papers did not receive the same honor and recognition. Even when they have been gathered and preserved, African American and women's archives frequently have not survived. Spencer and Douglas Johnson were among the first African American women who realized "the importance of and assumed responsibility for recording and preserving their own cultural artifacts," yet neither woman's papers are intact collections.[78] There is irony and sadness in the fact of their lost works, especially as both women strove to honor the memory of James Weldon Johnson through a memorial archive devoted to African American writers.

In the case of Spencer, several boxes of her manuscripts and correspondence were thrown away when she was away from her home convalescing with her daughter Bethel in New Jersey after an operation, most likely by a well-meaning friend of the family who wished to restore order to her home for the elderly woman's return. As her biographer J. Lee Greene writes, "During the months of [Spencer's] recuperation it is likely that many of her papers innocently were discarded."[79] Their absence creates a quandary. "The central problem," he states, "is that not only are valuable papers lost but there are fragments of several things which are probably useless if indeed the other parts are missing."[80] Even so, it may be wrong to presume that there was once a coherence to the author's individual works and to her archive that now survives piecemeal in different libraries and collections. Greene confirms this: "Certainly no one deliberately threw away any of her writings; but anyone unfamiliar with her methods of composition and filing would not know what was and what was not important. Her system was clear only to her."[81] Current scholars must acknowledge that Spencer's archive consists not only of her writing but also of fragments and gaps, some intentional, others inadvertent.

Looking to what McHenry calls "informal institutions" to recover readers, their reading materials, and broader notions of literacy, we may also recover a sense of the incomplete works by African American women authors, including those that have not survived or have not survived as discrete and coherent projects.[82] Literary groups like the Saturday Nighters and Spencer's Lynchburg circle have, McHenry notes, "historically been crucial to uniting black communities, illustrating the importance of a collective endeavor, providing a network of support for African American intellectuals, playing a constitutive role in the formation of American literature, and influencing the development of a black public sphere."[83] Spencer was instrumental in championing the idea of a memorial archive of James Weldon Johnson's writings. She not only sought institutional recognition for him but wanted to create her own monument to Johnson and their creative engagements in her manuscripts written in the decades after his death, exemplifying what Daphne Brooks describes as the fugitivity of Black women's thinking and the contrast between their cultural labor and the institutions designating cultural value—"libraries and universities, the publishing apparatuses and the awards councils."[84] In this sense we may regard Spencer's fugitive archive, a body of work that insists on "the unfinished," as a way of preserving Black feminist intellectual labor and "transforming it for new generations."[85]

"Motivated at once by private self-construction and public-minded group unity, the conscious building of black literary archives," Jean-Christophe Cloutier asserts, "defines the midcentury period between the New Negro movement and the Black Arts Movement."[86] Spencer's archives—that is, her unfinished, unpublished, manuscripts—came into being precisely at this moment, in tandem with but also as an alternative expression to the public Black literary archive. Her unfinished and unpublished work acknowledges the collective archival practices of African Americans, distinct from mainstream American institutional practices and authors. At the same time, Spencer defiantly engaged in a private, manuscript-as-archive practice in her writing, a radical expression of living and becoming.

It is ironic, then, that on the occasion of the dedication of the James Weldon Johnson Memorial Papers at Yale University in 1950, Redding's editorial "Black Art, White Audience" in *Afro Magazine* acknowledges Spencer as a major artist of the race.[87] Redding, whom Spencer befriended the decade prior to 1956, when he was named the James Weldon Johnson Professor of Creative Writing at Hampton University, complains that Black Americans' aspiration for better material circumstances has distracted their attention away from their artists. "And this is bad for them and bad for their artists," he notes. "Art is a solidifying, unifying force. It is the one level upon which, in America, people can meet on a plane of absolute equality."[88] His simultaneously expressing a desire for and condemning a black middle-class readership, lambasting "the black Babbitts" who were motivated by economic status and stability rather than the cultural authority of literature and the arts, betrays his contradictory views about elite modernist writing and mass culture.[89] Even as he acknowledges Spencer, his charge against the middle class as an economically driven unit echoes the Harlem Renaissance's treatment of women's lyrical poetry as apolitical. His statement conveys the contradiction of African American authorship in an era in which two options—an alliance with or a break from the "traditional," whether this was taken to mean a racial or a national tradition—severely limited the writing produced.

To Grace, Spencer sent this intentionally intimate, anticelebrity memorial of Johnson:

> In my new perspective of the whole affair I find comfort, and sanity, even, in a feeling of *continuity* that is the essence of life itself. Broun, Heywood [Heywood Broun], wrote of Gem's charm—charm with stamina. We have that still with us. Those now and in the future who never knew him in the flesh have for their own that better part, his urbane but intrepid spirit; his creative art forms in the pages left to them and the years. In the over 20 years I've known Gem I'm glad to feel how little his well-merited fame had to do with my deep trust in his integrity, or my love for Gem the person, not his fame but his personal gifts of sense percep-

tion, humor, genius, and sheer human goodness. These qualities make for high character and qualify for fame, but their complete absence is the hall-mark of too many persons called eminent. So Gem shall not be dead to me. I shall go on loving the two of you. This is my helpless contribution.[90]

"The days of grief have left me / I have no tears to shed," Spencer wrote in 1941, on the back of pamphlet providing a recommended reading list of modern poetry by Dr. James Southall Wilson, a professor of English literature at the University of Virginia.[91] After Johnson's death, Spencer published only one new poem. "At Easter, For Jim" was published in 1948 in *The Virginia Reader*, ten years after his tragic accident:

> If ever a garden was Gethsemane,
> with old tombs set high against
> the crumpled olive tree—and lichen,
> this, my garden, has been to me.
> For such as I none other is so sweet:
> Lacking old tombs, here stands my grief,
> and certainly its ancient tree.
> Peace is here and in every season
> a quite [sic] beauty.
> The sky falling about me
> evenly to the compass . . .
> What is sorrow but tenderness now
> in this earth-close frame of land and sky
> falling constantly into horizons
> of east and west, north and south;
> What is pain but happiness here
> amid these green and wordless patterns,—
> indefinite texture of blade and leaf:
>
> Beauty of an old, old tree,
> last comfort in Gethsemane.[92]

In the first stanza of the poem, powerful assonance is used to convey emotional anguish through the lengthened vowel sounds of "ai" "eh" and "ee": "Gethsemane" and "me," "against" and "sweet," "lichen" and "grief," and "tree." It is also powerfully present in the concluding couplet, which repeats with difference, the sounds now situated in opposite positions from their original placement in each line: "beauty" and "tree," and "Gethsemane." Assonance also appears in the middle stanza, in words like "peace," "here," "season," "me," "evenly," "green," and "leaf." The repetition of words and sounds throughout the poem builds meaning while delaying it, as the speaker's emotional progress and orientation to circumstance and context leads toward acceptance and the comfort that is to be had.

As if to trace grief and the stumbling comprehension of loss, the poem's lines contain varying meter and irregular stresses in five-, four-, and three-foot lines; there is no rhyme, and the effect of this is that assonance and repetition assume primacy, supplying the major structure of meaning in the poem's form. These techniques emphasize the speaker's distress and effort to accept the fact that her life continues and to find comfort in the living memory of the deceased.

"For Jim" focuses on orientation to time, on a sequence of events about to happen and on reconciling oneself to a profound transition from a time before to a time after. Jim in the garden on a recent visit, just weeks prior; Jim dead at sixty-eight, pulled from a horrible train- and car wreck. The idea of time in the poem is crucial, as it depends on the phases of the natural world and spring-time and the individual speaker's acceptance of loss through time's persistent motion. Yet the speaker is defiant in recalling and wedding individual memory to the faith and collective memory that is demanded of her to move forward. The line breaks in "For Jim" are powerfully rendered and indicate both pause and shift in thought and pause and continuity. The breaks underscore the formal organization of the poem through time. The orientation of the poem draws together past, present, and future, marking the continuation of natural life beyond the event. The speaker will remember, and she will call upon others to remember as well. That the speaker is the poet is appropriate in this context of living memory. Spencer will continue to write poetry, but she will not publish, or even finish, any of it. Instead, these longer works, written over decades, become living archives, a store of verse and lives that cannot be completed in the author's lifetime.

In this poem, Spencer's garden is a source both of agony and of healing. The vertical and the horizontal converge here, forming the image of a cross, the sky "falling" to Earth and to "horizons." For Spencer's speaker, the "compass" referenced is an instrument of orientation to time and place, "of east and west, north and south." The title "A Mood for Memory," a revision of this poem that has never been found, clearly conveys these geographic and psychic bearings.[93] The poem finds comfort in the "green and wordless patterns" and "indefinite texture" of "blade and leaf" in her garden, a natural living continuity without form, capable of providing an emotional resolution, from "sorrow" to "tenderness" and "pain" to "happiness." The transformation marks a survival of a loss so deep that it can't be put into words.

The phrase "in every season" is one she had used in a letter to Van Vechten describing her garden: "Our garden is enjoyed in every season—but it is smaller than most that are so named & at present weeds are knee-high. The persons who sometime look with pity at it then at us, would be unaware that one can part the weeds & come upon unexpected treasure."[94] The concept of time as continuity and time as finality captured in this phrase corresponds to the garden itself, its constant transformations and the inevitability of seasons passing and advancing death. Spencer acutely mourned her friend Johnson. Her withdrawal from her network of friends in the years immediately following his death in 1938 marked the close of an era of New Negro self-invention through the garden. Yet her writing cabin helped define a space for Spencer the writer in the subsequent decades. The pergola, set behind it and reaching across the garden, served as a link between its parts, between the writing cabin and the rest of the garden grounds. A physical manifestation of Spencer's metaphysical concern with the nature of time and knowing, the pergola represents both potential and actual space; it is a link between states of life and death, writing and cultivation. Derived from the Latin verb "pergere," to come or go forward, the pergola, grounded in the earthly human garden, affirms a connection to Earth and its ecology of life, which includes death. The story of Spencer's garden bears relation to her manuscripts produced from 1940 forward, in which the processes of time, change, and unfolding perspectives express her longing for the fruition of the public virtues she and other writers practiced in her literary circle and her home and garden. This enlargement had the potential to translate the communal virtues of the garden and Spencer's reading circle to the world.

What remained after Johnson's death was memory. And indeed Spencer spent the rest of her life memorializing her dear friend, insisting on placing his memory among the living, as she did in 1948. The poem, which was republished in Langston Hughes and Arna Bontemps's anthology *The Poetry of the Negro* in 1949 with the revised title "For Jim, Easter Eve, 1938–1948" and in numerous subsequent anthologies after that, mourns Johnson's loss in lyrical terms.[95] "At Easter, for Jim," emphasizes the relation between Johnson as a real-world Christ and the speaker. Publicly shared and dedicated to his memory, this poem represents Spencer's memorialization of Johnson.[96] Her early support for the James Weldon Johnson Memorial Collection of letters carried the "mood for memory" past the indistinctness of grief and into words—the letters written by Johnson and the host of other writers, including Spencer, whose works would join his there.

In draft letter that was likely intended for one of her anthologizers, she described one of her published poems, "I Have a Friend," as an attempt "to memorialize memory itself," in which the emphasis is "not had but *have*":[97]

> I have a friend
> And my heart from hence
> Is closed to friendship,
> Nor the gods' knees hold but one;
> He watches with me thru the long night,
> And when I call he comes,
> Or when he calls I am there;

He does not ask me how beloved
Are my husband and children,
Nor ever do I require
Details of life and love
In the grave—his home,—
We are such friends.[98]

In this draft letter, Spencer refers to her "dear critic," one woman's response to the poem in the local setting of Lynchburg: "I was sitting-in while a lovely lady explain [*sic*] to the group 'she means God.' I said later and *meanly* I was not excluding God."[99] This 1927 poem about "the sacredness of friendship" takes on new meaning as Spencer grieves Johnson. She told Greene, "of a real friend you don't ask a lot of questions. And if he dies, you still have that friend's influence on you."[100] To memorialize Johnson was, for Spencer, to contend with memory itself as a living practice in line with the Christian spirit that imbues the work and also to acknowledge the abiding processes of memory itself.

As the poem's original subtitle "1938–1948" indicates, Spencer's poem takes stock of the decade after Johnson's death. She completed the poem in late 1947 with the goal of seeing it to publication at the mark of the decade after his death. On November 4, 1947, she sent the poem to Grace Nail Johnson, who by that time had stepped into her role as the curator of his memory and was now always referred to in newspapers as "the widow Mrs. James Weldon Johnson." Grace recopied Spencer's letter to her and the poem, forwarding the copy on to Carl Van Vechten, who was gathering and soliciting materials for the memorial archive at Yale that had been decided on, finally—coordinated between Grace, other surviving family members, Walter White and the NAACP, and the universities at which he taught.[101]

Spencer's letter to Grace is a sort of preamble to the poem, a reflection on the decade since his passing that assesses the state of democracy on the world stage and voices a resolute postwar optimism:

> The world has now arrived, but not without mishap, at the year 1947—Although this says the calendar of most of the western world in the numeral, older cultures than ours, older religions than ours lay claim to a different age for Father Time. This item is apt because it is well to keep in mind what we owe to the long line of bright minds who survived a desperate past to finally make us heirs of their knowledge and skills.
>
> With the man fighting war "from pole to pole" tacitly over, we must take stock; to go over what humane supplies we have left, as reserves for the making of a democracy greater than man-kind has ever known.
>
> Hope is here. Even the people who are so good at hating, have it for themselves and their own material resources are here.

Manual Labor and the creative skills of manpower are here.

We have set ourselves the task of making obsolete old doubts and old fears, old acceptance of poverty, and of substituting for them the opportunity for each individual, to test his ability to translate hope, skills and resources into above subsistence living for all.

We make the plea for fixed opportunity for all persons beyond arbitrary prejudice of any one person or group anywhere. We ask this in the name of the greatest token of freedom ever written, The Constitution of the United States, with its twenty-one amendments—

The 21 amendments have now come of age and should cast their vote for its own documented principles.[102]

"Never really have I been so moved by the sheer poetic beauty of thought and word that inspired, (for such it is) this your thought," Grace writes Spencer in a letter dated November 15, 1947. "Thank you that memory sounds these depths and to think a decade marks the time. Incredible really; but that is the magic of time." Of the poem's setting in Spencer's garden, Grace remarks, "For all here who have been in your deepest affection this setting is . . . so sweet." She references what would have been her late husband's pride in "this creative impulse to set down with rare expression your very own thinking." Grace, in thanking Spencer, acknowledges both the poem and "the prose reflection" with its "deep philosophic insight—you say it all!"; it is, she remarks, "so timely and necessarily said." She also asks whether Spencer has thought about publishing it and suggests that she send it to Roy Wilkins, the editor at the *Crisis*.[103] Whether Spencer took that advice is not known, but her prose reflection was never published.

Spencer sent the poem in hopes, I believe, that Grace would ask her what she inevitably did: "Have you made any approach for publication?" Having consulted with Van Vechten, Grace suggested Spencer write Henry Seidel Canby at the *Saturday Review of Books*, providing the address and phone. Grace and Van Vechten reasoned that "if the *Review* carries it—Then it will be referenced in the Digest's etc. Hopefully." "Please have the poem published—Mrs. V. V. read it over twice aloud at home—beautifully. Carl kept it to copy and has asked me to request that you send him the original draft. So please get it right off to Mr. Canby, with the kind of letter you can write," adding, "Mr. V. V.—on returning your poem to me said:—'Dear Grace, this poem is most touching. I cried a little while I copied it. Be sure to ask Anne Spencer to send me the original for Yale.— Love, Carlo. Nov. 8, 1947.'" Spencer did send the poem off to Canby, but Canby declined to publish it.[104] Van Vechten had, according to Grace, suggested that Spencer entitle the poem "To James Weldon Johnson—For Jim—Easter Eve— (1938–48)," but Spencer did not take that advice. Such a title as Van Vechten proposed implied the formality of a memorial poem to a titled individual; Spencer's intention was decidedly different: a tracing of memory as an organic intimacy of correspondences.

Referencing Yale's university librarian James T. Babb, who succeeded Bernhard Knollenberg, Grace notes that she and Van Vechten made a "pilgrimage" just days prior to receiving her letter and that he "was impressed, establishing a quickened interest in 'us.'" Moreover, "a splendid young man—Mr. Donald Gallup sensitive and intelligent prepared has been assigned as curator of . . . [t]he American Collection, and [is] more than interested in the James Weldon Johnson Collection." She pointedly asks Anne, "Will you write something that may occur to you about the memorial library to J. W. J. at Yale? . . . Letters that may begin to come in expressing ones own thoughts about the Library founded by Carl for Scholarly Research—would naturally be enriched by thoughts that they might have to quote from; [it] . . . is . . . necessary to have in hand conscious feeling reflecting its purpose need importance etc. and for publicity purposes its place and significance."[105] Grace considered Spencer's reflection on the decade to be the start of a statement that more specifically referenced the James Weldon Johnson Memorial Collection, but there is no evidence that Spencer responded with such an elaboration.

"For Jim, Easter Eve" expresses Spencer's competing desires to achieve closure and to foster open-endedness that are manifested in the two archives of this time period. Spencer's garden, which centrally features in her 1948 memorial poem, became a place of memory. The poem itself represents a new beginning for Spencer's poetics, as she passed from her passionate friendship with Johnson during the New Negro Renaissance to the postdepression dawn of World War II. Her competing desires found expression in her garden, with its pergola a gateway to a larger human understanding of time, friendship, and mortality. Her manuscripts from this new era of writing following 1938 and until her death similarly express the competing desires of closure and open-endedness. Spencer, the interlocutor in the garden, devised more potent heroes for her writing, figures conveying both mastery and powerlessness, exploring both what had been lost and what had been created in the garden. This is the human condition, and it is also a practice specific to what Margo Jefferson calls a "black radical tradition of continuity *and* rupture."[106] "Striving to elevate the human toward the divine and seeking to call the gods down to earth," the heroes of Spencer's subsequent unfinished poems—John Brown, Abraham Lincoln, and Leroi Jones—manifest the tension between endings and beginnings, enabling her deliberation on the creative potential of transformation and on the profound powerlessness of humankind to evade mortality.[107]

CHAPTER THREE

"Virginia as Narcissus"

Anne Spencer's Southern Manifesto and the Place of Modern Poetry

Tradition is long use without written memorials.
—ANNE SPENCER, "Virginia as Narcissus"

—not Negroes who have no history no—black—it is
white who have not written theirs save mythologically
because of double lives—black & white prolifer—
—ANNE SPENCER, notebook

Spencer's networks outlived the Harlem Renaissance, stretching well into the 1950s. She continued interacting with this network of authors in an effort to keep Johnson's memory alive. At the same time, she continued her engaged reading of newspapers, journals, and literature and also worked on manuscripts in adamant privacy. While she increasingly withdrew from her active role in literary circles after Johnson's death in 1938, she was, "like everyone else, caught up in the war and the currents of interracialism that accompanied it," which she addresses through a regional lens.[1]

Composed intermittently between 1940 and 1975, "Virginia as Narcissus" is a memoir and a manifesto addressing the state of Virginia, Spencer's birthplace. As Chauncey Spencer clarifies in his autobiography, his mother "was born in Henry County near Danville, Virginia. Even though she was aware of the fact she was born in Virginia, Mother later listed her birthplace as Bramwell, West Virginia, 1882. Her reason for this was one of principle, Virginia had once been a slave state and West Virginia was not."[2] Bearing the various titles of "Virginia as Narcissus," "Virginia as Narcissist," "Narcissus as Virginia Power," "1620," and "Virginia as Narcissus: Or, The Southern Mind," the work, Spencer took pains to clarify, "does neither epitomize or symbolize Va. alone. Our whole country bears a part of what its an integer of. But as a whole we have a sane and lusty unbelief in our own godhead, or dogma read backwards." "Virginia as Narcissus" was informed by largely unpublished editorials Spencer wrote and also generated new ones. As she worked on it, she returned to some of the ideas she had written about or at least promised she would write about in letters to Johnson and Mencken. There is, for example, the outline of a letter to the editor titled "In Our Town / and its metamorphoses."[3]

"Metamorphosis" is an appropriate word for Spencer's investigation. As she signaled in her fragmentary telling of the Narcissus myth, it was Ovid's that she had in mind. Echo, the woodland nymph, is particularly significant for Spencer. Echo is far too divested of power, embodied presence, and voice to be a female intermediary like Sybil, but her appearance in Spencer's critique of tradition underscores both the objectification and the marginalization of women in Jim Crow. Spencer also no doubt identified with Ovid; they both had been exiled from their respective nations.

"Virginia as Narcissus" is a commentary on place as well as gender in the making of tradition. And the paper she wrote on provided active surfaces, dialogic opportunities. The bulk of "Virginia as Narcissus" exists as a draft in one of her notebooks, the notebook itself a recycled, secondhand day journal from the year 1927 that evidently belonged to a wealthy individual, who, according to the recorded events, spent a goodly portion of time vacationing in warmer climates. Spencer wrote around these notes, never in response to them; ever the recycler, her notes in this day journal span the 1940s to the mid-1960s and are not attached to the dates on which they are recorded. There is no evidence that Spencer knew the original owner of the day journal.[4] The stark contrast between these two writers' engagements, the one focusing on travel and leisure, the other concentrating on history and politics in the landscape of Virginia, underscores the seriousness of Spencer's project. Writing around the original author's notes, she speaks to subjects and experiences of far greater urgency. And in probing ideas of tradition, she undercuts the status of that original owner. As she continued the writing of the manuscript past the pages of this journal, Spencer used yellow legal pads and the back of the stationery of Francis E. Rivers, her son-in-law, and other notebooks.[5]

Spencer's physically composing this work on various surfaces is matched by her ideationally layering dialogues between Victorian, modernist, Southern Agrarian, and modern African American authors' views of freedom and power, bringing them to bear on contemporary Virginia as an "integer" of the nation while she considers the place of poetry in the national discourse. From the 1940s to the 1970s, Spencer continued work on this project. Of all the various stages of its thought as reflected by title, "Virginia as Narcissus: In the Best Southern Tradition," the one she gave to her biographer J. Lee Greene, is perhaps the most telling.[6] In an oral interview from 1973 with Greene and Garnell Stamps, a Lynchburg native and a scholar steeped in African American intellectual history, the ninety-year-old Spencer described her work's emphasis, referring to "Virginia as Narcissus" in the present tense as a living document that she had been working on for some time:

> I'm trying to do a thing on Virginia. Allen Tate, you know he was one of those
> signers of the manifesto. And that list has lost some of its signers who've gone

over on the humane side. But so far as I know Tate has stayed on it. And he wrote
an essay that wasn't readable for me called "Narcissus as Narcissus." But I profited
by it because I was trying to do this thing on Virginia. . . . And I said that's the perfect title. Virginia as Narcissus. I meant the white slave tradition of Virginia. And
I have Harriet Beecher Stowe's book there.[7]

Tate's "Narcissus as Narcissus," which was published in the *Virginia Quarterly*
in 1937, provides a reading of "Ode to the Confederate Dead," his best-known
poem, which is a southern version of T. S. Eliot's "The Waste Land" that reflects
on modern alienation and the role of older culture as a healing force. In this essay, Tate, known for his central role in the Southern Agrarian movement, suggests that an older southern culture is the antidote to modernist alienation.
This movement attempted to establish a "tradition" of life and writing through
an idea of naturalism that preserved the racial order of slavery while asserting
a pre-lapsarian, pre–Civil War innocence. When Spencer writes that "—not Negroes who have no history no—black—it is whites who have not written theirs
save mythologically because of double lives—black & white prolifer—" she has
this idea of tradition as reflected in Tate's essay in mind.

The Southern Agrarians' manifesto asserted a forward-looking social program of continued racial segregation. Langdon Hammer has pointed out the
contradiction of the Southern Agrarian anticapitalist stance and its support
for property ownership.[8] In "Virginia as Narcissus," Spencer characterizes
white southern ideas of the natural landscape ironically, supplanting them by
revealing their contemporary source of so-called tradition in "the white slave
tradition of Virginia." Spencer references historical and contemporary forms
of labor and landedness in the South in her representation of labor to leverage
her critique.[9] She rightly linked the Southern Agrarians' manifesto *I'll Take My
Stand* to Richard Russell, Strom Thurmond, and Harry F. Byrd's 1956 "Declaration of Constitutional Principles," or "Southern Manifesto," as it was informally
called, defending segregation, yet another assertion of "southern tradition."

In the decade following the publication of Tate's essay, African American
Virginians became increasingly politically organized, particularly in the state's
cities. As *The Negro in Virginia* observes in its chapter "City Life," the NAACP
played a shaping role in this political organization, "seek[ing] to improve the
treatment . . . of the Negro." Between 1938 and 1940, "the NAACP . . . tripled its
Virginia membership," during which time "its attorneys carried a test equaliza-
tion of salary case into the Norfolk Circuit Court."[10] In "Virginia as Narcissus,"
Spencer recalls that she "became a member in 1912 and became one amongst
the thousands who helped wag its tail at one dollar per head, no, not even one
for our local chapter kept fifty cents and the other fifty was sent on to 69 5th
ave—where dedicated men and women used it to do more for more people
with less money than our country had seen before—. . . they have so aided the

sight of unnumbered whites that when ever there is an ostensible vote against us in the South 1000s vote an encouraging nyet."

She addresses the spatiality and centrality of African Americans in this struggle in her prose work, using Virginia to locate the "place and purpose of poetry" in American life. It was an especially important inquiry at midcentury, as American poetry was becoming institutionalized—the stature of poetry asserted, its presence at the Library of Congress formally created, "American" poetry incorporated into the curriculum of colleges and universities. From the 1930s forward, the modern American poet developed in tandem with modern criticism.[11] Tate exerted an outsized influence on poetry. "An adequate assessment of Tate's 'politics,'" Hammer states, "would have to take into account the pragmatic, institutional authority he exerted in the middle and later phases of his career." Louis Rubin notes that "during the height of his career as Man of Letters (not as a poet; that came a little earlier), in the 1940s and 1950s, Allen Tate was a major and formidable presence in the American literary scene. His word could get books of poetry published, procure fellowships, set up literary awards and secure financial grants, arrange reviews, and assure academic appointments. There was no more influential presence in the province of poetry."[12] Here again, Tate's contradictions become apparent, even as they mask themselves: "Tate implicitly made formal rigor the sign of professional authority and a tough-minded, skeptical masculinity.... [T]hese symbolic values would win for Tate's formalism a privileged position in the intensively anticommunist literary culture of the postwar era. Tate's formalist principles and practice could be absorbed into English department pedagogy, under the rubric of technical expertise, as apolitical criteria."[13]

Spencer shaped her unfinished, unpublished work into a massive, lifelong document of refusal. Yet it was also a sustaining declaration of creative potential, both a living record of Spencer's relation to her physical space and a means of cultivating an intellectual and imaginative space for her writing. "Virginia as Narcissus" presents Virginia as shot through by the corrupting influence of the laws of slavery and segregation, by the violation of freedom, by the white power of a former slave-holding society in Virginia's legislature and its advancement of what she called "uncivil rights." At the other end of the spectrum in her representations of Virginia lies her 1927 poem "Life-Long, Poor Browning," first published in Countee Cullen's *Caroling Dusk* (1927) and heavily anthologized, which figures Virginia as a creative, accommodating, regenerating space in which one could write, build, and live:

> Life-long, poor Browning never knew Virginia,
> Or he'd not grieved in Florence for April sallies
> Back to English gardens after Euclid's linear:
> Clipt yews, Pomander Walks, and pleachéd alleys;

Primroses, prim indeed, in quiet ordered hedges,
Waterways, soberly, sedately enchanneled,
No thin riotous blade even among the sedges,
All the wild country-side tamely impaneled . . .

Dead, now, dear Browning lives on in heaven,—
(Heaven's Virginia when the year's at its Spring)
He's haunting the byways of wine-aired leaven
And throating the notes of the wildings on wing:

Here canopied reaches of dogwood and hazel,
Beech tree and redbud fine-laced in vines,
Feet clapping rills by lush fern and basil,
Drain blue hills to lowlands scented with pines . . .

Think you he meets in this tender green sweetness
Shade that was Elizabeth . . . immortal completeness!

In this poem, Spencer summons one of her favorite poets, Robert Browning, to present contrasting ideas of nature and order. The poem is built on the idea of the Victorian poet's encounter with a Virginia he never knew. His yearning to return to the English countryside and its gardens from Florence is described by a speaker who knows more than he does and pities him his lack of awareness of the beauty of Virginia. The speaker possesses a view of both and turns first to Browning's English garden, which is "prim," "quiet," "sober," "sedate"— "linear" as Euclid's geometric patterns, "enchanneled," "impaneled," and "ordered" (Spencer did not like geometry). The contrast of Virginia is striking in its animation, wildness and unexpectedness, a seeming disorder that is at once purposeful and arranged: "riotous," "rills," "canopied," "leaven," and "wildings" all convey an active order that is created by nature's movement (for example, a rill is a narrow channel cut into soil by flowing water; human beings, by contrast, the agents of what is enchanneled, which conveys stasis rather than motion.) The sweep of the speaker's vision is expansive and attentive, traveling through highlands and lowlands. The overall effect of such motion is nature's full-throated expression, which is aural, tactile, scented, and, of course, visual in its presentation: "wine-aired leaven," "notes of wildings," "reaches of dogwood and hazel," "fine-laced in vines," "scented with pines," "tender green sweetness." It is a poem, at bottom, about freedom and about the union of humankind through communion with nature, a chaste and consummate love of "green sweetness" between Browning and his wife Elizabeth Barrett. Appropriately enough the meter of the poem produces approximate, irregular iambic sestameter, with an abundance of trisyllables "rilling," if you will—cutting— through the poem's rhythmic pace. What is done to nature is done to human beings, the poem shows: clipped branches stifle humankind's relation to nature and as a result its capacity for expression. The poem's starting point calls attention to the idea of resurrection: the yew tree's branches are "clipt" in the English garden, but the tree's drooping branches, left unpruned, can reroot. Used at Easter as "palms" in church services, the branches are a symbol of new life. Browning's grief is misplaced, the speaker makes clear, for resurrection, true freedom, and consummated love can be found in Virginia, where nature's order supplants a stifling human order such as that found in the English garden. The speaker of this poem, like Sybil, sees the truth.

One of the subtitles of Spencer's manuscript refers to "Virginia as Narcissus" as a "testament of age" rather than of youth.[14] This work carried Spencer past the New Negro Renaissance period and its youthful aspirations for African American attainment of equality through literature and the arts. In referencing the testament of age, Spencer points to a long historical view of Virginia, both the distorted traditions attested to by a prejudiced legislature and the idea of Virginia as the origin of the American ideals of freedom and equality. Spencer moved past the attitudes and techniques of representation she had employed in the 1920s and early 1930s, undertaking a vigorous and broad intellectual history of labor and freedom.

In this work, as well as in her overlapping composition of the manuscript poems "John Brown" and "Leroi Meets Lincoln," Spencer reworks her prior ideas of nature and poetry from the New Negro Renaissance. What resulted was nothing short of a new, revolutionary poetics centered on the explicitly political nature of nature in the 1940s and beyond. This is a significant development for Spencer's poetics, because her nature poetry often has been viewed as representing a lyric sensibility, a female or African American personhood too individualized to encompass a broader sociopolitical frame of reference. "Virginia as Narcissus" conveys Spencer's frank sociopolitical assessment of her world. It was a world informed by the violent rupture of Johnson's death, the outbreak of World War II and its aftermath, including the Cold War, the virulent forms of segregation that aggrieved the soul on a daily basis, and the intensification of the civil rights struggle through three decades. "Virginia as Narcissus" summoned Spencer to undertake the task of forming a new poetics that affirmed her deepened commitment to poetry in a time of crisis.

Although "Virginia as Narcissus" is a prose work, it addresses both the emerging discourse of American poetry as tradition and the space-making necessary for expression outside of this controlling idea. It uses nature as a tool of political critique, not only interrogating the physically controlled spaces of segregation but also the limits imposed on the imaginative world of African Americans. The dictates limiting physical movement have far reaching effects, as they also regulate individual personhood in a way that shapes the collective identity of African Americans, decreeing from the outside how "they" are supposed to think and speak, what they should write about, and even how they should write about it. Spencer's existence within her writing therefore depends on its preservation as a manuscript, even as she addresses the power of segregation.

The expressive form of poetry Spencer repeatedly references in this manuscript is reflected in her embedding in it the manuscript poems "God never planted a garden," "Any Wife to Any Husband: A Derived poem," "Commonwealth," and the previously published "White Things" (1923). The result is an innovative space-making that operates not only within the manuscript of "Virginia as Narcissus" as it moves between poems, offering fresh and multiple contexts for them but also in Spencer's overlapping manuscript poems "John Brown" and "Leroi Meets Lincoln." The technique of refusing to end a poem or often, to distinguish between individual works enabled Spencer to create an ethical and aesthetic coherence out of seeming disorder.

Because Spencer did not plan to publish "Virginia as Narcissus," she felt free to develop an alternative take on poetry's form and subject. As she notes in 1948 with respect to modern poetry, "The newness of this or any subject presented in with a certain timing can lose its patina and grow old at the stroke of midnight—if we must depend too much on how recently? Or as we say, "what's new?"[15] "Objective poetry," she reflects, "grows old before subjective poetry does because refrigerators must be kept to date but the heart within us changes only for convenience." She criticized objectivity as mechanization, a refrigerator and its parts—cold—favoring the subjective heart as enduring warmth, human affirmation, and both living and lasting.

The manuscript is evidence that the radical, dynamic transformation of poets and their poetry at midcentury took place not only in the public sphere, where poets assumed a public persona, but also in personal spaces. Spencer's manuscript engages the very idea of a canonized poetry while refusing its standards in "a temporal alternative to progressivist myth."[16] In its critique and questioning of knowledge and its forms, its ability to represent individual and collective imagination, and its capacity for preserving or enacting social change "Virginia as Narcissus" makes space for possibility and for Spencer herself as author and poet and for others who do not possess equal status. This progressivist idea of time and history, she recognized, could lead to the institutionalization of poetry and the critical apparatus attached to it, which would have a devastating effect on African Americans and the literature they could produce for the public. Jean-Christophe Cloutier has observed that "literary criticism over the past decade has become richly attentive to the conditions that underwrite literary professionalization, yet the crucial role played by literary collections in 'making professionalization possible' remains obscure."[17] Spencer's "Virginia as Narcissus," precisely because it was experimental, incomplete, written over decades, and unpublished, conveys her nonalignment with national identity, spatiality, and political affiliation while also affirming and expanding space for Black cultural identity not limited by geographic location, uniformity of approach, or form itself.[18] Eve Dunbar has shown how African American authors such as Hurston, Wright, Baldwin, and Himes "used ethnography or ethnography-inspired writing . . . to destabilize expectations regarding the scale and content of African American letters."[19] Spencer's "Virginia as Narcissus," a study of the "white slave tradition" of Virginia, yields ethnographic knowledge that resituates African American authors' "regions of the imagination" in a global context. As she sought to confront African American alienation in the context of World War II, she also sought to make this alienation part of a global conversation about humankind in the world. Of Arthur Koestler's *Darkness at Noon* (1940), a novel about the failings of Communism, for example, Spencer observes , "Koestler saying, man is a reality, mankind is an abstraction—or may it make a truer appeal as *man is*. Even if multiplied circulatingly."[20] While recognizing that Koestler appeals to an abstract idea of humanity as an antidote to an urgent political situation, Spencer nevertheless asserts the physical, embodied existence of humankind. That physical experience was also the experience of segregation, its regulation of Black bodies, its attempt to reduce the measure of Black value, freedoms, ability to move, and to be seen and heard and its attempt to impose a nonhuman status on African Americans.[21]

"Virginia as Narcissus" represents a new form of writing about the more familiar subjects of her published peers, who, as Dunbar shows, "set about both documenting and reimagining a set of 'homegrown' experiences within a more worldly framework."[22] It rejects reductive categories of African American identity and writing and serves as a testament to her decision to embrace of Blackness, Virginia, the South, and Americanness. Her choices provided her with an agency that allowed her to criticize that was not available to her in the public sphere.[23] The unending manuscript affirms what Sonya Posmentier calls "the action of material and spiritual sustenance that is always under way in poetics, diffuse and partially expressed, never quite planted in one place or another."[24]

Spencer built her authority in "Virginia as Narcissus" through other writers who had depicted revolution and the story of the commonwealths of Britain and America, such as Tocqueville and Carlyle. She also took up American writers of the South such as Faulkner and Glasgow, aligning their perspectives with fascism's rise and continued segregation in the United States before and after World War II. There was truth to be revealed by confronting what Spencer called the "polite fiction of fiction."[25] The moral precipice that was World War II for Spencer was also that of the "southern mind."

> somehow by idiotic degrees the whole of the half sane world has let the threat of annihilation creep up down and over every-thing living, while they condoned this increase among weaker peoples, of everywhere nasty, virulent piles of hatred, virulent because wherever left the mushroom fallout from them was unconfinable.

Poison gas seeks its claims far areas: north, Midwest, west in USA; London Africa wherever—it cannot be kept at home. The people, the pile-builders, spread over the earth seeking one thing—tangible loot. Not the philosophy of peace in the old places; not the ability to feel aright the plight of the forsaken or to contribute at least one's complete empathy—which is a divine gift and to bring it back means we must bear it with us when we go.[26]

Hatred and annihilation will dog all of humanity, not just a portion of it, Spencer warns, invoking the atom bomb. Continuing in this vein, she compares fascism abroad and at home: "We can fear and despise (generic) Hitler. / Whom I just happened to meet the other day / The *youth* never lived to become a man because he 'pined away' for *love* (that extraordinary word use in each variant contexts) of his own image. Then unquestioned, he is followed by these seven states the law upheld, they become echo—and the myth becomes again a pagan religion—The only very-part of this story I write *this* for: that this area to which my human kin—and yours were brought may *become a man.*"[27] Humanity and homeland resonate from the American to the world context, as Spencer demonstrates:

> "Begin where home should begin, by teaching the use of necessary things without the abuse of any—but no, all children are now getting the short-end of the educational wishbone, and their litter-bug vandalism of spirit and hand is as shocking as it is understandable.
>
> This plight comes of adult depravity, or sham goings-on: In Virginia, selling a *double*-program education and prostitution thru a pretentious "Literary fund"—in reality a state ligourary [*sic*] trust; buried "funnies" cinema ads to allure old and young in highly unproper supine and clinch. Then in finale of this roleplay teach fascism and its *acceptance* to the young in veery public facility . . .[28]

Acknowledging the precarious and marginalized position of Jewish people, Spencer asserts their "gift" in the practice of recognizing a singular "living God":

> So that great people, the Jew, transmitted to this all of days the gift idea and ideal of the one and only *living* God. The fascists and other heathen people, taking over only that part of his domain which is mechanical enough to see touch and taste, have tried monstrously with thoroughness to eradicate the giver, even the *gift*. Think we can, of just one small section of these humans, who unable to conceive of anything beyond flesh and blood when finally the revelation comes thru they set out to slap the revealer. It is fantastic that the very pagans—"tattooed and woaded winter-clad in skins"—who could not think (spirit) up their own Jehovah, or his son Jesus Christ have little but hatred for those whose communion gave Father and Son to our word.[29]

Spencer believed that American authors had an important role to play in addressing these wrongs and contradictions. "So far as the manifesto novelists are in involved in this matter of opinion read their books. If *you* can find one of them written *not* by the head but by hand-determined artifacts and kitchen middens doing better than one can to take care of the chore by making money—you'll have to go back awhile to Chesnutt Cabell Glasgow—or if lacking book read these Apostles Acts the air is filled with their grammarians funeral—and what are they saying? If its Henry Ford's day, or a slavery steamer day their chorus is a negro can't learn to drive a car!"[30] As she notes in a reflection called "Some Literary People and the Negro" (subtitled "Agnes Repplier and Uncle Tom"), "Son, equality is not possible, but brotherhood always is."[31]

She was incensed by William Faulkner's travel abroad to Japan in 1955, particularly his comments about nations and loyalty: "Mr. F. in Japan: and: '—and I thought people should come to know one another' ++++ if there is anything that people of one nation can give to people of another nation, they should make the effort to do so."[32] She also notes his remark that "there is a lot of loose loyalty in this land. Even a little of it is too valuable to be ignored."[33] Most provocative to her was his claim that "disaster is good for man," for "if it does nothing else it reminds him who he is, what he is."[34] Spencer angrily rejoins:

No, Mr. F. it does not tell or teach him
it, disaster does not tell him he was not listening
It did not teach him he never hears—only shock *r*eminds him—

She further condemns his lack of candor in his fiction as well as his lectures:

Mr. F—and truth!
His people, his immediate people, just will not tell the truth about what they know about the negro, to which we know the big lie is added to and abetted by the negro himself. Their dialogues are concomitant but separate, the whites hush—hush when the housemaid nears; the negro listens hush hush when the employer holds forth against the NAACP—[35]

Like Pearl S. Buck, who had recently paid a visit to the state and had "told the ladies that they had no close knowledge of their own daughters," "Faulkner got a Nobel Prize for more of the same." "This demand for mental subservience from a people whose beliefs derive from sources of books about almost books, realism, How to Live, How to Influence, How to Eat. Even their religious textbook, the Holy Bible is subjected to watering down into the man who or David and Bathsheba—."[36] She considered writing a comparison, "M. Falkner vs. Mr. Archibald Rutledge," although she did not. Rutledge, poet laureate of South Carolina from 1937 to 1973, romanticized "plantation life"—black sharecropping—of the 1930s South in *God's Children* (1947).

While the works of Spencer's published contemporaries Gwendolyn Brooks, her friend Langston Hughes, Robert Hayden, and Margaret Walker often employed nature to the ends of a universalist perspective, Spencer chose prose to situate her subject emphatically in the South, in a specific region. Spencer rejects the universalism that might seem to characterize the female subjects of her published poems from the New Negro Renaissance by specifically relocating them to Virginia, in "the young girl I love."[37] In choosing Virginia and situating her female subject there, Spencer seeks to reclaim not just the region but nature itself from the duality of romanticism and racial terror. Through her garden, Spencer developed her own form of regionalism, one infused by epicurean ideals that Robert Harrison describes in *Gardens*: "The most important pedagogical lesson that the Epicurean garden imparted to those who tended it was that life—in all its forms—is intrinsically mortal and that the human soul shares the fate of whatever grows and perishes on and in the earth. Thus the garden reinforced the fundamental Epicurean belief that the human soul is as amenable to moral, spiritual, and intellectual cultivation as the garden is to organic cultivation."[38]

Spencer confronted the intrinsic mortality of life over the many decades during which she wrote "Virginia as Narcissus." Over the years of its composition, Spencer dealt with Johnson's tragic death, witnessed the diminishing health of her husband, Edward, and her own decline. But, as Harrison writes, "death sets things into motion, including our desires. It is the generative source of nature's ceaseless movement into form."[39] "Virginia as Narcissus" frames Virginia, Spencer's earthly garden, as poised to act—to move beyond its bounded concept of time into new forms of existence and new forms of writing. But Spencer also made clear Virginia's vulnerability: its very future depended not on the human face that found itself in the reflection but on humans finding and caring for each other and Earth. With the discernment of a poet, Spencer registers her faith in human care—the "keeper" of her manuscript poem "God never planted a garden"—and her devotion to humankind in her testament to Virginia.[40] In writing to destroy Virginia's myths, she creates a place for herself and others as caretakers of Earth, doing what Harrison calls "the painstaking, compensatory work of fostering the saving power of human culture."[41] Mindfully cultivated to serve these moral, spiritual, and intellectual purposes, Spencer's garden sustained the poet's imagination and the community of writers that gathered there in the postwar years. She was not alone: during the 1950s, the period of nuclear proliferation and the height of the Cold War, many writers with a national readership also carved out an epicurean regional stance, such as E. B. White, whom Spencer read.

She elaborates on her vision of a Virginian epicureanism in observing that "WE Va's normally are good feeders because as cooks we are straight men: no culinary oversoul stuff—we make butter base gravy with crisp lumps of goo in it—unstrained. With us, an egg is an egg and you can tell a potato's not a fromage. We haven't owned stoves long enough to forget how beef and pork taste from an outdoor pit or hearth."[42] The homeliness she conjures here does speak to a degree of shared culture, a culture of pleasure, it is true, but it is one that is formed by seeking distance from the corrupt state, as Epicurus did, and reestablishing a close relationship of the soul with nature.

Virginia was significant to the nation's story because, as James Freeman Clarke remarks in *Anti-Slavery Days*, one of Spencer's cherished and heavily annotated books, "The seeds of freedom and of slavery were planted in this country in the same year": "the May Flower brought the Pilgrim Fathers to Plymouth," and "a Dutch ship entered the James River in Virginia with twenty African slaves."[43] The 1940 Works Progress Administration historical guide *The Negro in Virginia*, to which Spencer was invited to contribute by Sterling Brown, its editor, affirmed J. Saunders Redding's 1939 view that the urban North did not represent African Americans at large:

> The deep-seated feeling that the Negro problem will be solved in "Negro America—the Nation's own back yard"—rather than through "armchair conferences in the North," evidenced by the coming of many national organizations to the South for conferences, has stimulated among Negroes, particularly in the cities, race pride, an increased interest in civic affairs, and a willingness to cooperate in programs that seek not only to inspire definite objectives but to campaign for them. Civic leagues, city forums, and round table conferences in every city draw a large number of Negroes who feel that mass pressure rather than "patient waiting" is needed to solve many of the problems that confront Virginia's largest minority group.[44]

The authors of this work explicitly remark on Virginia's literal and symbolic status as a birthplace: "Virginia, 'mother of the Nation,' has nurtured the roots of more Negro families than any other State." These families were widely dispersed, but migrants carried their culture with them.[45] Roscoe E. Lewis, supervisor of the project under the Federal Writers Project of the Works Progress Administration states in his preface to *The Negro in Virginia*, "It is appropriate that the first WPA State book on the Negro be produced in Virginia; for here the first African natives were brought and held in enforced servitude, and here also, more than two centuries later, freedom for some 5,000,000 of their descendants was assured on the surrender grounds at Appomattox."[46] The final pages of The *Negro in Virginia* state: "To Virginia's shores the first black man was brought and enslaved; on Virginia soil his freedom finally was assured. By the sweat of his brow the Virginia Negro has paid for that freedom. This is his home, for the strength of his muscles has gone into its building. The cleared forests, the rolling farmlands, the bridged rivers, the thriving cities and towns, the stately mansions are mute testimony to his labors. Work has been his heritage, and his hope is that he may come some day into a fair share of the fruits of his labors."[47] Simultaneously referencing the pastoral tradition of America and the labor required to create this tradition, *The Negro in Virginia* calls attention to the land shaped and cultivated by African Americans in a seemingly universal description of land and nature, thereby telling a story about African American labor, visible in the landscape that so far has been "mute."

That labor is also represented by the monumental tome *The Negro in Virginia* itself, unique among the works produced by the Federal Writers Project during the Depression for several reasons, including the fact that it was completed. In her excellent recovery work on this period, Joanne V. Gabbin establishes the central role Sterling Brown played as national editor of Negro affairs in the Federal Writers Project: he used his network of African American scholars to see *The Negro in Virginia* through to publication, with the authorial voices of its African American authors intact.[48] Gabbin describes the challenges Brown faced, ranging from guaranteeing equity in employment of African American writers to the inclusion of "Black subjects in the American Guide Series" at all.[49] The objective was to produce "a portrait that sketched the Black American as a participant and not a problem."[50] Brown found that "he was powerless to ensure the hiring of qualified Blacks outside of his immediate staff and that attaining a fair treatment of Black material was fraught with difficulty."[51] Most challenging, "Brown's work, especially with the state guides, was hampered by partisanship." He "insisted on integrity and truth in guide material" but "was often confronted by the flagrant use of stereotypes of glaring misconceptions concerning disease, mortality, crime, and illiteracy among Blacks."[52] As he notes in his 1937 historical guide to Washington, D.C.,

> from the preservation of the color-line in the District grave consequences arise. Educationally, segregation means the maintenance of a dual system—expensive not only in dollars and cents but also in its indoctrination of white children with a belief in their superiority and of Negro children with a belief in their inferiority, both equally false. Politically, it is believed by many that the determination to keep the Negro "in his place" has lessened the agitation for suffrage in the District. Economically, the presence of a large number of unemployed constitutes a critical relief problem; the low rate of pay received by Negro workers lowers the standard of living and threatens the trade-union movement. Socially, the effects of Negro ghettos are far-reaching. One cannot segregate disease and crime. In this border city, southern in so many respects, there is a denial of democracy, at times hypocritical and at times flagrant. Social compulsion forces many who would naturally be on the side of civic fairness into hopelessness and indifference. Washington has made steps in the direction of justice, but many steps remain to be taken for the sake of the underprivileged and for the sake of a greater Washington.[53]

This passage, Brown's concluding paragraph of the essay, is striking not only for its candor but for its measured representation of segregation's ills that conveys his vision for a rational order and harmonious world that doesn't yet exist. As a consequence of the essay's candor and his challenging the condescending and explicitly racist depictions of African American cultural life in various state guides such as Mississippi's, Brown was placed under investigation by the federal government.[54]

The Negro in Virginia, composed by an all-African American writing and research staff of fifteen run largely out of research offices at Virginia's Hampton Institute, with consultants on "Negro affairs" throughout the state, was the informed antidote to these distortions. Spencer was one of the consultants.[55] Her role led to formal collaboration with scholars at Hampton and initiated her enduring relationship with the institute and scholars who circulated through it: Arthur P. Davis, who taught at Virginia Union University in Richmond in the early 1940s and was born in Hampton; J. Saunders Redding, who joined the Hampton faculty in 1943; and more peripherally, William Moses, an architect and professor at Hampton. Spencer's consultancy was important because there was a predominating fraternal influence in Brown's network: many were members of the Omega Psi Phi fraternity, a historically Black fraternity established at Howard University in 1911, including Brown, Davis, Redding, and Moses, who was also president of the Hampton chapter of the NAACP.[56] All four men created referential apparatuses that featured Spencer, from their edited anthologies and critical histories to the map of Virginia Moses designed on the front and back endpapers of *The Negro in Virginia*, which featured Lynchburg through an illustration of Spencer: "Anne Spencer—Poems and Flowers," reads number thirty-five of the legend to "A Historical Map of the Negro in Virginia." A tiny dress-clad figure holds a piece of paper and appears to address people and flowers on an outdoor stage.[57]

A letter from Spencer to Brown from 1936 provides evidence that she was invited to participate in the writing of this monumental volume by her friend. She writes: "Dear Mr. Brown: June the 18th, I received your letter from Mr. Braxton and other literature regarding the projected work on the American Negro Guide, and asking if I would lend my aid in the Virginia part of the job—or about that. Judging from your program in outline, I think I could do it, and would like to try. There is of course much else I need to know about working details when you come to that part of it."[58]

Brown himself insisted on his "adoption" by Virginia, from which he drew much of his folk material for his poetry collected in *Southern Road*. A beautiful coffee table book on Virginia given to Spencer by Brown for "Xmas 1930" is inscribed to her and signed "From a Virginian who insists he's adopted whether Virginia wills or not. Sterling A. Brown."[59] The Virginia project, which finally got

(35) Anne Spencer — Poems and Flowers.

William Moses, detail, "Anne Spencer: Poems and Flowers,"
from "A Historical Map of Virginia," in *The Negro in Virginia* (1940).

under way in 1937, continued for three years, spanning from when James Weldon Johnson was encouraging Spencer to write her prose novel to after his untimely death in June 1938.[60] Recognizing, as did Brown, the significance of *The Negro in Virginia*, which "essentially told the story of the Black man in America," Spencer continued the project in "Virginia as Narcissus."[61]

As it turned out, *The Negro in Virginia* was "both a standard bearer and an anomaly": few other books emerged from the Federal Writers Project that were focused on the history of African Americans and authored by African Americans, yielding a realistic and informative representation.[62] Brown's editorial power within the national institution was slight, but in the Virginia project he was able to draw on a network of African American Virginians whose collaborations extended beyond the project. Spencer was recognized in Virginia through this work and subsequent projects, such as Brown's anthology, *The Negro Caravan* (1941), Arthur P. Davis and J. Saunders Redding's *Cavalcade* (1971), and Arthur P. Davis's *The New Negro Renaissance* (1975), the last of which, significantly, republished Spencer's poem about lynching, "White Things," for the first time since 1923.[63] This place-defined network of African American Virginian authors, led by Brown, continued to address the struggle over authority, contextualization, assigned value, and ultimately the political significance of African American history and culture in the nation.

Chapter 25 of *The Negro in Virginia*, dedicated to "Arts," begins with Spencer's verse "Dunbar." The author of this chapter begins with James Bland (the originator of "Carry Me Back to Ole Virginny") and devotes a whole paragraph to Spencer in a fast-paced catalogue of African American artists:

> Of the contemporary Negro poets, Anne Spencer of Lynchburg has been heralded as Virginia's most outstanding. During both her school days and her career as a teacher, she scribbled verse, but, as she confesses, "I never thought that folks would call it poetry." On a visit to Lynchburg, James Weldon Johnson, the Negro critic, advised Anne Spencer to "put a back and a front to those sheets and send them to a publisher," a task that she has "never yet gotten around to." Johnson used five of her poems in his anthology, *The Book of American Negro Poetry*. Few poets have been praised so highly and have published so little as Anne Spencer. "Why, anyone can write a dull poem," she explains, "but not everyone can grow my flowers."[64]

This description clearly built off of James Weldon Johnson's introduction of Spencer in his 1922 preface to *The Book of American Negro Poetry*, in which he asserts that her poetry's "opulence" "may infuse a much-needed color, warmth and spirit of abandon into American poetry."[65] But the author of the chapter in *The Negro in America* goes beyond Brown's description in characterizing Spencer's poetry as rare, perhaps rarer than the hybrid flowers she grew from bulbs.

In his 1939 call for African American writers to return "to earth" and to "earthly people," Redding assesses the extent to which African American poetry of the modern era serves as a conduit to nature and the folk and declares Langston Hughes's blues poetry of Negro life profoundly limited.[66] Redding concludes his study with the poetry of Sterling Brown from *Southern Road* (1932), the counterpoint, in his view, to Hughes's treatment of the folk. Brown's poetry is "gratifying new work" that draws on folk material but "differs from the old."[67] He affirms James Weldon Johnson's evaluation of Brown's work in his preface to *Southern Road* that Brown's treatment of folk material works to "deepen . . . its meaning and multiply . . . its implications." John Henry and other such folk figures are updated in Brown's realist poetry, which represents their complex and modern condition; they aren't simply diminished folk figures of the past but are voiced through politically relevant, earthly people, such as Big Boy Davis.

Redding's folk are located in history and bear political significance; they are not a romanticized, ahistorical folk that feel rather than think. An intellectual culture of the folk, he suggests, could be more effectively conveyed through its modern-day contextualization, which granted a political existence to rural African American life. The incomplete Federal Writers Project endeavor to provide African American history by state and region concluded with the depression years. But the situating of African American mass culture in the South and in nature was continued by African American writers in the following decade of the 1940s.

"Reapers of . . . Misery": Writing and the Ecology of Place

"In the 1940s," George Hutchison has observed, "literature came to be not just a vehicle for delivering environmentalist or conservationist messages. Its relationship to the environment might be ontological, the processes of its utterance those of nature itself, forces in the ecosystem. Inherent in such a notion is the inextricable relationship between nature and culture, that nature is not culture's 'other'—nor, say, its romantic origin. Culture may be a natural product of human beings, but it also has effects in the natural world—that is to say, it is part of the ecology of a place."[68] The attitude was, he points out, Whitmanian, but with a significant difference: it called for the ethical transformation of a collective human society, not just of individuals. This mindset characterizes a distinct outlook shaped by World War II and the years following this cataclysmic event.

A poem authored by Spencer in this period that revisits the form of the short poem, which she had used early in her publishing career with "Dunbar," titled "God never planted a garden" affirms this lesson of body and soul, culture and ecology, invoking both the Cold War and domestic segregation. Ecology for Spencer means placing nature at the center of an inquiry into the relation of living things and humankind to Earth. This inquiry takes on special significance in the advent and aftermath of World War II in the connection between nations and the sense of a shared ethical obligation of them in a global ecology. It was a developing national conversation with significant implications for African Americans in the American nation. The poem demonstrates this concern for global and domestic ecology:

> God never planted a garden
> But He placed a keeper there;
> And the keeper ever razed the ground
> And built a city where
> God cannot walk at the eve of day,
> Nor take the morning air.[69]

Spencer wrote this poem in the mid-1950s, in the midst of generating ideas for "Virginia as Narcissus" while confronting the separatist resistance to school desegregation exemplified by Senator Richard Russell and the other participants in massive resistance. The "Southern Manifesto" was the southern states'

Anne Spencer photographed by Jimmie Ray, circa 1948 (Anne Spencer Papers, Anne Spencer House and Garden Museum Archives).

official reaction to the 1954 *Brown v. Board of Education* ruling that in law if not in practice officially ended segregation. A senator from Georgia and a virulent segregationist, Russell was held in high regard by his peers for his technical knowledge of procedure, which he used to advance the segregationists' refutation of the federal ruling. Spencer mentions him and others in her manuscript. "God never planted a garden" similarly references the poet's concern for Earth in the hands of a human "keeper"—the atom bomb and segregationists. These global and domestic contexts are cataclysmic.

In "Virginia as Narcissus," Spencer recalls that

> we used on Sunday Mornings (after the young part of our family was grown and
> gone and no longer had to set the going to SS pattern; and besides, our bones
> ached) listen by radio to a southern religionist governor teach what we had to
> guess was a business man's bible class. It was remarkable how close his didac-
> tic voice and wave-length personality lay to the Tribune's late McCormick. This
> particular Sunday, he rode off in all directions—as we didactic ones are prone to

do—his subject was a "natural." Extolling, from his words, flower-garden making "only the Anglo-Saxon has exercised the art of gardening." This, with the Lord God making—according to his own accepted textbook—a garden, and walking in it in the cool of the evening![70]

This recollection provides the background to Spencer's "God never planted a garden": the narcissism of Anglo Saxon "superiority." As for Spencer's garden of the manuscript poem, we are made to understand that humans plant a garden and they are the keepers of God's Earth. The body and the soul live and die together.

The Editorials

In "Life-Long, Poor Browning" Spencer acknowledges the restrictive and expansive space of the poem, simultaneously distinguishing between the garden of human beings and nature, God's creation. In "Virginia as Narcissus," Spencer emphasizes African Americans' intellectual and imaginative freedom and the power of poetic thought to provide a corrective to southern myths and their false institutions. Immediately following the profile of Spencer, *The Negro in Virginia* acknowledges the power of poetry for many in a chapter on the arts penned by Brown: "In every city and hamlet of Virginia are would-be Negro poets who find solace simply in 'putting their thoughts on paper.' Lawyers, ministers, business men, teachers, and students write poetry, which—whether privately published or printed in newspapers—gives satisfaction to the writer."[71] Brown adds that African American newspapers have not only provided a publication outlet for Black American poetry but have also "played a vital part in the intellectual life of every community."[72] Spencer's many letters to the editor of newspapers, also written in this time period, demonstrate her intellectual engagement, while the fact that they remained unpublished testifies to the restriction of public discourse. The critique she offers in these unpublished editorials calls attention to the limitations of what can be said in mainstream, published, and regulated discourse. Her editorials underscore the values and circumstances that produce literary professionals and show how modern poetry itself has been institutionalized.

The conceit of writing a weekly column for a newspaper forced Spencer to write, creating a pointed outlet for her prose. Her friends Langston Hughes, Georgia Douglas Johnson, and J. Saunders Redding all wrote regularly for African American newspapers with national circulation, and James Weldon Johnson had had a column called Views and Reviews at the *New York Age* from 1914–16.[73] Spencer was full of fire, burning to write her own weekly editorials. And she would write them, even though they would not be published.

The editorials grew out of Chauncey's stationing with the U.S. Air Force at

Patterson Field Air Base, just outside Dayton, Ohio, where a series of personal attacks on him were published in the *Ohio State News*, a Black newspaper, between 1944 and 1945. As Chauncey remarks in his memoir *Who Is Chauncey Spencer?*, as the employee relations officer for the air depot, a position never before occupied by an African American, and with a mandate to implement Executive Order 8802—mandatory integration of the armed forces—he found himself caught between white superiors who advised him to "drag [his] feet" if he wanted to keep the job and African American employees who expected to advance merely "because they [were] Negroes" on the basis of "special favors."[74] The *Cleveland Call Post* noted Chauncey's resulting "heroic accomplishments" in this role: "In 1940 there were twenty-three Negro janitors at Patterson Field. In 1944 there are six-hundred Negroes working in all capacities."[75]

Although he would receive "decoration for exceptional civilian service from the Secretary of the Army" in 1948, in late 1944, as Chauncey puts it in his memoir, "condemnation followed [his] commendation" for achievement.[76] "As long as there was an all-Negro Air Corps," he writes, "there would always be a bottleneck in the upward movement of the Negroes."[77] After a lengthy libel suit brought by Chauncey, the *Ohio State News* was found guilty and forced to pay restitution to him. Yet even though he won the libel suit, his reputation had suffered as a result of the innuendoes and accusations. "Caught in the middle," he could be questioned easily by both African Americans and whites.[78] The editorials Spencer wrote explicitly voice the disillusionment and outrage of the World War II years in which African American servicemen defending the nation again faced racial discrimination, both within the military and upon return home. Chauncey had witnessed this discrimination firsthand. His success story as a pilot obscured the despondency and frustration he felt about the limitations imposed on him and others as second-class citizens.

Chauncey and his mother came up with the idea of sending the editorials to the *Pittsburgh Courier*, which had grown to be one of the top Black newspapers of the 1940s and 1950s from its founding in the first decade of the twentieth century, with a distribution of over a quarter of a million nationwide and several regional editions. They picked this newspaper for a couple of reasons. For one, a reporter from the *Pittsburgh Courier*, Al Dunmore, who had covered the integration of Patterson Field for the paper, followed Chauncey through the trial, "assisting me with coverage and supporting me in my fight for integration and my reputation."[79] For another, the paper and its editor, Robert L. Vann, had been following Chauncey ever since his founding of and membership in the National Airmen's Association, and it advocated for congressional recognition of African American aviators. Chauncey Spencer and fellow pilot Dale White had first met Vann in 1939. The idea was that Spencer would send the pieces she had written "to the *Pittsburgh Courier* as a weekly feature" that would be called The Indicator, but, as Chauncey noted to Green, "knowing mother we felt that she may decide—'I do not want to write any more'—after several publications so we decided to keep them in our possession for later use."[80] So, in the end, the editorials were never sent off to the newspaper.

Spencer's desire to tell it like it is fueled these drafted editorials. She had even written to the *Ohio State News* in defense of Chauncey, when a column "dragged in his family" in the accusation that he was a flunky at Patterson. Chauncey cites the letter:

> Again this long spite crusade would have gone its way with no word from me in his behalf. He is a man. He has been raised—raised is right—to tote his own weight; raised not with people in a house but parents in a home. You, and your henchmen actually seem to have a morbid talent for not letting bad enough alone. That is where I come in.
>
> In your last release you reached back behind my son and dragged in his family. I suppose this is another one of your ways to help the Negro people! Yes, we are average American humans. Folk who work hard; avoid any special limelight when we can do so; respect others as we ourselves demand respect—something to glow about when save, for the Grace of God, we could be putrid. We pay our taxes, cast our ballot for our rights. We know, too, that rights and duties are the twins born to every true citizen. We like it that way.
>
> This is a long letter, but not so long as the sum total of the attacks I now resent which your paper has unfairly made week after week. I hope your sixth sense will reveal the duty of a good newspaperman, and let you print this.
>
> —Anne Spencer[81]

The matter of who could critique the nation and the risks to livelihood following from such political critique were bound up in this decision to sign the pieces C. E. Spencer. Yet the name obviously references Chauncey. In the first of these editorials, "C. E. Spencer" invokes the Acts of the Assembly of Virginia of 1853–54, "an almost dead copy" of which she notes kept company with "the rather junky piles of books I grew up with" (this book can be found in Spencer's library collection at the University of Virginia) to discuss the recent passage of a resolution made to Congress by the Virginia House of Delegates "to permit Southern states to remove racial discriminations 'in their own way.'" The author calls attention to the absurdity of the state's legal code of that time with the example of a tax on dogs in Culpeper County, Virginia: "Article 12. No slave, free negro or mulatto shall, under any pretence whatever, have, keep, or own—a dog, or dogs—; and in case—it shall be lawful—to order said dog or dogs to be killed, and at [the justice of the peace's] discretion—to punish the owner with stripes not exceeding thirty-nine lashes." The editorial is laced with satire, referencing the "august body" enacting this policy "in the 78th year of the Commonwealth." "Virginia as Narcissus" continues this inquiry:

Acts of the General Assembly of Virginia, Passed in 1853–4, 78 yr of the common-wealth; and the wonder grows, were these lawless laws ever rescinded or did they just become in shame quiescent thru the years? Were they yet alive as Acts of the Assembly these men when the lightning struck and killed them, April 9, 1865? Were there, even then, one or two voices in this Gomorrah raised against them? As now gives heart wherever dastard law is voted the event is heartened by a ro-bust opposition however small—

The editorial was written in 1948. Its intentional scope of nearly one hundred years, found here and in the other unpublished editorials, characterizes Spen-cer's post-1940 explicit engagement with the nation's mythology and its pol-itics. I quote another one from 1948 in its entirety that shows the range and depth of her historical knowledge and that highlights her commitments:

The books and papers of the day in which we live are so italicized by words like Freedom, Liberty, Democracy, and Civilization, that as in like instances, famil-iarity may breed contempt. Are we too casual about the whole thing? We are if we think that what is—or almost is—has always been. It seems nearer the truth to believe—if our national life is truly progressing, that the strength of our polit-ical character today is our grown-up weakness of past years, just as in the future historians, no doubt, will regard the world of tomorrow as their Present having come into its maturity: that history is a very bad book indeed if the quality of hu-man material which goes into its records is not somewhat improved from decade to decade. I read a review of Beard's recent book called "The American Spirit." The first words of the piece asked the question, How old is the word civilization? It is a young word, it seems; was really born about the same time as the Constitution of the United States—born of the necessity for such a word, if, we can believe, Dr. Samuel Johnson rejected the word for his dictionary in 1772 despite Boswell's pleas. A French writer first uses it, Paine, and Jefferson knew him and seized on the essence of what civilization could mean—putting in motion here the urge in America and in France for progress in human welfare.

One then, may safely say that "Our Twentieth Century Liberties" are a com-posite of all life can mean when we make the comparatively just claim to being a civilized people: we have bought—but have not quite paid for—a document called the Constitution of The United States of America. We have bought the doc-ument, as we say, on credit and half the price is paid. We made our blood pay-ments: at Boston Common at Valley Forge at Yorktown—on land and sea. That was half the price. But that being done the young nation sat down awhile to lick a few sores, and write a few works; a few immortal words, as our opening dictum to a document significant and eternal—like the one at Sinai: "We, the people of the United States—to form—establish—insure—provide— promote . . . wings of lib-erty to ourselves—but half the price, these were the last democratic words to appear in a people, just emerged from, but still so close to Boston Commons, to Valley Forge, and Yorktown—places at which they had paid in blood, half the price for their precious liberties—that vigilant fear was a part of their daily lives.

or Jefferson, or Franklin, or Mason, or the rest; but it was not stronger than Washington and Jefferson, and Franklin, and Mason, and the rest. The combination of what the signers were was the Compacts' grace and disgrace: perhaps if these great minds had stopped and written no word more after they had agreed to set down as from Sinai, —We, the People of [t]he United States, in order to form a more perfect union, establish justice, insure—provide—promote the general welfare, and secure—. But their eyes were the human eyes of their time and the words were written into Article 4; Sect. 3 that were to soil the pages of history for the next seventy-eight years: "no person held to service—in one state— escaping—but shall be delivered up—to whom—labor may be due. But even then, near the end of the 18th century, the makers of this noble paper were beginning to write works in other places showing that an Angel was troubling the waters of their minds—Jefferson, "I tremble for my country, when I remember that God is just"; Washington, in his will, devising freedom for his retainers. The way even then was beginning to be made straight for "Our Twentieth Century Liberties.["]

The Monroe Doctrine phase stopped European imperialism in its westward prowl because our adroit termination of the war of 1817, in the weakest phase of America's existence made the war mongers pause—pause until we were again stronger. Chilled hearts all over our country were feeling at last an expanding touch of sun, and with it the courage to declare for freedom.

Rock-minded John Brown was being hanged for his too active belief that it is good to kill that good may come of it; Mrs. Stowe was writing her Book, one which as definitely as "Mein Kampf," and to better purpose shamed a nation into war; Garrison was being stoned, but printing, printing; Lucretia Mott, Sojourner Truth, Frederick Douglass, Wendell Phillips, Daniel Webster—speaking, speaking, for woman suffrage, against human bondage; speaking, in words so true & notable that the years have left them essentially intact. The poets writing, Longfellow, Whittier; and the Whitman from Camden, N-J, saying what he wanted to say about blood, and sweat, and tears, and brotherhood, saying it before Winston Churchill was born, in a new word sequence, more like chapters from Isaiah, less likely the poet laureates. And on Nov. 19, 1863, a homely gaunt man of great beauty at Gettysburg, making literary history because, perhaps, he chose as opening phrase to his 267-word speech—four scores and seven years ago. Who can say? Small things, and great ones, have moved toward us to make the mass history of the present.

History can be a very bad book and if the quality of the human material that gets into its pages is improved from decade to decade. . . . [W]e are making our final payment on the Constitution of the United States; that we are paying in full for this instrument of freedom, which with its now twenty-one amendments has at last come of age and casts its own vote for the Twentieth Century liberties of mankind; and under the sheltering branches of this Tree of Liberty the young shall be taught that duty is freedom & that discipline is liberty. Their liberty is rooted so deep in the life of the human race that a small wind can set it moving. And brave men, and the mothers of men keep coming on, to build its cities anew, to plant again, to alight anew its torches.[82]

The first 1948 editorial also relates a friend's account of travel to Reno, Nevada, where a clerk accepts the traveler as a patron by night but turns her away by day: "What had been debatable by the moon, was clearly exposed by the sun." Reno, being a "pin-ball town given over to gambling wheels and religious spiels," did not stand on principle as a matter of course, but it had nevertheless adopted a policy of segregation. Reaching its conclusion, the editorial observes, "No, Culpeper, Virginia, 1854 and Reno Nevada, 1948 are not far removed either in distance or in time. The Southern states have all along been permitted to remove racial discrimination 'in their own way.' And their own way amounts to just a relentless around-the-world infiltration of their own inhuman brew of poison gas.'"[83]

The Southwest, purportedly free of such prejudice, is shown to have been infiltrated by the poison of racial prejudice and its immoral and contradictory basis. Moreover, Spencer underscores both the randomness and insidiousness of so-called tradition—"in our own way"—so frequently invoked by Virginia lawmakers to assert state rights in matters of equality and the according or denying of civil rights to African American citizens. There was no tradition. This affirms what Spencer writes in her notes for "Virginia as Narcissus": a tradition that is written down is invalid, demonstrating the opposite: an overt assertion of unequal rights. True tradition, for Spencer, as the first epigraph to this chapter suggests, is a long-standing practice that is not recorded. "So this malpractice is not tradition, + is not in truth claimable as such. It is in uniquely this daemon. It is written down. The evil thing is archived that it might actually be kept alive."[84] The "malpractice" began in slavery and was continued in the modern, twentieth century by Virginia's 1924 Racial Integrity Act and other segregating practices culminating in the Southern Manifesto. Her manuscript makes this clear: "In this century of slave emancipation so far, the southern mind has shown its deternation [sic: determination; her intentional, and satiric, vernacular usage] to reconcreta [sic] slavedom policies by 2 atrocities Plessy V—and rep[eated]. Jim Crowism of spirit and body," she wrote.[85] While Spencer believed false tradition could only be kept alive if was it written down and archived, she maintained that memory, as her poem marking the ten-year anniversary of Johnson's death indicates, had to be kept alive through practice, through a present-tense companionship.

The editorial sheds light on her poem "Commonwealth."

> Editor News Sir: You wanner bet?
> The Block Optimist
> I like to lie awake in the dark make what's wrong of life so otherwise
> Change wrong to right but the
> Grinning Adversary is there to counter
> What is right?
> All that is not wrong.
> How do you know
> Another man wrote it in a book
> Is that the only man?
> Is that the last book?
> Well, if it gives no pain
> That dawn was just the one
> The sun forgot.[86]

The speaker, who describes herself as a "Block Optimist," challenges the "Editor News Sir" and "Grinning Adversary" with a desire to right wrongs. The pat answers to the questions posed by the speaker convey the unjust and authoritarian use of a totalizing knowledge in dictating what the meaning of life is. "How do you know / Another man wrote it in a book" underscores Spencer's belief in the invention of corrupt tradition through the written word, an assertion of power and privilege archived for posterity. The dawn itself is made out to be "the one / The sun forgot." The corrupt written word, by extending this logic to the idea that the opening of the new day is forgotten by the agent of its creation in the natural world, calls attention not only to the absurdity but also the danger of this "reasoning."

As Spencer's address of "Editor News Sir" suggests, the engagement between African Americans and newspapers could be productively antagonistic. This poem certainly provided Spencer with an outlet for her thoughts, giving her a way to interrogate commonly held and profoundly wrong positions on knowledge, books, human beings, and nature that were evident in Lynchburg and beyond. Spencer wrote editorials directed to white newspapers as well: the *Lynchburg News*, the *Saturday Review*, the *Richmond Times-Dispatch*, the *Daily Advance*. In these editorials, Spencer takes up the discourse of race generated by whites on civil rights, correcting misinformation and providing alternative perspectives. Passing as male, Spencer on occasion asserted regional authority through "his" knowledge, including experience of place. She also occasionally leveraged her subject from an anonymous and ambiguous racial designation—perhaps taking inspiration from James Weldon Johnson's protagonist in *The*

Autobiography of an Ex-Colored Man, a book in the Spencer family library.[87] The anonymity offered safety and even sanity—even if the piece was not published.

Spencer continued writing these editorials, from the late 1940s into the mid-1960s. In a letter addressed to the editor at the *Lynchburg News*, for example, she writes: "Sir—the vaunted kindly tradition of Virginia can be, and usually is, just so much mish-mash except as that exchanged between the salt of the earth, here or anywhere else." She continues by invoking the same article from the Acts of the General Assembly of Virginia that she references in the editorial written for the *Pittsburgh Courier* but in a way intended to educate the primarily white staff and audience of the newspaper: "So here you have the red and black not by Stendhal but a creation and its perpetuation by white men who had so lately themselves fled them down the years to freedom."[88] As she writes in "Virginia as Narcissus," "Anselm: To Wm the Red / 'Treat me as a free man and I devote myself and all that I have to your service but if you treat me as a slave you shall have neither me nor mine!'"[89] Referencing the class system and the necessity of a realist gaze on the condition of any laborer's desire for advancement, she calls attention to the social order of slavery and segregation that characterizes the American context.

"Virginia as Narcissus"

Spencer devised her ambitious project as a means of orienting herself to the discourses of nation and democracy. "Virginia as Narcissus" is a learned work with a vast range of references to intellectual history, philosophy, religion, revolution, and the American encounter with freedom, and slavery.[90] Chauncey Spencer recalled that his mother "always said about the matter of Virginia, 'Virginia is a great state. This is where democracy was born. It died here, too!'"[91]

It was to be a learned work of the scope and proportions of Sir Thomas Carlyle's life works, which Spencer owned in a ten-volume set, and it drew from his spirit as well. Spencer, underlined his declaration that "work . . . is communication with nature."[92] Drawing together literary sources as various as the Greek myth of Narcissus, William Makepeace Thackeray's *The Virginians*, and Charles Darwin's *Origin of Species*, she provides a contemporary critique of her state's continued segregating practices. The 1956 "Southern Manifesto," which led to the passage of laws that cut off funding for public schools that attempted to integrate, fueled Spencer's writing of "Virginia as Narcissus: Or, the Southern Mind," a corrective manifesto to the "massive resistance" stance in Virginia and the South and the hypocrisy of southern claims to possession:

> The Southern mind in its search for an unknown God, has found him in any
> moneyed object little or big, or restricted use—restricted to I me mine we us
> our—

This spirit obtains in the foundation when any churches schools libraries, parks—if the thing looks expensive, handsome out go their arms around it—however its got—the use is limit to even their poor whites by kindly ostracism; to us by open, insulting laws set down with unreligious fervor—-S.M. [southern mind, Southern Manifesto] brings the charge, granted of mal use of those premises. Teachers wonted their salt—sitting there, just a spitting distance from their other life from which they had fled—these men, set down here and passed into history a thing in modern parlance too vile to be called a law.[93]

Contemplating the metamorphosis of Lynchburg as a former librarian and educator, Spencer annotated her books to rework, appropriate, and correct prior studies of the nation. In her copy of Alexis de Tocqueville's *Democracy in America* (1835–40), Spencer notes in 1955 "Prophecy: 120 years later" alongside this paragraph in chapter 18, titled "Situation of the Black Population in the United States, and the Dangers with Which Its Presence Threatens Whites":

It is true, that in the North of the Union, marriages may be legally contracted between negroes and whites; but public opinion would stigmatize a man who should connect himself with a negress as infamous, and it would be difficult to meet with a single instance of such a union. The electoral franchise has been conferred upon the negroes in almost all the states in which slavery has been abolished; but if they come forward to vote, their lives are in danger. If oppressed, they may bring an action at law, but they will find none but whites amongst their judges; and although they may legally serve as jurors, prejudice repulses them from that office. The same schools do not receive the child of the black and of the European. In the theatres, gold cannot procure a seat for the servile race beside their former masters; in the hospitals they lie apart; and although they are allowed to invoke the same Divinity as the whites, it must be at a different altar, and in their own churches, with their own clergy. The gates of Heaven are not closed against these unhappy beings; but their inferiority is continued to the very confines of the other world; when the negro is defunct, his bones are cast aside, and the distinction of condition prevails even in the equality of death. The negro is free, but he can share neither the rights, nor the pleasures, nor the labor, nor the afflictions, nor the tomb of him whose equal he has been declared to be; and he cannot meet him upon fair terms in life or in death.[94]

In the introduction to this work, Spencer also wrote in the margin, "1831–1781=50."[95] Spencer here calculated how many years had passed since the Revolutionary War's last battle and Tocqueville visited the United States and made these observations.[96]

In her heavily annotated her copy of Thackeray's *The Virginians*, Spencer links Thackeray's fictional plantation directly to George Washington: "She widow Curtis: And he, G.W., inherited 50 thou / grand [sic] of slavery sweat- / thru her- the first / money fortune in the / Dominion—tho the win / ning may have lost him / the other one—the love / of his life—"[97] She writes "notes for VA as Narcissus" by a pivotal passage in *The Virginians*, in which the aunt of the protagonist offers a moral corrective to the judgments issued against him for his friendship toward an Indian woman who "helped me, and was kind to me."[98] His aunt "railed at all the world round her" and "unveiled to her nephew . . . a strange picture of life and manners" in which religious tradition undergirds selfish acts and also drives out pleasure: "A sermon in the morning: a sermon at night: and two or three of a Sunday. That is what people call being good. Every pleasure cried fie upon; all us worldly people excommunicated; a ball an abomination of desolation; a play a forbidden pastime; and a game of cards perdition; What a life!"[99] Spencer offers a similar negative evaluation of goodness in a much earlier, undated letter to Grace and James Weldon Johnson, probably from after 1931, when the second edition of *The Book of American Negro Poetry* was published:

Darling Grace 'n Gem,

Egad this is a white man's country—thank God! How momentous the months have been since we were together we all know—but nobody, except the Russellites and the Creator, knows what it all *means*. I was reared to believe—and it is still mother's gospel—that one to be good must be *unhappy* to the point of salvation. So, vicariously, if in no other way, we are all marching in the "sacred Direction."[100]

Her copy of Darwin's *On the Origin of Species by Means of Natural Selection* was marked in key passages, beginning with its first epigraph from Whewell's *Bridgewater Treatise*: "But with regard to the material world, we can at least go so far as this—we can perceive that events are brought about not by insulated interpositions of Divine power, exerted in each particular case, but by the establishment of general laws." "Whose laws?," Spencer wrote, and then erased it.[101] Her initial stance as a reader of Darwin demonstrates a suspicion of the controlling narratives of tradition in science and the law. As she annotated her copy of James Freeman Clarke's *Anti-Slavery Days*, she updated the argument for the 1950s. As Clarke wrote, "Slavery was abolished not by disunion, but by the power which opposed disunion. . . . [I]t was not abolished by those who wished for disunion, but by those who were determined at all hazards and by every sacrifice to maintain the Union." In the margin here, Spencer writes "Sen. Russell," indicating that the same reasoning applied in the situation of desegregation.[102]

She took the idea of interposition from Darwin's epigraph and altered it to create a new coinage—"interimposition"—as a pointed, witty critique of the application of laws, a term she uses in "Virginia as Narcissus":

> found subsistence by Indian fare and food—Columbus found something that
> wasn't lost—
> we blacks—sent by God, and brought by the devil—were delivered here long
> before Russell's folk began to people
> For the same reason that hinter state Georgia commonly referred to in my mind
> as the Australia of America: chock full as *my* country is of remittance men,
> religionists, interimpositionalists—This word dialogically alters Darwin's
> *early* in the history of the English.
> —except that nowhere else is there greater determinism toward the thing
> sought than Va. evinces in her attempt to stabilize her face in the pool for all
> to admire. In part, this has been so successful that, in initiation there of the
> real, and . . . unilateral
> Your editorial of yesterday is far beneath your inmost thought you do not pity
> little colored children. You mention, and castigate local negro leadership you
> deflatter us. No one of us is a leader.[103]

Spencer also drew words for use from the glossary Darwin provided, which she used in "Virginia as Narcissus": "imago," "the perfect, generally winged reproductive state of an insect," and "loess," "a marly deposit of recent (post-Tertiary) date, which occupies a great part of the valley of the Rhine."[104]

Spencer annotated Darwin's discussion of correlated variation, one of the many places in *Origin* where he made the case that natural and artificial selection parallel each other: "Many laws regulate variation, some few of which can be dimly seen. . . . Color and constitutional peculiarities go together, of which many remarkable cases could be given among animals and plants," Darwin writes, relating an example of Virginian pigs selected for survival that he had been told about by a group of Virginia pig farmers. "One of the 'Crackers' (*i.e.*, Virginia squatters) added, 'We select the black members of a litter for raising, as they alone have a good chance of living.' . . . Hence if man goes on selecting, and thus augmenting, any peculiarity, he will almost certainly modify unintentionally other parts of the structure, owing to the mysterious laws of correlation."[105] "Any variation which is not inherited is unimportant for us," Darwin adds. Spencer circled "us," an indication of her deep suspicion of the discourse of science as an assertion of absolute reason and of laws that came out of this discourse.[106] Fascinated by hybridization, Spencer carefully studied it not only in the bulbs she planted but in how it was approached by Darwin and used in contemporary political discourse to argue for segregation.

Spencer alludes to the relevance of the various sources she consulted over the decades of composing "Virginia as Narcissus" in one of her outlines for the work:

Virginia as Narcissist
By
Mary Wythe Caution in Collaboration
With
Thomas Babington Macualay and others
Last Will and Testament to the people I love; mostly Virginians, Too—
    "Mix 'Em."[107]

"Mary Wythe Caution" (marry with caution) references the 1924 Racial Integrity Act, which racially designated babies at birth as either black or white and eliminated Native American designations and names; in a bit of wordplay, her "mix 'em" (a mixing she notes had characterized Oberlin, "the first decent elementary school of the South," and Hampton, "which pioneered in educating the American Indian and American negro together until the Indians were claimed as siblings and unproved forbears by certain ladies in waiting") takes the place of what she elsewhere occasionally refers to as "M.E.," "the mind's eye," or "me," by which she means the narcissistic tendency of southern restrictions: "In your caste system the w.m. [white man] occupies the primary secondary tertiary place.[108] Spencer recalls that "in Va the year that the social integrity bill was passed was precipice year—Jim Crow wasn't enough."[109]

The pen name also references Virginia's Wythe County, where Raymond Arthur Byrd was lynched in in 1926. A World War I veteran—he had served in the 807th Pioneer Infantry in France—Byrd had an extramarital affair with the daughter of the farmer for whom he worked. She bore a child and refused to say she had been raped. Byrd was nevertheless charged with a statutory offense, imprisoned, and lynched by a mob who dragged his beaten body through town and hanged him from a tree by a church. It was a source of embarrassment to the governor of Virginia at that time, Harry F. Byrd Sr., that the two men shared a name.

But Spencer's focus wasn't simply 1924–26. Virginia's stance against school integration through "massive resistance" was established by Harry F. Byrd, by this time a senator, who invoked the state's antimiscegenation law as the central reason for defying school desegregation. When in 1958 the resistance was ruled unconstitutional, the General Assembly of Virginia then repealed the state's compulsory school attendance law and gave counties and cities the power to decide whether to provide public education. Spencer, a lifelong educator in her various formal and informal capacities, was incensed. She recognized the deep and lasting impact of these policies on racial relations in Virginia. Most cities and counties proceeded with integration, but in a number of places, private schools for whites were established with the financial support of both the state and local governments, which had the effect of drawing whites to the suburbs and leaving Black schoolchildren in the cities of Virginia.

On top of that, Spencer worried about how integration happened in only one direction:

> Now that "Pub[lic] schools are equal" why should the only answer be that of "mixing" the colored children into the white schools why not use the turn-about statement of mixing the white children into the "equalized" colored schools? Since some of the latter are so big the kids are rattling around like dried peas in locust pods where at least one ideal that of space has been realized—[110]

The first page of her manuscript states:

> I leave to my heirs forever my united country; the United States of America. And my especial niche in my country—the young girl I love Virginia. But because even now I am "busy dying" these words are to remind you The sort of gentle men and gentle women who'd not rest till safeguard for slave catching was written into our constitution So when it is affirmed that Congress can kill any one amendment we merely reply they have already done so— / What follows is a testament of love (or cure)[111]

There was a precipitous urgency to the testament, because, as Spencer remarks, "the monotonous ever lugubrious culture of our southland is as arrested as a stalled car: the habit of waiting for a federal or 'up north' push for itself is both automatic and unconscious. Besides, the aid is always denied." Looking backward, Spencer reflects on the perspective of time past: "An important piece in a . . . magazine asked on its cover . . . "Should public schools be secular?" when the query might better have been, "Should public schools be public?" I have said in my testament of youth (as this is one of Age) that I owned no regalia + was loath to join cults social or religious, But I had seen my men and women join groups fostering much pesade and a parment but they follow patternus Americana while supporting [racial division]." As she observes elsewhere in "Virginia as Narcissus," "The average negro teacher May be bravely articulate about integration in private with a peer—to make his associate quip *with us* you'd think he invented integration"). Spencer was emphatic that schools should be public and that integration should not amount to the reluctant admission of a few Black students to white schools. She imagined a full-fledged integration, but she recognized that Black teachers were probably too vulnerable to publicly demand this. She continues: "The best we could offer—is the best of our selves—the NAACP; that does not stand alone but is a unit of all who have since Christ believed in a perveous [sic] humanity." Elsewhere in the manuscript she writes: "Va is im-pervious." The dilemma of Virginia and its schools was also the dilemma of rights, of humanity.[112]

In 1959, when the bulk of "Virginia as Narcissus" was composed, Edward Murrow broadcast "The Lost Class of 1959," featuring Virginia's school closures, on national television. Spencer notes:

> Murrow among the preachers who dared God to be on the side of the ~~dark~~
> mythic people even the dark ones—
> Those who in the face of God with all their might and swore by the hell that
> sired them
> Man-maker make white[113]

In her depiction of Virginia's resistance to school desegregation as a national shame, Spencer draws in her 1923 poem about lynching, "White Things," which was published in the March issue of the *Crisis*. She had never forgotten this poem. When it was first published, James Weldon Johnson had written her a short, powerful letter: "I must congratulate you on your poem 'White Things.' It is splendid."[114] Reading Thomas Babington Macauley's complete works ("Macaulay: 'don't confuse myth with Claudius Narcissus,'" she notes) again reminded her of "White Things":

> Most things are colorful things—the sky, earth, and sea.
> Black men are most men; but the white are free!
> White things are rare things; so rare, so rare
> They stole from out a silvered world—somewhere.
> Finding earth-plains fair plains, save greenly grassed,
> They strewed white feathers of cowardice, as they passed;
>> The golden stars with lances fine
>> The hills all red and darkened pine,
> They blanched with their wand of power;
> And turned the blood in a ruby rose
> To a poor white poppy-flower.
> They pyred a race of black, black men,
> And burned them to ashes white; then,
> Laughing, a young one claimed a skull,
> For the skull of a black is white, not dull,
>> But a glistening, awful thing;
>> Made, it seems, for this ghoul to swing
> In the face of God with all his might,
> And swear by the hell that sirèd him:
>> "Man-maker, make white!"[115]

Spencer incorporates a revision of the lines "to swing / in the face of God with all his might / . . . 'Man-maker, make white!'" into "Virginia as Narcissus": "and fling in the face of / God with all your might / Man-maker, make white!"[116] The shift in address from third person to second person, the explicit condemnation of the "you," is striking, voicing outrage against the assault on black humanity.

Spencer uses the Narcissus myth to emphasize that "soul-making is a slow, tedious process too precious to be wasted."[117] "White Things" traces the soul making that is undone by the "blanching" "cowardice" that destroys "a race of black, black men . . . in the face of God." The environmental destruction, which saps Earth of its color through bold insistence—changing "greenly grassed" plains to "fair," "the blood in a ruby-rose / to a poor white poppy-flower"— culminates in the "pyred . . . race of black, black men," who are "burned . . . to ashes white." "Pyred" and "sirèd" provide the internal rhyme that encapsulates this poem's devastation, for the action of the lynching is carried out not by God but by a "ghoul" who defies God's law, replacing it for man's law. The "face of God" provides a counterpoint to the skull swung before him, part of a man who had been made in his image now rendered "a glistening, awful thing."

Man's law, the swinging skull, the defiance of a natural order that is asso-ciated with God, and the demand to "make white" all the world convey the faulty perception of white power. The emphasis on "red" in "pyred" and "sirèd" links the victim and victimizer through the color of blood. The focus on white-ness, on self-image, on intentional isolation carries over from "White Things" to "Virginia as Narcissus," intensified by the myth of Narcissus, who "seeing his own reflection in the pool of a fountain loved it and lost it and there remained lonely but echo echo echo," as Spencer writes in cascading script. "Speaking his speech, thinking his thought (senator Russell) Narcissus was a gentleman, At least a slightly feckless one and naturally he owned an echo."[118] Calling forth the Acts of the General Assembly of Virginia yet again, Spencer notes,

> I often think if I were a preaching minister I'd like to teach with this or that text from the Holy Scriptures. The favorite selection, tho, is from Genesis—"and the *spirit* of God *moved* on the face of the water." And from The Beloved, "In the beginning was the *word* and the *word* was God. Two texts in one to *Bind* into [within] the human heart to confront its own mendacious words, and, acts of self-adulation. For the first time in any religion there was a moving God; instead of a movable god. For the first time in any religion God became actual communi-cant to Man: the word.[119]

From a position of moral authority, Spencer, in her projected sermon, empha-sizes God's spirit as the face of the water. The myth supplanted this spirit, re-placing it with Narcissus's search for his own image.

In a further reckoning of the sources that informed the composition of "Virginia as Narcissus," Spencer went so far as to make a credit-debit list that stretched through the intellectual life of Rome, England, and America. Brown-ing, and Carlyle, occupied the credit side; Macaulay, as well as Byrd, occupied the debit side:

Credit:
Browning
Hamilton

Moors—mistake not going Duke of Alva's creed

...

Sequoia

...

Carlyle vs. [Macaulay]

Debit:

...

Faubers [Orval Faubus]—put in thumb pulled out plumb—big boy am I

Hand

Santayana

Wave of the future people—belong Matt. Arnold's Sweetness and light—

Kasper and Pound not import., just slight trauma

...

Byrd

Kilpatrick, Dabney

Macaulay

Noteworthy among these names is the sequoia, a tree, on the credit side. As she writes elsewhere, in an unfinished thought, "The most uncelebrated brain in America should be Sequoias."[120] Spencer asserts the primacy of nature, Earth, over humankind.

Under the pen name Mary Wythe Caution, Spencer created an outline of truths for the design of "Virginia as Narcissus":

Chapt. 1.—origin of codex of prejudice called tradition:

Argyle [slave ship]: 2. Captivity had restored to him the noblest kind of liberty— all about

3. he became as one inspired with new wisdom and virtue [...]

10. Never to be absurd to oneself is never to be completely *alive*.

11. Essence of Kant: The problem is to estimate what the *Babe* trailing clouds

12. of glory *already knows*, and what he *can* know—"from the infinite to the finite"

13. —no doubt Kant's aversion to travel per se was the longer tour yet his preoccupation with the mind of man in that longest of trips from the womb into our world—

Green's *Short History of the English People*, she points out, "warns us that much of Palgrave's Hist. of English common[wealth]—is helpful, if read *with caution*— enough not to consider it a source of primary authority, so in the south fable and History make high-colored propaganda for our section." The "high-colored" propaganda of commonwealth history applies to the South and its perceived tradition as well. She elaborates: "Wm Byrd ... and cap'n [John] Smith ... in between is not too much viable." She takes her critique into the twentieth century, mentioning the Virginian writer Ellen Glasgow, whose fiction she describes as "the very essence of these New World folk in their dominating situation" and James Branch Cabell, who she states "recognized the odor" of segregation and "years later with another holy gesture" wrote *Let Me Lie*. "Meritorious and meretricious as words poles apart or as people close together are always lying there ready to spring, never together in action each alone," that is, "meritorious" and "meretricious" should be poles apart in principle, but in practice they are not.[121]

For the conclusion to "Virginia as Narcissus," which remained unfinished, Spencer wonders, "—if the African slaves and the indentured debtors + criminals had not been slushed into Va early in 17th century The dangling adventurer and other remittance younger son would have gone out into nowhere along with the Croatans—no colonists no Tom Paine no Alex Hamilton, no Aaron Burr for another 3 centuries and this land could have by now used its own common sense to begin a Perfect Land No, Banish the thought. We accept our universe in time and place—or space."[122] With an ironic jab, Spencer writes: "End of book—Tom Paine on the appearance of right—...—Tom Paine meant what he said." Spencer means that Paine himself contradicted the principles of liberty that he espoused. In a different part of the manuscript, Spencer writes, "So. Tradition 'A long habit of not thinking a thing wrong gives it a superficial appearance of being right' Tom Paine."[123]Observing that there is "no religion but people," Spencer remarks that "in nature's economy: nothing is lost—try as we do, It nature cannot be wasted—but its changes are catastrophic," linking this post–atom bomb idea with her observation that "Columbus found something that wasn't lost."[124] To this, she adds: "End: Every human decency is pleading here for itself in essence; the somewhat that the world has had so too little of—friendship. Better even than brotherhood when that word cannot—as it often does not—become twin to friend. I am reminded of my five-year perfectly grandson who introduced a playmate as ["]This is my girl friend"! Brother, or friend both can atrophy" (the page on which this note appears is ripped, cutting off the end of this last sentence).[125] In a prophetic conclusion, Spencer writes: "Let us end these things, these parts now and forever and if in the mind of God we have time set there be naught save Future in which men deal justly with men after the true deserts of each and not by the color of the face of mankind—"[126]

And, in the final, penultimate lines of "Virginia as Narcissus," leaving space for elaboration on her acceptance of "time and place—or space," she states:

To be born in a free State—
[space]
finis: if this is the twilight of the gods, it can only mean that God himself shall
    arrive[127]

Making Ends: Acknowledging the Unwritten as Tradition

In an undated draft letter to Mr. Basler at the Library of Congress, written sometime in the early 1970s, Spencer wrote, "I don't negate my poems—they are me in the years here they are my conversation with myself."[128] Humble and defiant, Spencer's assertion that her poetry constitutes her existence while "here" on Earth indicates its essentiality. It is the spirit of place, the language of the imagination; it is, at last, life itself. Spencer makes this space for herself and her writing and for black women's writing by extension through the writing of her manuscripts.

By 1970, Spencer began thinking of turning "Virginia as Narcissus" into an essay, as she wrote editor John Ferrone at Harcourt.[129] Spencer and Ferrone corresponded over several years, with the author promising and making excuses along the way; Ferrone's letters were charming, as evidenced by her replies in which she insists she will put together a collection of her poems, which she hoped would be prefaced by Sterling Brown.[130] "There are several pieces of paper around here with that salute on them but with a new pad and a childs stout-looking pencil and a mental shove from Pop and God I may make ends meet—literary ones." She explains her vision for the book: "With your permission our book's make-up gets the idea of format from EBW's 'Second Tree From the Corner'—suggested but no attempted likeness save form—and many have put flotsam & jetsam in a pile after salvage—." Spencer then enumerates the format:

1. Virginia as Narcissus should go in—essay from birth to now called
2. Immediate Genealogy—the best chance this side of Heaven
3. Title: Poems by Anne Spencer[131]

Spencer's description of "Virginia as Narcissus" as an essay "from birth to now" is wonderfully ambiguous, admitting both the author's birth and the state's. She acknowledges the incomplete and eclectic gathering of odds and ends necessary to comprise the book. The outline indicates both her ambition and her ultimate refusal to share her work in its stages of experimentation or to finish it at all.

That Spencer did not complete and publish "Virginia as Narcissus" yet worked on it for decades indicates her devotion to a cultural world hostile to her vital conscience, her individual perspective through which she conveyed and searched for a collective society of humankind. Bearing in mind Hutchinson's observation that "culture . . . is part of the ecology of a place," we must also attend to the fact that it may remain hidden from sight, expressed incompletely in the intermediary form of an African American woman author's manuscript of public critique.

"Virginia as Narcissus" was never abandoned, but it was never coherently or completely written either. After a period of extensive prose experimentation from 1940–55, Spencer returned to writing poetry. It was, she found, a more appropriate form for her vision than prose. While the urgency of truth telling could be conveyed by both forms, poetry accommodated multiple forms of experience and expression simultaneously, allowing for the voicing of different stages of experience, awareness, and memory. But, as I show in chapter 3, the "John Brown" manuscript preserves its multiple frames of experience precisely because it remains incomplete and unpublished, functioning as a *practice* of memory and tradition as Spencer defined it—incomplete because "unwritten," a living archive of memory representing both communal practices and Spencer's evolving individual imagination.

CHAPTER FOUR

"John Brown"
An "Epic of Democracy"

> Think it not thy business, this of knowing thyself; thou art an
> unknowable individual: know what thou canst work at; and
> work at it, like a Hercules! That will be thy better plan.
> —THOMAS CARLYLE, *Past and Present*

Spencer's epic project on John Brown grew in tandem with and out of "Virginia as Narcissus." Exploring the commonwealth of Virginia also meant tracing West Virginia's division from it. The two states were the source of Spencer's two selves, one born in Virginia, a slave-holding state, the other in West Virginia, a free state. To recognize and think through John Brown's history and action and its significance in American history was to think through her own autobiography and the significant role of both Virginia and West Virginia in her upbringing and sense of self. Brown became an abiding presence in Spencer's meditations. He was her companion guide through the shifting twentieth-century American landscape. Spencer called him "J-no."

As her guide, Brown enabled her to transform her previously published poems into a living archive of memory. "J-no" lived in Spencer's imagination continuously from 1940 through to the last years of her life. She wrote notes for the poem on every possible surface for more than thirty years, sometimes with the heading "NBJB" (nota bene John Brown), other times simply with "J-no." Evaluating the one hundred years between 1859 and 1959, from Brown's insurrection at Harpers Ferry to the intensified atmosphere of civil rights integration and the South's massive resistance, Spencer aligned Brown's refusal of slavery with her refusal of inequality. Through the persona of John Brown as hero, martyr, and marching soul, a defiant, justice-seeking spirit even beyond death—she explores the dynamic relation of rupture and connection in African American environmental experiences in her home state of Virginia, a battleground for desegregation, over two centuries.

As we have seen, the loss of Johnson and the advent and aftermath of World War II led to an epochal shift in Spencer's writing after 1940. Segregation and economic hardship persisted for African Americans even in the face of the connection between nations and the sense of a shared ethical obligation among them in a global ecology that came in the wake of the war. It was a developing national conversation with significant implications for African Americans, even as they were largely excluded from it. Embracing the idea of long poems as "a textual process of 'betweenness,'" I interpret Spencer's "John Brown" as a dynamic and nuanced negotiation of epic's conventions, a response to its restrictive tradition and elite social structures.[1] Because it was unfinished and unpublished, Spencer was able to easily move between cultures and conventions as she wrote it, making use of the real time of memory enacted by her writing of the manuscript over decades, and to present a female consciousness *within*, not outside, its form. This movement is significant for its representation of African American environmental experience, and Spencer's epic should be seen as a unique contribution to what Posmentier has shown to be the "lyric ecologies" of Black literature in its responses to both natural and human-made disasters.

Spencer's "John Brown" manuscript is an epic's unfinished journey to claim its rightful status in the national culture, insisting, along the way, not simply on justice and equality for African American citizens but on the necessity of a specifically female virtue as guide. Spencer worked from a painting that had become part of the national lore: Thomas Hovenden's 1882–84 *The Last Moments of John Brown*.[2] Hovenden's painting was reproduced in *The Negro in Virginia*, the work for which Spencer was invited by Sterling Brown to serve as a consultant and in which her role as a Virginian featured prominently.[3] Clarke's *Anti-Slavery Days* (1883), one of Spencer's heavily annotated books in which notes for "John Brown" appear, describes the scene:

> We remember how when John Brown was being led to execution, he remarked on the beauty of the scenery. He saw on the way a colored woman with a colored infant in her arms. He took the colored infant in his arms and kissed it. Only a few months after that, I was riding through Virginia woods by moonlight, and a regiment of Wisconsin soldiers were marching by, singing, "John Brown's body lies mouldering in the ground. His soul is marching on." And his soul was marching on. It marched on until the whole South was redeemed.[4]

This lasting image was a fiction, as Villard's 1910 history of John Brown notes. "No little slave-child was held up for the benison of his lips, for none but soldiery was near and the street was full of marching men."[5] Nudelman confirms that Brown's hanging was a "military spectacle" in which the sentimentalism evoked by the image of father, mother, and child played no part. "Surrounded by 1,500 cavalry and militia, he was executed. According to *Harper's Weekly*, by the time Brown reached the field, 'the military already had full possession. Pickets were established, and citizens kept back, at the point of bayonet, from taking any position but that assigned to them.'"[6]

The sentimental image of Hovenden's painting figured Brown as a morally righteous patriarch of the American family and expressive of a liberal humanism affirming the morality Brown's antislavery stance.[7] As John Stauffer points

Thomas Hovenden, *The Last Moments of John Brown* (1882–84) (Metropolitan Museum of Art).

out, empathy was a driving force of the religious modernism of the radical abolitionists that Brown himself represented.[8] "Empathy greatly facilitated the convergence of black and white identities among these Radical Abolitionists," he writes, reminding his reader that "empathy . . . has aesthetic roots."[9] The intimate experience of viewing a painting or reading an epic could create empathetic bonds.

In her poem Spencer focuses on the enslaved woman and her baby. Rather than depict an equality that is bestowed upon African American mother and infant, Spencer grants them agency and subject status, sentience rather than sentiment. Her central image of this mother in her "John Brown" asserts a self-possessed humanity, effectively shifting the emotional bond of sympathy in the painting to empathy in her poem. In "A Dream of John Brown," one part of the larger epic, Spencer explicitly references this image:

About you and this mission
You saw their faces, the scared, angry, puzzled crowds
Black and white
Whole milled around by the thousands

I've been on the swing for eons of time. Where are those poor
creatures? Heaven is so empty!
One incident down there pleased me a lot
A very brave slave woman came near enough to hold up her
    Baby for my blessing—
Who am I to bless so I kissed the child's soft cheek
You have of course the picture in your files
Some aide to an aide in the newly formed manner
    Suggested
I be beheaded. I'm glad that was ignored
I need a rest to make this long trip
Acting accordingly to the best trained judgment of their
    Yet to be born, Pentagon, the piety of the different sorts,
The greed of slave, catches slave-aristocracy, the anxiously upheld
now litany of slave populations
They have finally got rid of all the Lord's way,
On the trip around and up.[10]

In another representation of Brown's kissing the child, Spencer writes,

Dear God you know me well not to be pious—no mouth full of praise, pris +
    passamenterie,
So then this
Gallant strange woman suffice [saffire?] brown
Her face for my
Blessing, I leaned
To its tender, small
face—and kissed it—
much to my own benefit—[11]

The "pris + passementerie" references the nation through what Spencer calls
"regalia" in her autobiographical statement for *Caroling Dusk* ("I have no academic honors, no lodge regalia").[12] It leads into the subsequent notes, where
the nation is figured as a white woman, who more correctly can be seen as a
symbol of falsity. And in this verse from 1970 a black man is beholden to white
woman wielding power and falseness simultaneously:

The ebony laddy
who likes ladies
that area of female who blush blush
can red white or blue
if she has but to say
prism prines or passamenterie—[13]

As the epic of John Brown is translated to a woman's body, prophetic vision is bestowed on Spencer herself, an authority unlike the power-corrupt white woman. In the process of writing it, Spencer transformed her previously published poems, revising them and recontextualizing them within the framework of the epic along with new poems emerging out of the manuscript's composition. In this new context for her poems, Spencer moves from lyric subjectivity to a framework in which her grief and suffering as a Black woman gives way to judgment. The poetic speaker bears witness, recounting events from the past to shape future generations.

Her poem "Po' Little Lib" is one important example of how she recontextualized and revised previous poems as she wrote "John Brown." Spencer reuses a phrase from this poem, an unpublished work composed in the early 1930s and a favorite of Walter White's, in "John Brown." The two poems exist alongside each other in the same notebook, although written in different decades and phases of the poet's life.

The phrase is "air turns leaf into lance." "Po' Little Lib" was originally titled "Tragedy," prompting a consideration of spatial as well as emotional scale with its subject, ostensibly a spider, who is "Liberty."

> Half-inch brown spider,
> Black-spotted back
> Moves thru the grass,
> White-sheeted pack
> m.-o.-v.-e.-s thru the grass, O God,
> if it chance
> for the drought driven air turns leaf into lance
>
> Run, escape wee one you're free
>
> How delicately she re-knits
> Her vast pain
>
> Chance did set her free.
> What bound her again?[14]

In conversation with her biographer, Spencer stated that this poem concerns women's liberty. The spider assumes the burden of the pack, the minute and delicate yet "vast pain," as she continues on her quest, even if it means death. In "John Brown," this image of women's liberty is woven into the epic fabric of humankind's liberty, the phrase "leaf into lance" reappearing in a draft fragment of the poem from about 1972:

> Reply in full to the half-question of a prescient Friend—
> Note for JB

—then, they caught me dead—if they could think at all—dress from French for
  the lady Saville apalled the gents
who went to the quarters at midnight the slave post holding their pants
I was far from dead
I was swinging passel of goods
It take[s] a full canyon
I pained my wife and family—
Our good deeds hurt somebody as will
will as what is
not good: one truth came slant
the bondman with
shackles in flux as the
slave + slave hold[ers] never
stop
until
suddenly there
was Orion constellation
your blacker constellation
+ welcome bad[e] me stop
and
anyway Heaven I thought
would be crowded- a big
man like me pushing thru
finally. Father I missed you—Orion is
drought-holden
air turns leaf into lance

chance death
is a fair far man
With a strung out
Universe of stars his
Tracking so
so conveniently
I swing with him to sea[15]

Here, it is Orion's constellation that is "drought-holden," the air turning "leaf
into lance." The image is a powerful one, with the air capable of creating a
weapon out of the natural element of a leaf.

The witnessing speaker infuses the "John Brown" poem with a visionary perspective that cross-cuts time, introducing a female perspective that is universal rather than limited. In one of her many rejoinders to her world, Spencer
notes that "looking has so little to do with *seeing*."[16] This observation becomes

even more poignant in light of Spencer's great difficulty with her eyesight in her advanced years, as insight took on the imperative to tell, to prophecy humankind's future. Not only does Spencer revise and transform earlier poems in "John Brown," but her vision as a Black woman in it echoes and updates with the wisdom of years her biographical portrait for Cullen's anthology—the "taboo" of "being a Negro woman." Adjacent to a note for "John Brown" that was written in 1962, at age eighty, she observes, "for, thank God, it has been years since I was a female, now, at 80 I'm just a woman." "The academic essentials are surely a pivot in liguorary fund language—of truer esthetics, ethics, and logic."[17] In this description, written almost thirty-five years after her self-declaration in *Caroling Dusk*, she calls attention to the external definitions of black women, marginalized regardless, designated "female" but not worthy of any other title in her younger days. As her white fellow citizen Murrell Edmunds wrote Greene concerning the climate of Lynchburg, a "deeply conservative (pardon my euphemism!) Virginia city": "Suffice it to say . . . that in those days when I knew her, it was considered improper and socially unacceptable for a white person even to address a Negro as 'Mr.' or 'Mrs.' or 'Miss,' and, although Lynchburg was a city with numerous 'Poetry' clubs and circles and workshops, her name did not appear on their roles [*sic*], nor among their activities."[18]

Spencer intervenes in epic's telling, presenting not just an alternative narrative but a multivocal, Whitmanian "epic of democracy." While establishing her moral vision and authority as a poet, she invokes a transformative present that is a call to a future state of being. The poem is both an exploration of lyrical subjectivity and a telling of the nation through the lens of African American experience. The epicist herself appears in this history, merging it with her individual, lyrical experience. Posmentier suggests that "environmental catastrophe brings to the fore not only crises of representation but crises of preservation."[19] Yet the archive itself is most often associated with a conservative and conserving institutional impulse that maintains rather than transforms knowledge. Spencer's manuscript epic creates, by contrast, an alternative archive of knowledge by providing both personal and large-scale responses to the social and environmental history of violence and rupture experienced by African Americans.[20] "John Brown" provides a history of environmental rupture and human consciousness itself as it processes experience.[21]

The epic form fell out of favor in the broader literary establishment during the second half of the twentieth century, the period in which Spencer was writing "John Brown," but as R. Baxter Miller notes, Black authors were conducting an "epic search" for an appropriate hero and for a way of describing humanity through epic.[22] The epic form was compelling to African American authors both because it was a public discourse and because it provided an idea of literary history from an African American author's point of view. What is more, the epic affirmed the idea that there is an intrinsic meaning of history *in* poetry: poetry could tell a history that a historian could not. The epic form represented a commitment not simply to history but to its telling, an undertaking in which the poet is given prominence. A dynamic form that references the past, the imperative to tell, and future promise, epic may also advance the democratic and universal impulses of truth and beauty and the poet herself by establishing her prominence as an epic writer and her authority, which she lends to her vision of the subject.[23] Because it is a moving form, epic eludes precise definition, and this is part of what makes it so appealing as a category of literature to Spencer.[24]

In his original preface to *The Book of American Negro Poetry* (1922), Johnson acknowledges the "sustained work" of the epic in the previous century by African American authors Frances Ellen Watkins Harper, James M. Bell, and Albery Whitman.[25] But the new century and Johnson's anthology emphasizes different forms that herald the New Negro: investment in a lyrical subjectivity through poetry.[26] Writing in the epic form at midcentury, Spencer aligned herself with the long tradition of epic in African American writing in a renewed commitment to universal themes and also to modern African American experiences. She recognized the primary role of poetry in telling this modern history.[27] Moving away from the lyrical subjectivity that characterizes her poems of the New Negro Renaissance, Spencer instead chose a form of poetry that functioned as public discourse. Using the epic, she explicitly addresses approaches to tradition and innovation in a national literature, particularly questions of subject and form, by advancing African American experiences as central to the modern, twentieth-century epic. Such a move confirms Lynn Keller's observation that in the late twentieth century, "the very institutionalization of the expressive lyric" that "obscured the increasing importance of the long poem" in fact "fostered the long poem's development by heightening poets' consciousness of the need to seek alternatives if poetry is to regain cultural importance."[28]

Epics create an entire world, assuming a sweeping formal scale in the length of the poem and the stature of its subject. Spencer's "John Brown" projects forms of beauty and heroism nobler than those that currently exist in her world. Although the conventions of epic dictate a male speaker, a public figure, and a state-sanctioned storyteller, Spencer presents herself as the epic bearer who witnesses the narrated events. She provides a vision of morality, intellect, and poetry itself. The emotional scale of epic, ranging from stasis to rage, from glory to mourning, projects a distinct cultural memory that carries time from the past to the present and toward the future. Her entire library, her history as a reader as well as an individual in this history, is brought to bear in "John Brown," demonstrating her cultural attainment and her moral authority.[29]

Stephen Vincent Benét's *John Brown's Body* (1927), which won the Pulitzer Prize for poetry in 1928, issued a challenge to African American writers:

Oh blackskinned epic, epic with the black spear
I cannot sing you, having too white a heart,
And yet, some day, a poet will rise to sing you
And sing you with such truth and mellowness,
—Deep mellow of the husky golden voice
Crying dark heaven through the spirituals,
Soft mellow of the levee roustabouts,
Singing at night against the banjo-moon—
That you will be a match for any song
Sung by old, populous nations in the past,
And stand like hills against the American sky,
And lay your black spear down by Roland's horn.[30]

An African American epic would voice an imaginative world with the potential to wed blackness to the nation. Benét's poem proved important to African American authors because it countered modernist projects like that of the
Southern Agrarians. It was, moreover, popularly *and* institutionally successful.
The Pulitzer Prize it earned demonstrated that Benét's literary project was recognized as American poetry by cultural authorities. Projecting a national conscience through a diverse cast of speakers, the poem lent itself to dramatiza-
tion. In subsequent years, it was turned into a radio play (1939) and adapted for
the Broadway stage (1953). Yet in its mainstream iterations, *John Brown's Body*
cast no black actors in the work, undermining the democratic virtues of the
poem and evincing the enduring practice of segregation in American popular
forms. Spencer found the Broadway production, starring Tyrone Power, Judith
Anderson and Raymond Massey, objectionable. In her notebooks, she writes,
"There be theatre fashionables who sit through 'JB' who've never peeped into
the room where sit the protagonist himself and his 3 damnable, almost typical friends."[31] The play was in large a white Yale production, from its musical ar-
rangements by Fenno Heath—which were supposed to be spirituals—to its director and actors.

Certain flaws of the productions of *John Brown's Body* are also in the poem.
The voices of slavery and emancipation in the work are conveyed by diminished stereotypes of loyal slave Cudjoe and rebellious slave Spade. No doubt
African American authors recognized in Benét's success the costly effect of
an epic of the Civil War in the hands of a white author. Du Bois described the
quandary of audience and the resulting cost to African American art in *Dusk of
Dawn* (1940) on the eve of the World War II: "No authentic group literature can
rise save at the demand and with the support of the group which is calling for
self-expression.... [T]he New Negro literature was forced to place its depen-
dence almost entirely upon a white audience and that audience had its own
distinct patterns and preferences for Negro writing."[32] African American writ-

ers looked to Benét's work in their 1940s projects not simply because it issued a call for a "blackskinned epic" but because of its negative example, its exhibition of the force of a white audience that "had its own distinct patterns and preferences" for African American subjects and writing.

The poet Robert Hayden responded to Benét's call, he recalled in interviews.[33] The working title for his first collection of poems, written from the late 1930s through the mid-1940s, was "The Black Spear." Of these poems, Hayden's "Middle Passage," published in *Phylon* under Du Bois as editor in 1945, was meant to be this black-skinned epic: it complicated the call in appropriately democratic but not deracinated ways, even though the central voices of Hayden's work were not black.[34] The poem exhibited the scale but not the voices of a black-skinned epic.

Spencer's "John Brown" poem raised the stakes of the black-skinned epic in American poetry, responding to the democratic call with her hero. While her poem also centers on the voice of a white man, it extends Brown's historical journey from Harpers Ferry to African American experiences and consciousnesses: the Great Migration, World War I and World War II, and the emerging civil rights movement. Her note that "a friend is one I often need but seldom use—their presence is en[ough]" refers to the persona of Brown that she creates in her epic manuscript.[35] This friendship makes room in the poem for Spencer herself, for her intellect and her experiences. The poem represents an expansion of Spencer's voice and authorial stance, reassessing and revising national memory by making space for black women in the "epic of democracy."

Brown's October 16–18, 1859, raid on Harpers Ferry, a key historical moment in American history, was at the time an ambivalent symbol of freedom because it was a violent rebellion, not just a war of words or an abstract argument against slavery. David Blight describes the event as "a strategic disaster" that "with time emerged as the most catalytic and successful symbolic event in the history of the antislavery cause."[36] As Du Bois remarks in his 1909 study, *John Brown*, which was published on the fiftieth anniversary of the raid on Harpers Ferry, "ever since [Brown's] violent murder of the border ruffians who were trying to force slavery on Kansas and his attempt to seize the armory at Harper's Ferry so as to arm the slaves, there had been bitter debate as to how far force and violence can bring peace and good will. This is a question that can never be completely answered for all circumstances and for all time."[37] It is recognized as an event of violent rupture in American history and the history of slavery, and it has captivated the attention of a host of writers ever since, who have debated the ethics of violent rebellion.[38] Works of art depicting John Brown and his raid on Harpers Ferry have compelled reflection on this historic moment.

Spencer's portrayal raises issues of equality in the twentieth century, and through it, she ruminates not only on the violent rupture of this historical moment but on the many instances of rupture in African American experiences of the New World. At the same she offers an evaluative reading of the present that also imagines a future.[39] The centenary of Harpers Ferry in 1959 was poignantly relevant to the continued quest for equality. The expanded temporality of archival manuscripts that resist stability is reflected, Cloutier argues, in "the creation of a document, its preservation by the author, and its repurposing into a new temporality, often through a new vessel (a novel, a story, an essay, a song, a photograph, a letter, a statue," which has the effect of articulating a "back-and-forth temporality."[40] Such an expansive and unstable manuscript as Spencer's "John Brown" describes and enacts the environmental continuities and ruptures that characterize Black creative, fugitive, and radical existence.

The personal memory of the loss of her infant son, John, shaped Spencer's rumination on John Brown; her "J-no" persona captures both the "no" of refusing slavery and the death of John in the first month of his life.[41] Spencer's surviving children were born in 1901, 1903, and 1906; John most likely was born in 1904–5. There are no birth or death records in this period for him, the result of a brief federal policy that did not require recording them.[42] But Spencer's notes on the back of letterhead from the city court of New York, where her son-in-law was employed, reads: "A Dedication . . . To my loving unpatient children in alphabet: Alroy, Bethel, Chauncey—we intended to name the other one John to break it up—."[43] John, who had died of diphtheria, was the last Spencer child born on Holiday Street in Lynchburg, where Edward and Anne lived after marrying in 1901, before Edward constructed the house at 1313 Pierce Street, finished in 1904. Most of Lynchburg's black citizens, including Edward's parents, lived in this "old home" neighborhood, which bordered the James River.[44] In her notebooks from the 1960s, Spencer recollected on the year the city water was tainted and nearly every family lost a member to typhoid: "No friction needed we either / had a core approach Miss Lizzie whose death was the first in our family: that summer there was a typhoid death in every house on our block they were the people who warned the rest of us not to drink the city water, each evening. They went to Miss Jennie's well to get a good their good clean water to drink."[45] Chauncey was the first Spencer child born at Pierce Street, which was located in a different part of town, the "Camp Davis" neighborhood, on higher ground.

John Brown was an abiding persona for Spencer who functioned as an active repository for memory, allowing her to document the widespread environmental experiences of African Americans in the nation over the course of a hundred years. Over the decades of its composition, the observations moved from John's death to the poet's confrontation of her failing eyesight and overall health and her own mortality.

The very fragmentation of "John Brown," by far the most extensive of her existing unpublished works, produces a textured experience of Spencer's writing through and over time as she faces her mortality as well as the losses of John,

Johnson, and her husband. Notes for the work appear everywhere in her manuscript writings from 1940 to 1975, in her notebooks, in comments for other works, and in annotations in her books. Emerging alongside "Virginia as Narcissus," the "John Brown" poem moves from the autobiographical testament of "Virginia as Narcissus" to a dialogue about faith and action. Her notebooks for "Virginia as Narcissus," which cover the period from 1959 1972, contain a late note, dated July 1972, for "John Brown": "Father, every day / that I was away / I loved you more / than my life / Yes Son I know / and I love you / as My Life."[46] Spencer's physical experience of writing the fragmented manuscript of "John Brown"—in the face of failing eyesight and a partially removed tongue—yields, at last, this acknowledgment both of incompletion and of the mortal self.

"Any Wife to Any Husband: A Derived Poem" appears just prior to Spencer's 1972 notes for "John Brown."[47]

> This small garden is half my world
> I am nothing to it—when all is said,
> I plant the thorn and kiss the rose,
> But they will grow when I am dead.
>
> Let not this change, Love, the human life
> Share with her the joy you had with me,
> List with her the plaintive bird you heard with me.
> Feel all human joys, but
> Feel most a "shadowy third."[48]

Explicitly referencing Robert Browning's "Any Wife to Any Husband," the poem emphasizes "derived" as verb and adjective, highlighting the idea of the poem as both a process of extension and modification and a product. Like "Creed," the poem features a balance of interconnected parts: wife and husband, halves of a world, transformed by a "shadowy third" that is absence and presence.[49]

An Epic of Betweenness: Beginnings and Sources

The Spencers' visit to Harpers Ferry not only produced "Creed" but another poem about John Brown. This second poem is not found in her manuscripts. Spencer told Greene that this poem was rejected by Cullen at *Opportunity* magazine.[50] But she did write another draft poem titled "Harpers Ferry" in the early 1940s. It marked a fresh attempt to acknowledge John Brown in verse:

> This is where I'll build
> His house
> His sweet memorial Home
> Where the wide open
> Arms of the unidentical

Gates of my [a]re bought and
Paid for country wrap it
Round and hug him down
At least 2 ½ Gates
Does the not some part of One
Of late seem retractive
Renegade? A little less
than clean
Chanced upon and make it
Spell tawdry cheap?
But the House must be built!
Log, adamant cement and
Stone the same—
Yield I do to Bessemer steel
For the new word stone[51]

This preliminary work engages ideas of place and placement. The speaker's emphasis on place aligns with her dedicated quest to create a memorial for John Brown, a material and metaphysical marker, and her own quest for home and at-homeness. Through "Gates," "Log, adamant cement and / stone," the poem highlights relations and bonding agents, whether actual or ideal. The poet-speaker conveys her important role in activating memory with the imperative "But the house must be built!" Her actions, her efforts to build a psychic and physical home of the spirit, one that can be found in the relationships human beings establish with each other through their faith in God, are made equal to those of John Brown.[52] The poet's most heroic role, then, is to encourage relations—to supply "adamant cement"—between people "for the new word stone."

From "Harpers Ferry," Spencer devised the more ambitious project of developing the epic persona of "John Brown" in a grand design. The scale of the poem exceeds that imagined for the epic by Samuel Taylor Coleridge, who had remarked, "I should not think of devoting less than twenty years to an epic poem. Ten to collect materials and warm my mind with universal science. . . . —the next five to the composition of the poem—and the five last to the correction of it."[53] Spencer devoted over thirty years to "John Brown." It was not an easy undertaking. As Keller remarks, "Earlier women poets did not possess the cultural authority that would legitimate their attempts at epic, that would allow them to narrate the sweeping 'tale of the tribe' or to produce extended philosophical meditation." Moreover, she notes, "women rarely figure in discussions of the long poem."[54] Spencer recognized that a black women's intellectual tradition must be considered in discussions of a national literature and that both recovery work and intellectual grounding were necessary.[55]

The poem effects a dynamic and nuanced recoding of epic's conventions through its unfinished and unpublished manuscript status, and Spencer's engagements with historiography, formal tradition, and cultural experience demonstrate the way in which epic is always in process, its conventions always being revised.[56] One way she revises its conventions is by shifting the emphasis from the hero in isolation to the potential collaboration among the marginalized.[57] Keller notes, "In their long poems, women enact various models of relationship with the dominant traditions."[58] These enacted models remake epic from a traditional heroic narrative to a search for communal principles and virtue through an alternative, polyvocal remembering. In Spencer's notes she references such a collaboration under the heading "Poetry":

> One word that takes care of it: preposterous: it has a permanent basis in angles
>   and curves never laid—revolt never planted but here it stands there it thrives
>   never and forever, timeless in time! Excitable, calm, dependable It can be a
>   word a life: a word "Open
> Harriet Tubman
> John Brown
> She got away with it
> John Brown did too
> Look out + up—he is still swing
> Space-out for . . .
> And up with the constellation
> *Orion*
> In the constellation[59]

The speaker doubles the pair of Tubman and Brown with poetry and the constellations in the night sky, "the angles and curves never laid," the "revolt never planted but here it stands there it thrives never and forever, timeless in time!" "Out + up" and "swing[ing]" introduce the spatial and temporal motions of Spencer's epic, which reaches back in time not to provide a timeless memorial but a moving arc of memorializing that propels change.

It reaches back in time as far as Ovid's *Metamorphosis*, one source among many that Spencer uses that come from not a single, uniform tradition but from plural traditions that are made one by her.[60] Spencer's choice of Ovid as a source for "John Brown" is evocative, since Ovid transformed Homer and Virgil by interrogating the idea of national greatness. The *Metamorphoses* opens with a description of Earth's creation and its corruption through successive generations of humankind up to the "Age of Iron," where Ovid's story begins. As Marguerite Johnson points out, his epic imparts the truth that "as the offspring of the Age of Iron, we must endure and struggle against corruption, brutality, and injustice."[61] This present state is not sustainable; humankind must inevitably transform itself, both to survive the intolerable present and to make the future better. In "Harpers Ferry," Spencer figures this transformation in metals, from iron to Bessemer steel. The image of iron melded to create Bessemer steel reappears in the "John Brown" poem, suggesting that Spencer is linking Ovid's "Age of Iron" with the irons of slavery. The fallenness of humankind in her poem references the corruptness of the American nation that owes both to slavery and continued inequality.

Spencer's vast reading provided not just companionship but the means through which to ponder her place in intellectual traditions and in the world, which in turn provided her with a dynamic way of approaching her epic, and Carlyle was an especially important influence.[62] For Spencer, the works of Carlyle offered a foundation for the poet's cultural authority, creating an experiential framework for her epic that is based on reading.[63]

On the flyleaf of volume 10 of Carlyle's *Complete Works* (1882), she writes:

> The iron men need no curtain
> Neither Gustavus, nor Cromwell nor
> I, Jno. [John] Brown—we, we are
> Bessemer steel!

Her note conveys the specific relation of Carlyle to the "John Brown" epic and its metaphor of forging iron into steel. Its reference to the "iron curtain," moreover, reveals the years in which it was authored.

This volume, which contains Carlyle's *Past and Present*, was annotated by Spencer with the note "p. 36: Schiller" in red-colored pencil. As I mention in chapter 1, Spencer's 1927 poem "Creed" is drawn from Schiller's play "*Don Carlos*," parts of which Carlyle translates in part 2 of the chapter "Schiller at Dresden" in his *Life of Friedrich Schiller*. "Sire, your creed is also mine," states the Marquis de Posa to King Philip.[64] Carlyle translates the entirety of act 3, scene 10, to make his point about right conduct and heroic behavior. Here is How Carlyle describes the significance of this scene:

> With the Marquis de Posa, he [Schiller] had a more genial task. This Posa, we can easily perceive is the representative of Schiller himself. The ardent love of men, which forms his ruling passion, was likewise the constant feeling of his author; the glowing eloquence with which he advocates the cause of truth, and justice, and humanity, was such as Schiller too would have employed in similar circumstances. In some respects, Posa is the chief character of the piece: of a splendid intellect, and a daring devoted heart, his powers are all combined upon a single purpose . . . the universal interests of men. Aiming, with all his force of thought and action, to advance the happiness and best rights of his fellow creatures; pursuing this noble aim with the skill and dignity which it deserves, his mind is at once unwearied, earnest and serene. . . . There is a calm strength in Posa, which no accident of fortune can shake. Whether cheering the forlorn Carlos into new activity; whether lifting up his voice in the ear of tyrants and inquisitors, or tak-

ing leave of life amid his vast unexecuted schemes, there is the same sedate mag-
nanimity, the same fearless composure: when the fatal bullet strikes him, he dies
with the concerns of others, not his own, upon his lips. He is a reformer, the per-
fection of reformers; not a revolutionist, but a prudent though determined im-
prover. His enthusiasm does not burst forth in violence, but in manly and enlightened energy: his eloquence is not more moving to the heart than his lofty
philosophy is convincing to the head.... There is something so striking in the
idea of confronting the cold solitary tyrant with 'the only man in all his states
that does not need him'; of raising the voice of true manhood for once within
the gloomy chambers of thralldom and priestcraft that we can forgive the stretch
of poetic license by which it is effected. Philip and Posa are antipodes in all re-
spects.[65]

The Marquis de Posa points out the king's circumscribed worldview by referencing the "creed" of humankind rather than the doctrine of religious sep-
aratism the king thinks he subscribes to: "Philip thinks his new instructor is
a 'Protestant'; a charge which Posa rebuts with calm dignity, his object not
being separation and contention, but union and peaceful gradual improvement.... Posa... attacks [Philip's] selfishness and pride, represents to him the
intrinsic meanness and misery of a throne, however decked with adventitious
pomp, if built on servitude and isolated from the sympathies and interests of
others."[66]

Posa's assessment aligns with Carlyle's evaluation of the French Revolution
in his best-known work: a thoughtless and morally bankrupt society will inevitably fail. Carlyle defended reason and order—domestic order, duty, and
destiny—declaring that such order would prevail, whether through reform or
revolution. As he argues in his 1841 *Heroes and Hero Worship*, chaotic events
demand heroes, dynamic individuals can take control and direct spiritual
energies.

Carlyle's offers this translation of the Marquis de Posa's confrontation with
the tyrant King Philip:

MAR: 'Tis not myself but Truth that I endanger
....
Right conduct has a value of its own:
The happiness my king might cause me plant I would myself produce; and
     conscious joy,
And free selection, not the force of duty,
Should impel me. Is it thus your Majesty
Requires it? Could you suffer new creators
In your own creation? Or could I
Consent with patience to become the chisel,
When I hoped to be the statuary?

I love mankind; and in a monarchy,
Myself is all that I can love.
....

What the king desires to spread abroad
Through these weak hands, is it the good of men?
That good which my unfetter'd love would wish them?
Pale majesty would tremble to behold it!
No! Policy has fashioned in her courts
Another sort of human good.

Spencer marks the lines "I love mankind; and in a monarchy, / Myself is all that I can love." This passage underscores the moral question of whether revolution is required to effect social change or whether reform alone can accomplish it, a topic that concerned Carlyle because of the potential for anarchy and chaos to disrupt order. He remarks that

> had the character of Posa been drawn ten years later, it would have been im-
> puted, as all things are, to the "French Revolution;" and Schiller himself perhaps
> might have been called a Jacobin. Happily, as matters stand, there is room for no
> such imputation. It is pleasing to behold in Posa the deliberate expression of a
> great and good man's sentiment on these ever-agitated subjects: a noble monu-
> ment, embodying the liberal ideas of his age, in a form beautified by his own ge-
> nius, and lasting as its other products.[67]

Carlyle maintains that reformation can redeem the best principles of an ordered society and strong, wise government. He approvingly remarks on Schiller's art, which itself represents "a noble monument" as "lasting" as the liberal
principles it embodies.

Although Carlyle's *Complete Works* might seem like an odd choice of source
text for Spencer, especially given the callousness regarding slavery and the
rights of the enslaved that he voices in his infamous essay concerning "the Negro Question" (1853), I believe she noted but read past his limitations because
she found his concern for social and ethical matters compelling, particularly
his argument that past events could shed light on the present. Spencer adopts
this Carlylian stance in her evaluation of the American condition in "John
Brown."

Carlyle himself is also the source of a modern and expansive understanding of epic that Spencer emulates.[68] As Phillips writes, "Carlyle would in fact become famous for expanding the definition of 'epic'" to include "the sense of 'a
composition comparable to an epic'—a work that does epic work even if it does
not exhibit a traditional epic structure."[69] Carlyle's discussion of Marquis de
Posa, who was, he found, "the deliberate expression of a great and good man's
sentiment on these ever-agitated subjects" of creed and humankind, his speech
and actions "a noble monument, embodying the liberal ideas of his age, in a

form beautified by his own genius, and lasting as its other products," opened up a space in which Spencer could develop her epic.[70]

Carlyle's concerns reflected a shift in inquiry over the course of the nineteenth century from study of the individual to that of national culture, as Spencer was aware. Carlyle explicitly revises Alexander Pope's "know then thyself, presume not God to scan" in *Past and Present*, (1843), in the section titled "The Modern Worker." Spencer marked this passage:

> For there is a perennial nobleness, and even sacredness, in Work. Were he never so benighted, forgetful of his high calling, there is always hope in a man that actually and earnestly works: in Idleness alone is there perpetual despair. Work, never so Mammonish, mean, *is* in communication with nature; the real desire to get Work done will itself lead one more and more to truth, to Nature's appointments and regulations, which are truth.... The latest Gospel in this world is, Know thy work and do it. "Know thyself:" long enough has that poor "self" of thine tormented thee; thou wilt never get to "know" it, I believe! Think it not thy business, this of knowing thyself; thou art an unknowable individual: know what thou canst work at; and work at it, like a Hercules! That will be thy better plan.[71]

In red-colored pencil Spencer underlines four times, "like a Hercules!" and writes, "Know, then, thyself. Presume not God to scan / The proper study of mankind is man. —Pope." Carlyle's emphasis on work rather than self-study reflects the mid-nineteenth century "shift from an author-based literary history to a culture- or worldview-based one . . . as well as an increased awareness of the intellectual and economic systems that manipulated the work and reception of authors, even those of the rank of Homer and Milton."[72] Spencer's "John Brown" in turn reflects Carlyle's focus on work. She represents Brown's actions as work on a heroic scale, and she regarded her own epic writing as work that approached Carlyle's scale of analysis and range of literary considerations and that was to be taken seriously.

In Spencer's as in Carlyle's outlook, the matter of work and faith are connected, with work representing an energy directed toward the achievement of deeper spiritual understanding. She notes his observation that "democracy is everywhere the inexorable demand of these ages, swiftly fulfilling itself. . . . [A]ll things announce democracy," a demand he questions by quoting his character Herr Teufelsdröckh from *Sartor Resartus*, who notes that "democracy, which means despair of finding any heroes to govern you, and contented putting up with the want of them, . . . is of kin to atheism, and other sad Isms: he who discovers no God whatever, how should he discover Heroes, the visible temples of God?"[73] For Spencer, though, the democratic principle was innately connected to faith in God. Although Carlyle was doubtful about democracy, his emphasis on heroes as moral leaders of an age was formative for Spencer's distinct argument about John Brown, whom she viewed a dynamic hero directing the spiritual energies of moral reform during the American "Age of Iron." While Carlyle's emphasis on "good government" and his skepticism of democracy would not allow him to see Brown as a hero, Spencer recognized in Brown's actions the potential spiritual rebirth of the American nation. The craven government that supported slavery was to blame, not Brown, for the loss of life at Harpers Ferry; a new age of faith and moral rectitude could establish its democratic principles.

Spencer's manuscript poem "Mortal Sin is Not Unbelief" confirms this judgment of Brown:

> Mortal Sin is Not Unbelief
> not if your last word:
> not if my last fears + cares/ come.
> I gave up my sons, wife home years + land— [I gave up mine too]
> Not your ~~lost pain~~ your word nor your soul's tears
> Can warm the ice of an iced fire
> And wandering man had at last
> to desire when the trap
> flew open and I went down
> —on the whip-lash thong—
> my grey-white face turned to blood + flame[74]

On the inside of the program where she recorded this poem, Spencer notes: "Our unbelief has naught to do with day songs were the deed short like thong and the trap that word comes came thru; the time to act within our fears." Contemplating the sacrifices of Brown, Spencer aligns them with others', perhaps the poet's own: "I gave up my sons, wife home years + land—[I gave up mine too]." The alignment of these experiences prompts further inquiry about reform versus revolution in the social order.

Over the course of the last thirty-five years of her life, Spencer, spurred on by Carlyle's reflections, searched for the meaning of the heroic in an imperfect democracy, as evidenced by decades of the draft poems titled "Generals." An early fragment inquires,

> Who makes a General?
> Himself makes a General . . . with
> of course a bit of coddle from the universe
> A snip off Orion—a smidge from[75]

Here Spencer uses the myth and constellation of Orion as a reference point for her exploration. A general is self-generated in creating a singular vision and plan of action, but he creates himself with "a bit of coddle from the universe / a snip off Orion," meaning that human beings exist in a larger universe of existence.

The status of Orion as a formidable hunter and powerful agent infuses the work with a figure of autonomy that contrasts with John Brown. Orion's strength does not compare to Brown's, as Brown's is for the cause of love, while Orion's is undisciplined, an exertion of power for the sake of power that find him boasting about the annihilation of mankind and the rape of a young woman.[76] In 1969, referencing Apollo 11's mission to the moon, Spencer writes, "God: I have heard you thru John of Johns, the greatest, —because most selfless. The tale was not stranger to me. I was there all the way with well, not Orion's place I was never favorable to a serving mans group foolish blend for a woman—but among the stars he is our greatest honor—not too much of Equipment no blast-off—no souvenir you know it all, too. He would you with him but cannot add to your knowledge—wish you, no, intelligent but say—the train of suffering . . .."[77] Here Orion is "our greatest honor" to the stars. Although he requires little in the way of "equipment"—just a lance, not a rocket—he "cannot add" to John's knowledge.

Yet Orion can be used as a gauge for humankind's self-knowledge. The mighty, the powerful, and the rapacious man Orion is defeated by the small, determined, and defiant scorpion and the various women of the myths who place it there to bring about his demise. The measure of his greatness, a power conveyed by brightness in the sky, is borne out in his relation to other stars in the heavens. When we view Orion in the context of its placement among the stars, its brightness does not exceed Vega's. When we view it in relation to Earth and the sun, it is an instrument through which to measure passing of the year. In November, the constellation Orion rises with the sun, marking the end of a year; Brown was hanged on December 2. When John Brown moves on from Orion, he moves on toward Vega, the once and future North Star, proximate to Earth and brighter than any other star (besides the sun). The "swinging" of this shifting star, like the "swinging" John Brown's body, which measures the continuity of his spirit, means a return of his ideals through which to make a "new world," even as the poet herself measured the passing of years and the imminence of her death.

Spencer's emphasis on Polaris—often referred to as the North Star—as seemingly fixed in place but yet moving over time came from lines from Benét's poem: "Sometimes there comes a crack in Time itself. / Sometimes the earth is torn by something blind. / Sometimes an image that has stood so long / it seems implanted as the polar star / is moved against an unfathomed force / that suddenly will not have it any more."[78] From his travels past Orion and toward God, "Father," Brown is able to consider Earth from a scale of time and perspective that both diminishes and enlarges it.

A much later fragment of the "Generals" poem invokes the inquirer herself. Spencer asks,

What causes in force—makes a General? I ponder this. I know what he is: a man
  who exceeds himself—and far off (icy) as a polar cap he In mind holds but
  his own one thought, never weakened, never displaced
But the force creating his polar cap kept so unlike
Other men?
In my century of life I have
Looked given to us step by step
Up the stairway of the ages

The authority of witness in this thought piece establishes an equivalence between poet and general: both possess singular vision, virtue, and tenacity, the strengths of a moral vision.

Another fragment probably written in early 1960 brings Spencer closer to this moral vision as demonstrated by John Brown. Here Brown's death for the cause of humanity is a "GOOD" that "pays" the debt of the South to equality and to freedom, as Spencer connects the Liberty Tree with Brown's gallows tree:

A General the probable:
Swords or gallows tree for a cause
Acclaimed GOOD pays South . . .
Or a day after he pays

In one of her notebooks, she writes, "For the roots we are go deeper than the gallows thereof the curled vine reaches beyond all suns but thine, head-crowned."[79] Having conducted research on the Liberty Tree, Spencer contrasts this tree with what she imagined as John Brown's gallows tree. Her spatial trajectory covers humanity's root to God's crown, along which she searches for their meeting point, extending her emphasis on relation.

And finally, in her most complete version, written on her son-in-law Francis E. Rivers's letterhead from the city court of New York and dating to around 1960, Spencer offers the poet's perspective of the general:

He wills to have
One star. —His wrong
Made right
The older the wrong
Better the fight
This star is a fixed star
So much the better
The nails are somewhere
Find the casuistries
in growth smash of
pull drive or but annihilate—no

talk no sophisticate
[later]
no Alps no slaver
go—
My generals stopped
Indeed but ate
Fear for the
Belly's sake—
Each man was a man
Carried his own
Logistic said at the
Beginning what was to
Be said—the driver for me
As I sit here is[80]

Spencer contrasts star and fixity with the speciousness of reasoning marked by the word "casuistries," here used to reference the evasion of ethical matters. The speaker-poet finds herself in a courthouse of justice where casuistries must be annihilated, either by extirpating false reasoning or hammering home the truth, "one star / —His wrong/ Made right / The older the wrong / Better the fight / This star is a fixed star."

"Things starkly different / Can equate," Spencer writes, in one of the last drafts of this work, from the final years of her writing life:

Generals
Things starkly different
Can equate:
If love is stronger
Than death
So is ignorance
Add, peace & . . .

In this reflection, Spencer shows how an ostensible truism can turn out to be false. It seems evident that starkly different things can equate, but the poet uses the statement to mock the false moral logic that relies on it to evade equality. The "fixed star" is the general's resolute determination to expose a compromised truth—one that claims relation but uses it to maintain inequality. Spencer's John Brown poem traces this motion of the stars in relation to the truth.

Yet another source was Walt Whitman. It is not clear whether Spencer was familiar with his "Year of Meteors," which represents 1859 as a year of irrevocable changes, one of which was John Brown's raid, but it is clear that she saw herself as collaborating with Whitman in the project of democracy: "'I will accept nothing which all men cannot have the counterpart of on equal terms.' Is it possible now, or can it be possible in the near future for our nation as a people to take a stand with Walt *Whitman*. If we answer yes: we need not be clear as to ways and means, but we can be *resolute* in purpose. We can as one for all, and all for one, see the program thru, our best national defense is finding a *moral* equivalent for physical war, making even greater personal sacrifices to maintain a high level of liability for the most people possible."[81] Spencer approves of Whitman's clarity of vision from which both empathy and activism derive. In "John Brown," Spencer directs her individual genius to the ends of a new epic informed by her views of Whitman and of democracy.[82]

Emerson also was important to Spencer's understanding of the poetic process as she penned "John Brown." Spencer wrote Roy Basler at the Library of Congress in 1972 that "my poems . . . are me . . . in the years here they are my conversation with myself." In this same year, she told John Ferrone at Harcourt Brace that "I try to tell my truth as I *do* accept the truth of those who have reverence for it." These statements attest to her attention to internal truth and also her desire to create lasting work. In the writing of an epic whose goal is to speak transcendental truth, "study and attentive experience go together," writes Phillips.[83] Spencer cherished her multivolume set of Emerson's works, recollecting that one of her teachers at Virginia Seminary made a gift of them to her after her graduation. "Dr Bolling sent me 4 vol. set of Emerson, which I still have," she wrote.[84] The generation of scholars and teachers following Emerson and the transcendentalists "saw their purpose focused not as much on creating an ordered society through classical education as on finding truth that each individual student could grasp and explore."[85]

The "John Brown" epic is, for Spencer, a gateway between the classical, conserving epic of the nation and more expressive forms of it—ones that could offer expansive commentary on the nation's "half paid" purchase of "our liberties," as she remarks in a draft editorial from 1948. The "gates," a trope for a half-opened freedom first introduced in "Harpers Ferry," was still with Spencer as she wrote some of the last lines of the John Brown poem twenty-five years later, just prior to her death. Spencer balances Carlyle and Emerson, creating a world of reference through their ideas and through Whitman's *Leaves of Grass* and Ovid's *Metamorphoses*. "John Brown" is a continuously shifting, new poem for a new century, a new world, in which new judgments were needed.

Judgments and New Worlds

James Freeman Clarke referred to John Brown as "an Old Testament hero," thereby conveying his ambivalence about Brown's violent actions that led to the loss of human lives.[86] Villard was disposed to the view that "it was the man on the scaffold sacrificing, not taking life, who inspired. The song that regiment after regiment sang at Charlestown dealt not with John Brown's feeble sword, but with his soul. It was the heroic qualities of his spirit that awed them, his wonderful readiness to die with joy and in peace as so many of them were about to die for the nation and the freedom of another race."[87] In her heavily annotated copy of Clarke's *Anti-Slavery Days*, Spencer comments, "If Jno Brown was God's angry man Garrison was God's furious angel," which appears next to Clarke's statement that "Garrison held to his purpose to the end—the purpose he announced at the beginning. He was thought by many to be too harsh; too severe; too denunciatory. And certainly he chose his words with the careful purpose of making them shock and sting. His programme was this: 'I will be as harsh as truth, as uncompromising as justice. . . . I am in earnest; I will not equivocate; I will not excuse; I will not retreat a single inch, and I will be heard.'"[88] Spencer's annotations convey her alignment as a poet with Brown's uncompromising adherence to truth.

Spencer's high regard of Garrison's unequivocal stance was matched by her low opinion of Frederick Douglass. In her notebook, she writes: "—F Douglass wasn't a hero—to say I married a white & black to compliment both races was a lie & he was not solving a social problem, he was compromising."[89] She allied herself with Brown and Garrison because of their willingness to be revolutionaries and take action rather than simply offer appeasements, as Spencer believed Douglass had in his *Life and Times*. In his written record, John Brown delivered a "final, wonderfully prophetic and imperishable message to the 'million hearts' of his countrymen," Villard pronounces in his book, providing in full the note Brown handed to one of his guards on the way to his execution: "I John Brown am now quite *certain* that the crimes of this *guilty land*: *will* never be purged *away*; but with Blood. I had *as* I *now think*: *vainly* flattered myself that without *very much* bloodshed; it might be done."[90]

Brown's final note has been read as reflecting the extent to which, as Nudelman notes, "a theological emphasis on Christ's love as a model for human compassion failed to account for the crisis [of slavery]," compelling "those responsible for narrating the war," including "politicians and poets" to conjure "a punitive God who exacts obedience in the form of human suffering."[91] Brown's hanging was doubly symbolic. "On the morning of his execution, Brown spoke not in imitation of Christ's selfless love but with the unrelenting voice of his own Calvinist God: in his last public utterance, blood was not the medium of sympathy but of retribution. On the scaffold, Brown represented both a suffering slave population and a guilty white nation. Because he was a white man, the act of self-sacrifice doubled as an act of penance; to suffer in concert with slaves was also to pay a historical debt for the injuries whites had inflicted on slaves."[92] During Spencer's lifetime, this perspective that underscores Brown's execution as punishment of the white population for its sins was more apparent to African Americans than to whites, as her writing demonstrates.

For Spencer and her contemporaries contemplating the centenary of John Brown's attack on Harpers Ferry, the rebellion was clearly one of whites against Blacks in school desegregation.[93] It was impossible not to remark on the century past, with its momentous changes. The *Second Century*, a Black publication, declared that "the second century of Negro freedom requires that we re-think our dramatic history, fortify our spirits with the new spiritual insight, reorient ourselves in terms of economic realities, and launch a program with immediate and long-range goals. History has spoken, declaring that America's fate was and is the Negro's destiny."[94] The magazine reasoned that the second century should begin a hundred years after "victory," not the "proclamation" and acknowledged "their voices after 100 years."[95] It referred to "the war of freedom and the great defense of freedom" (the Revolutionary War and the Civil War) and asserted that "there is no way for America to engage in defending liberty save by extending it—here and around the world. And the Negro himself again must become the spearhead. As we approach the year 1963 a new awakening is urged. America's fate once more may become his destiny, but this time with the spokesmen of the race playing a larger and more positive role."

In another judgment, notes from 1972 that begin "NBJB," the poet avers that false pride and narcissism interfere with the "divine / experiment" that makes Earth unique:

> For only Earth as an ___ is allowed
> within its strand to manage
> and, at present, to mis-
> manage itself—as a divine
> experiment (you have found many
> such tests—I keep the
> power small on Earth
> You + your earth
> father found many
> such tests in your
> Holy book
> Earth people are my *house*
> only the space, lands are
> all-mind operated—[96]

God announces here that "Earth people are my house" and that Earth's space and lands—meaning nature and the natural landscape—are directed by God. The dialogue between Brown and God as father speaks to the dramatic scope of the poem, which concerns the nature of freedom, humankind's incomplete fulfillment of the quest for freedom on Earth, and the forgiveness of mortal sin through belief. In another manuscript fragment, John states,

You said, Father—
I could never desire
Utterly any thing
So captive as Heaven
Or beautiful
As my Earth
What of your words
Words semantically are
Ambiguous as am I
Tide
And—? [sic]
She Earth and Heaven
Stay—they are
Elegan[t] gallery + stage
Why do you think man
Must die
You must stay here
With me that blushing
Dawn when I share
Say
Good John Brown
Man is entirely
New again:
The bright, all new
Children of your
God have grown to
A newly peopled world[97]

In her notebook, Spencer notes, "Words are semantically ambiguous / The earth and heaven stay—they are elegant gallery and stage," which Spencer repeats here.[98] Like the "green and wordless patterns" of "For Jim, Easter Eve," like her poem "Creed" with its idea of relationality, Spencer aligns acute skills of observation with a truth that inhabits not words but Earth and heavens. As she witnesses nature and the passing of time in the epic, she simultaneously compresses her visual experience of the ordinary into the poem and expands its significance to the galaxy, to the stars beyond Earth. As she writes, there was "no way out but up." This fragment proposes as a resolution to the inevitability of death the rebirth of humankind, God's children, the achievement of "a newly peopled world." In a draft note from 1959–60, Spencer remarks:

My inspired scriveners gave Heaven gold the best they had in and turn-about. Heaven gave to Ear[th] the best it had the completed planet: soil, rock forest, clear streams, uneven litoral, men who desired to see their maker and adore him!

That too was all owed them. But being mere men they sometimes double-crossed
their maker and themselves

John—pitiable of course—but it is weak to weep.[99]

The constitutional founders, historians, and legislators (scriveners) of humankind let down their end of the pact with God and heaven. This note was written
in the same time period as Spencer's focused work on "Virginia as Narcissus"
and shows the interconnectedness of the two manuscripts.

Interrogating freedom, Spencer uses the status of "bondman" to contrast the
servitude of British migrants to America with the enslavement of Africans, referencing their forgetfulness of that bond status. Her circa 1968 observation that
"the bondman with / shackles in flux as the / slave + slave hold[ers] never / stop
/ until" develops into her 1972 reflection labeled "JB," in which she comments
that "the bondman is already a loose-man himself he has / Worked free / While
the slaves / Are stapelia + stamped / Evermore / Together / They are . . . roped
/ With Spiritual imagined folk / Evermore, / Evermore to the other: So Father, since no one comes here close it and" ("and" marks the end of the manuscript page).[100] Stapelia, low-growing spineless succulent plants from South
Africa, are made a plural collective, while the "bondman" is an individual, singular, loosed on the world. "Stamped," roped together, linked "evermore to the
other," the enslaved and their descendants have not experienced a labor that is
"free." As Spencer notes in a different notebook, "Appomatix was a victory for
the South—a way out into the world, physically and mentally. But because not
enough of them have believed it they are still hesitating at the gate they hand
to ankle wearing slave coffles."[101] The gate here, as in the earlier "Harpers Ferry"
poem, is the threshold between "chattel" and free status. "Evermore" provides a
temporal equivalence to these relations: slavery marks the point of no return, a
humankind evermore unequal, nevermore equal.

Green describes "structural-thematic concepts of time" in "John Brown"
that "emanate . . . from one of the poem's three main speakers: the poet (dream
time), John Brown (human time), and God (cosmic time)."[102] But time in the
poem is maternal; much more space in it is given over to women's experiences
than to men's. Spencer's highlights mothers in relation to humanity and the
cosmos. They, with Spencer, represent an archive of memory and a living moral
vision. It is this heightened yet fugitive status of women that enables Spencer
to write a poem about Ruth Brown, the mother of John, in the midst of her
notes on "J-no."

The manuscript poem "Ruth Brown" introduces Brown's female survivor
and the song that marks his memory:

Ruth Brown more brown
Than a name
Less brown than the

Man,—at the farm
The song in her throat
And the wreath on
Her door
O Lordy, long gone +
The wreath and the song evermore,
Nevermore[103]

The poem forges relations: it moves between Ruth Brown and John Brown, between mother and man. Tradition and truth intersect with memory, the wreath and the song functioning as memorials to John, yielding a contrast to his physical loss. Ruth survives her son; his memory is in between the states of "evermore" and "nevermore," the song "in her throat" and wreath "on / Her door" representing an unfulfilled, incomplete expression of John Brown, who is simply and yet indefinitely referred to not by name but as "the / Man." It is a threshold existence and an incomplete memory, pushed through to future and fuller states of existence by speaker-poet herself. Spencer further asserts connections between Ruth Browns, between John Brown's mother and the rhythm and blues singer Ruth A. Brown, a Virginia native.[104] The relations of mother to son, of white woman to black woman, move between time, history, and culture. Ruth A. Brown emblematizes this link between women, mothers, and memory, connecting "song" and the dwelling places of memory from centuries apart.

Spencer recorded some of the final lines to the "John Brown" poem in 1974, a year before she died. Her poem "1975" anticipates Earth's embrace of her in return for the life it has given her, one of struggling through the human condition, and lays out the way the poet and her poem will come to be understood:

Turn an earth clod
Peel a shaley rock
In fondness molest a curly worm
Whose *familiar* is everywhere
Kneel
And the curly worm sentient *now*
Will *light* the word that tells the poet what a poem is[105]

The counterpart to this vision of return to Earth can be found in a nearly unreadable fragment of the "John Brown" manuscript. Writing blind, Spencer jots words that loop over each other and down the page, answering the poet's imperative to speak her truth and assert her place in the world:

JB—the East—a pr[illegible] at surviving world [illegible]
The Western world has (esp. America) *organized* itself back into a corner
There is no way, except *up*—*out* of its frittetaria [*sic*] of fear
Chains, slink and pull—pull

To get out except up +
Nobody *down* can
Say briefly where up is—[106]

This assertion of her truth, her place, permits her to engage in global and cultural analysis regarding East and West, the entrenchment of American fear that holds the nation in place and human lives in inequality, and, at last, the resolution that can only be found in the ordered cosmos—"out" and "up."

The "Found" Epic

In 2002 the Lynchburg *News and Advance* announced that the John Brown poem had been "discovered": Chauncey, aged ninety-six, and his wife, also named Anne, "brought to the public Friday what may prove a remarkable literary discovery," the story reported.[107] At a ceremony recognizing the poem and poet's importance, Garnell Stamps, a friend of the Spencer family, local civil rights activist, and retired English schoolteacher, "presented five yellowed notebooks containing about 200 lines of Spencer's unfinished epic poem, 'A Dream of John Brown on His Return Trip Home.'" U.S. congressman Bob Goodlatte and Lynchburg mayor Carl Hutcherson attended the event. Spencer's son Chauncey had high ambitions for the poem: he wished "to see the work authenticated, chemically preserved and housed in the Library of Congress." The poem was described by its scenario, since this, rather than the lines of the poem itself, offered coherence: "The piece envisions Brown . . . returning to speak to God after his death." Stamps, not incorrectly, observed at the time of Spencer's epic projects that "she said she was going to write five or six!"[108]

But there was the matter of projected ideas that had not been realized. "Anne Spencer died in 1975, and the unpublished 'A Dream of John Brown' was her last work," stated the newspaper feature. Failing eyesight and advanced age certainly made the completion of this project more difficult. "Spencer's granddaughter, Carol Spencer Read, said her grandmother ceased all other projects on the advice of her doctor to spend the last of her failing eyesight on the poem."[109] A Spencer note from circa 1974 confirms this: "A statement no excuse / This week mine to go far / Orders + no phone."[110] Yet the poem itself was a reckoning with loss and the poet's own mortality, representing both an ongoing store of her responses to the decades of hoped-for change—the measure she relates in her editorial "Our Twentieth Century Liberties"—and the finality of her life and writing. The power of John Brown as hero also provides a stark contrast to the powerlessness in which the speaker's sight is compromised yet is observant enough to see its diminishment. This is conveyed in "Another April," a poem that probably dates to the mid-1960s. It is unusual among Spencer's lyrical works: a sixteen-line self-portrait:

She is too weak to tend
her garden last year, this
year—and old.
The plants know, and
cluster, running free.
The wisteria, purple and white,
leaps from tree to martin-
box dragged down by globes
of the fragrant wet petals
to shore up, strengthen the vine, then
drops to touch Earth, to shoot
up again looping, hanging,
pealing out "April again!"
April is here! . . .
And the window from
which she stares needs washing—[111]

Here the poet reflects on the passing of time, growth and depletion, and natural order versus the human endeavor to control gardens (and perhaps verses), offering a different sense of nature and time than in "Life-Long, Poor Browning." Indeed, this poem is its counterpart, as the speaker looks out the window of death rather than of birth and life. In "Life-Long, Poor Browning," the speaker celebrates the untamed, native, and vital beauty of the Virginia landscape, but in "Another April," she laments that while nature in is "running free," she is not; she is unwillingly contained. She must acknowledge at one and the same time impermanence and continuity: the garden, defiant of the gardener in her advancing age and physical frailty, continues beyond her mortal life. The synesthetic experience of nature, visually and aurally expressive, contrasts with the speaker's occluded view from her dirty windows. Her verse, too, witnesses birth and death on either side of the windows; the speaker cannot help but find her lines as weak and impermanent as her frail body even as she acknowledges the ceaseless leaps of the natural world. "Running," "leaps," "drops," and "shoot" assert continuous motion, and vivid aural articulations appear in the "peals" and "shoots." Most tellingly, the plants "know," conveying an intentional defiance of order. "Another April" expresses the speaker's awareness of the relentlessness of time, which is defined by birth and death, "dawn and twilight," rupture and continuity.

It is possible that John Brown, Spencer's abiding persona and intimate friend, was a secret she kept from her family as well as the public in her advanced years. Chauncey and his wife stated that they "found the notebooks [in] boxes of the late poet's belongings. They were struck when they saw what the notebooks contained—the only mention of the John Brown poem, aside from conversations with family members, appeared in a 1977 book written about Spencer's work."[112] That book, of course, is Greene's *Time's Unfading Garden*. Notes from an interview with Spencer mention "generals—what makes a general—John Brown & Hannibal—poems she is writing."[113] Spencer wrote to Greene, "John Brown moves me to tears when I think of him & u; hardly do you see a moral & physical hero made up together." Spencer placed Greene in the company of John Brown and other "moral and physical" heroes, but she did not share her notebooks even with him.

"There are many kinds of epic in the archive," and there are many kinds of archive, from the institutional Library of Congress to an author's privately kept notebooks.[114] Spencer kept her "John Brown" poem in manuscript form because it offered her a way to record not only the twentieth century's quest for freedom but her responses to epic over the second half of her life. She had witnessed two centuries: "To have one's foot planted in the 19th century and the other firmly advanced in the 20th, is quite a straddle." In a separate note, she reflects, "It is important that John Dewey—and we oldsters have straddled 2 centuries and lived thru them all."[115] "John Brown" provides Spencer's lifelong reflections on the meaning of poetry, place, time, reading, and writing. Through this poem, she aspires to poetic greatness. There is a lesson to be learned from the mother who witnesses and speaks not only as historian but as a cultural authority in a changing landscape that is temporal, geographical, and metaphorical: the grounds of virtue. "John Brown" is Spencer's epic memory, her "Testament of Age," an evaluative instrument measuring the cultural practices surrounding epic and the social practices of memory.[116] While enacting the classical logic of heroism and the monumentalizing of public memory that represents the conventionalized epic form, the poem also activates reflection through communal and individual mourning.

The undertaking of an epic poem takes over a poet's life—everything the writer does becomes part of the epic.[117] Phillips describes "a desire on the part of many (if not all) Americans who engage with the epic tradition: a desire to beat time, to transcend history in the name of something greater."[118] John Brown, Spencer's abiding companion for the duration of the poem's composition—which was also the duration of Spencer's remaining years of life—helped the poet achieve a stride and rhythm for her existence on Earth. The experimental, expansive, and unfinished form of her epic poignantly carries forward her subject: freedom. Its delicate balance between inside and outside—the story of unattained liberty and the poet's witnessing of the events—creates a moving archive of memory. Telling a national history over time and geography, the voice of Spencer's "J-no" both conveys the adamant rejection of slavery exemplified by her hero and presents the unresolved fulfillment of democratic promise.

The paradox of her unfinished manuscript epic of freedom and democracy is also the paradox of poetic experience, which is "the poet's desire for a moral and ethical justice; her vindication or revelation of it through the poetic expression of its lack," as Helen Vendler writes.[119] The poem's lack of final coherence, its discovery and announcement to the public notwithstanding, attests to the author's and African Americans' vexed relationship to American national literature's development in the twentieth century. It constitutes a form of dynamic knowledge, Spencer's own, precisely by remaining a manuscript. Its archival state offers a living record of Spencer's imagination.

As we have seen, in the years between 1940 and 1975, Spencer experimented with public forms such as epic as a means of expanding her imagination just at the time she stopped publishing. Staging her consciousness through John Brown at Harpers Ferry, Spencer explores the distinctly American crisis of slavery and equality through historical and personal experience, using shifting expressive modes to observe and critique the nation. Forced to confront its past and present in the modern century, American poetry had the potential to assume more democratic forms, as "John Brown" attests. In the final chapter, I show how Spencer positions herself as a witness to Black Arts poetry and activism in 1969 through Amiri Baraka, formerly Leroi Jones, who, as Spencer's persona in her unfinished poem "Leroy Meets Lincoln," establishes a participatory role for Spencer in a new world of poetry.

CHAPTER FIVE

"Leroi Meets Lincoln" / "Bastion at Newark"

Anne Spencer's Black Aesthetic

In this place here where 3 worlds meet

—ANNE SPENCER, "Leroi Jones meets Abraham Lincoln"

It started as a poem about Lincoln in 1959, but it became a work about thresholds: encounters between Lincoln, the poet, and a decade later, Leroi Jones (Amiri Baraka) in the city of Newark that documents Spencer's evolving aesthetic over the course of the momentous decade from 1959 to 1969. The poem, and Spencer's aesthetic, reaches its fullest expression in the wake of the rebellion that erupted in Newark in 1967 and the subsequent arrest and trial of poet Leroi Jones. Over this decade, Spencer moved from issuing judgments to calling for action.

Variously titled "Lincoln at Newark," "Abraham Lincoln meets Leroy Jones," "Leroy Jones meets Abraham Lincoln a composite," "When Abraham Lincoln met Leroy Jones," "Leroi Jones meets Lincoln," it was originally titled and at times is still called "Bastion at Newark." In the habit of making her abiding personae intimates to her witnessing, Spencer adopted an abbreviation for "Leroi": "L-ro." From J-no to L-ro, Spencer's nicknames indicate the extent to which these characters were evaluative personae, friends that accompanied the poet in her increasingly isolated life—particularly after her husband's death in 1964. Including Lincoln, these three men draw together the "three worlds" that meet in the circle of humankind referenced in this chapter's epigraph. Yet Spencer herself is also a crucial part of this circle. In a significant development of the "no" of "J-no," the "ro" of "L-ro" signifies not simply refusal and deprivation but revolution. By positioning herself as a witness to Black Arts poetry through Leroi Jones (Spencer at times spells his name "Leroy"), she brings herself into relation with a "potent and alive" Lincoln and the "brightly clad figure" of Leroi outside the Newark courthouse. The poet as witness calls for a movement from reform to revolution, claiming a role for herself in a new decade of poetry.

In *From the Dark Tower*, Arthur P. Davis remarks that African American literature from 1940 to 1960 is characterized by an inescapable paradox: it was the result of both continued segregation and an emerging faith in the prospect of its dismantling. "There is great creative motivation in a movement, which brings all members of a group together and cements them in a common bond. And that is just what segregation did for the Negro.... The mere suggestion that integration was possible in the not-too-distant future tended to destroy during the fifties the protest element in Negro writing."[1] He contrasts the protest ethos of Melvin Tolson's and Gwendolyn Brooks's early works (*Rendezvous with America* [1944] and *A Street in Bronzeville* [1945], respectively), which are informed by a protest ethos, with their later works, which "turn back on protest in favor of technique."[2] While he acknowledges Brooks's return to political engagement in works like *In the Mecca* (1968), Davis's view is that aesthetics and politics are at odds, an idea that has limited understanding of Spencer's published poetry.

Brooks herself acknowledges the many questions about poetic expression asked by African American writers and aspiring poets alike in 1970. In her brief introduction to *The Poetry of Black America* (1973), she observes that "many blacks, those who want to create one poem only, *and* those who want to write poetry for the rest of their lives, are asking for help. Their questions are poignant. *How* do I make words work for me? Are there ways, is there *any* way, to make English words speak blackly? Are there forms already that, with a little tampering, will encase blackness properly, or must we blacks create forms of our own? If we must create forms of our own, how shall we go about this work? Is length helpful—should blacks write epics? Or will blacks find that they need to forge poems 'bullet'-size (with bullet-precision?)"[3]

The recognized need for poetry was matched by a vigorous discussion of its form and purpose. Spencer asked herself similar questions in the ten years between 1959 and 1969. Her selection of publicly oriented personae and poetic forms for the "John Brown" epic and "Leroi Meets Lincoln" enabled her to poetically mediate between a protective, conserving position and an adamant, combative one. While retaining her faith in democracy, Spencer sought a form of poetic expression that would engage the emerging discourses of civil rights and African American poetry, from the works of Tolson and Brooks, who, with Robert Hayden, were the public faces of African American midcentury poetry, to those of Leroi Jones, who represented a new, defiant form of expression. If African American writing in the years leading up to Davis's remarks occupied a paradoxical position, it was because African American experiences of the decade were themselves paradoxical. The 1960s were retrogressive and transformative years, with continued violence directed by the state at African Americans in Watts, Newark, and many other cities across the nation. At the same time, events such as the appointment of Gwendolyn Brooks as poet laureate of Illinois in 1968, succeeding Carl Sandburg, demonstrated an increased regard of African American poetry in national discourse.[4] In this period, Spencer was thrilled by the emergent Black Arts Movement, symbolized for her by Leroi Jones, which she hoped would be able to highlight the lack of social justice and the nation's unfulfilled promise of freedom. At the same time, she was troubled by the creation of national monuments celebrating emancipation and freedom while segregation continued. In this decade of an evolving poetics, Spencer sought to distinguish memory as a physically asserted possession of the powerful from memory as a subversive and sustaining practice of the marginalized. Spencer's monumental archive of unfinished manuscripts thus "maps ... the countercultural hopes of a present to come."[5]

In February 1959, Spencer reflects,

> Abraham Lincoln if he lived today would be one hundred and fifty years old. And that is how old he is. Lincoln is the only united American who, O King, will live forever. Forever will merely but surely mean so long as we need him.
>
> As far as our country is concerned Lincoln is also only indispensable *man*. He is the improbable man, doing the impossible. The others were good men in a group—Lincoln is one man—doing what one man cannot do. He does it in the human way as a human being. When he has to act and speak adversely he so acts and speaks overlooking immediacy to see the human end of the thing considered.
>
> Today he is potent and alive The age in which we grovel too[6]

By "and that is how old he is," Spencer means that Lincoln's actions and moral vision, which saw past "immediacy," were "potent and alive" because he could see "the human end of the thing." Lincoln "still lives," she later notes, because of his actions, and what he left for us: an example of a living practice of morality, of action, and of movement.[7] "Lincoln is not quick to gamble, as some others are, with the sanctity of human life but he does believe more in the sanctity of human aspiration; the belief saves him. He still is here with us. Salvation, too, can be ephemeral and must continually be restored."[8] The poet aligned herself with this example of living practice, perhaps also wishing that her insights would still live.

She referred to him as "my Lincoln." In the last years of her life, she recalled how she and Edward, after marrying in May 1901, had had to wait for a honeymoon for many years. When they finally took it in 1916, they traveled to Washington, D.C., where they saw the siting of the Lincoln Memorial, its massive marble statue of Lincoln that was completed in 1920 and dedicated in 1922. "Several times on return visits there were moments but no such thrills even looking at my Lincoln there is the feeling that too much is expected of money capacity—must we buy all our seeing and feeling?" she wrote Greene.[9] Here, as in "John Brown," Spencer referred to the "bought for" "feeling" of liberty, conveying her mistrust of the statue as a thing that becomes a substitute for authentic feeling—the human practice of liberty it is meant to honor. The statue, as grand as it is, as symbolic as it is in its materials drawn from various states and regions of the now unified nation, represents memory as *possession* rather than as a *practice* by individuals and their actions.[10] The risk involved in looking to an unmoving statue as the articulation of national conscience and human progress is that the dynamic relation of human beings in the present and how they put the nation's ideals into practice are forgotten. Spencer takes up the ballad form alongside the epic form of "John Brown," using ballad to invoke a different version of public memory from that conjured by epic, one that is popular rather than elite.

Working from a compelling visual image, as she did with "John Brown" and earlier poems such as "Creed" and "At the Carnival," Spencer drew on the statue of Lincoln in Newark, New Jersey. "Bastion at Newark" establishes the setting of what will become "Leroi Meets Lincoln." At the center is the statue of Lincoln, situated in front of the Newark courthouse, cast by Gutzon Borglum in in 1911, where three (or sometimes, in her notes, four) roads meet. While the idea for "Bastion" may have come from a photograph of the statue that was published in the February 1920 issue of *Crisis* magazine, Spencer had personal connections to Newark that made the statue important to her. Her younger daughter, Bethel, had been appointed court clerk at Newark, as Spencer shared in a 1967 letter to Grace Nail Johnson: "*She is Court Clerk in Newark*—24 mile drive every day—bought a quaint old house with large grounds, her heaven but it is not home for me nor Pop."[11] Spencer convalesced with Bethel in New Jersey on several occasions in the 1960s as her health deteriorated, and yet she insisted on living alone at 1313 Pierce Street. A little less than five months after Spencer sent Grace this letter, the five-day Newark riots—or rebellion, as its African American citizens referred to it—took place.

In her poem, Spencer brings Lincoln into the present moment of civil rights and the Black Arts Movement to advance her developing aesthetic, linking her works to Black Arts Movement writing such as Baraka's. Drawing on the trope of "Bessemer steel," which burns out the impurities of iron ore to make a stronger material, Spencer "melds" Jones and Lincoln: "—born / Far apart in Time, and space / And manners / They met and wedded—no— / Melded—they call this pro- / Pinquity unavoidable: no place / To travel but the Circle—that / Is the Law. / For us the doom. / Whatever happens must happen here." Spencer takes up justice and American ideals through two men of conviction and calls attention to their convergence in the circle of humankind. This convergence of history displaces the specious timeline of progress that she called "Southern tradition" in "Virginia as Narcissus," replacing it with a layered picture of American and African American purposes, fates, and obligations in a single ecology of human practice.

By the mid-1960s it seemed as if Newark had forsaken its African American residents, who remained in the city while whites moved to the suburbs.[12] Slumlords demanded rent for uninhabitable buildings, and African Americans encountered systematic racism when they attempted to find better places to live. Moreover, an entire neighborhood was subjected to urban planning that did not include its residents in the process, failing to acknowledge the human lives

Gutzon Borglum, *Seated Lincoln*, Newark, N.J. (1911).
Photographed by Arnold Genthe circa 1916 (Library of Congress).

that lived there. This urban renewal project that was proposed in early 1967 and whose goal, according to local African American residents, was "Negro removal" threatened to displace 150 acres of Black residences to make space for a medical school.[13] What African American residents of Newark experienced was a locally specific version of a national problem with fair housing practices. A series of laws passed between 1948 and 1949 liberalized lending practices, introduced mortgage insurance, and extended mortgages to thirty years, paving the way for postwar suburban development.[14] But African Americans were left behind. Prospective renters and buyers who were African American were turned away from properties in virtually every major metropolitan city.

Baraka was at the center of a grassroots project of self-determination and the defense of Black livelihood in Newark, making him a powerful example to Spencer and also one with whom she could identify given her deep attachment to her local agitations in Lynchburg and her identity as a Virginian and a southerner. She regarded Baraka's endeavors as a writer and as an activist working for the advancement of Black and Puerto Rican Newark's claims to political representation and autonomy in the majority-Black city as an exciting, empowering development of Black selfhood within the nation and its literature. Through the drafts of "Leroi Meets Lincoln," Spencer imaginatively recreates her nation and the idea of belonging, addressing the crisis in Newark and considering Black experiences there in relation to her own poetic project. As Eve

Dunbar reminds us, the Black Arts Movement "serves, at the very least, as a discursive opening for us to consider what the proactive embrace of black art versus cultural translation looks like. What might a call for cultural resistance and nation making within a nation look like when carried out through black artistic imagination?"[15] Spencer's "Leroi Meets Lincoln" explores the possible routes of this new form of expression in her poetry.

Spencer was well aware of the dire situation in the North from her two daughters' experiences in the New York–New Jersey metropolitan area. Her son-in-law Francis E. Rivers, her daughter Alroy's second husband, became the highest ranking African American judge when he was appointed to the city court in New York in September 1943 and elected to it November 1943.[16] From 1930 on, when he was elected to the state assembly, Rivers was active in Republican politics in Harlem. During the 1930s, he worked to put two laws on the books, both of which were signed into law by Franklin Delano Roosevelt: the first was to create a municipal court in Harlem and the second was to allow renters to forego paying rent to landlords until housing violations had been corrected. He served continuously on the bench of the city court from 1943 to 1963. Rivers was also an active member of the NAACP Legal Defense and Education Fund and served as its president from 1965 to 1970.[17] In these roles, he served as a local and national advocate for the rights of African Americans seeking homes.

Downtown Newark burned from July 13 to July 17, 1967. City police had pulled over, arrested, and severely beaten an African American taxicab driver on July 12. His injuries were so severe that he was sent to the hospital—but by a back route, so that gathering crowds of outraged citizens would not see his wounded state. As in other conflagrations such as Harlem in 1935, the absence of the man who was arrested was taken to mean that he had died in police custody, creating widespread outrage that was an expression of the totality of institutionalized racism. Daily threats to African American livelihood in all forms found expression in these three days of uprising.[18]

Among those arrested was Amiri Baraka, who then was known as Leroi Jones. As Jelani Cobb writes, "Amiri Baraka was pulled over during the riots and severely beaten by Newark police officers, one of them his former high school classmate,"[19] suffering injuries that required stitches. He, along with the two other men who were riding in his VW bus, were charged with unlawful possession of two firearms, which he claimed were planted, and he was also charged with resisting arrest.[20] His trial took place in February 1968. At sentencing, Baraka's judge read "Black People," a recently published piece by Baraka, into the court record in its entirety as evidence of his fomenting of violence.[21] No matter that he had written the poem after his experience in police custody. The city prosecutor described it as "a diabolical prescription to commit murder and to steal and plunder." Jones responded "I'm being sentenced for the poem.

Is that what you're saying?" The prosecutor claimed that the poem's "similar evidences . . . cause one to suspect that you were a participant in formulating a plot to ignite the spark on the night of July 13, 1967 to burn the City of Newark." Jones responded, "You mean, you don't like the poem, in other words." Recalling the experience forty-five years later, Baraka reflected, "That 1967 thing was like a reckoning. I used to get held by the police for going to a poetry reading. The police would take the script out of my hand. That's like living under some kind of fascism."[22]

The trial of Baraka also marked a defining moment for Spencer, who serves as its witness. On February 14, 1968, the first day of the trial, she notes that "today there is a wreath" in the lap of the Lincoln statue outside the courthouse. She continues:

> This morning as usual the Sheriff's "wagons" and those from the State Prison at Trenton, of the Penitentiary and the Reformatories were coming in to park just back of the Statue[.] From the Reformatories boys 17, 18 or so years of age from the other cars men hand cuffed holding their hands in that defenseless fashion in front of themselves some chained one to the other in groups of up to 10 men going to the various criminal courts in the building—from September to December 31st this court was having criminal cases; since January civil cases, and most of them are Negroes—Of the heavy, backlogged, criminal calendars the majority are Negroes with now and then big embezzlers, white murders [sic] for mercenary reasons, white on gang, white on domestic reasons while the indictments on which the many Negroes appear are small thefts, narcotics and when theyre really angry and frustrated assault and battery, most of these trivial offenses should have been disposed of in the lower courts[.]
>
> Anyway, also today I saw two brightly clad figures walk down the steps of the building past Lincoln, I was attracted to them because of the way the wind was blowing the cotton garments and it was cold! I then realized they were Leroy [sic] Jones and his wife in African dress. They stopped and she took the baby from him so that they could wrap him in her striped shawl and they walked on purple, yellow, green, orange and brown waving in the wind. He is appealing from a conviction of 3 to 5 years in the State Prison for having carried a weapon in his car during the riots last summer. He says the police stopped his car and while he was being searched planted the gun in his car.
>
> At the time he was being sentenced last summer the Judge read some of Jones poems [sic], to those present in the courtroom, commenting that the poems were revolutionary in content—thereupon a melee, a free for all broke up the sentencing. Jones was taken to State Prison where he spent one night and day and was then placed on bail pending his appeal.[23]

While appearing to have been based on an actual event and on a photograph of Baraka and his wife descending the courthouse steps that circulated

Leroi Jones / Amiri Baraka, wife, and child leaving Newark courthouse in snow.
Photographed by Neil Boenzi (Neal Boenzi / *New York Times* / Redux).

in the newspapers, Spencer's witnessing is both improvisational and expansive, an interpretation of the events by the poet who sees into the future from the past. Using Baraka's trial to interrogate Lincoln's place not so much in history as in memory, Spencer uses the very substance—bronze—the statue is made of to reference its humility and authentic expression:

> We know but cannot learn.
> Whatever we know (passes)
> Here in this place where four
> roads meet for pause and
> do not there is this statue in
> at the apex of the public square
> there is a statue in a public sq. of bronze it is fashioned,
> pure, without need to glisten.[24]

Spencer associates the statue's bronze with purity: it is memory as practice. "Without need to glisten," this statue of Lincoln contrasts with the inauthentic "bought and paid for" idea of liberty introduced in her "John Brown." Recalling her observation that "too much is expected of money capacity—must we buy all our seeing and feeling?," we may conclude that this bronze statue, through its materials, contrasts with the Lincoln Memorial: it advances memory and feeling. However, at the same time, she points to the potential for the statue to produce the opposite result.

An area flat, without
Any natural pile of
Earth called hill
No place for energy.
The four roads could
Be plotted and worked
Quickly—no energy.
Just the site to plumb
Down this massed inertia, insensate,
Man of bronze.
Memory of him would hold
The roads in bastion—too
Easy for flat roads meeting
Here, dallying not crossing![25]

Lincoln, as "massed inertia," here prevents interconnection among the roads: "memory of him" preserves the division. The spatial and temporal swinging arc of John Brown, the central figure of his dream and return, stands in stark contrast to the unmoving Lincoln, set in a place with "no energy," unmoving because of the human choice to "hold" him in memory rather than continue his legacy, his vision.

Spencer the poet thus assigns herself the task of advancing his conception. In notes for the poem from after 1967, Spencer ruminates on the image of the Lincoln statue in Newark:

> This massive copper Lincoln was placed here at the [corner] in Newark New
> > Jersey where [Springbell] ran into the arms of 2 other street[s] and the 3
> > turned for a bad look into
> > The atrocity ghetto ^going toward^ of row and St. This tale is not easy history
> > with Mr. L.
> > For he was lately emerged from a far greater violence but closer, sheer topical
> > news route still there is an urgent pressure
> The night darker a flicke[r] came on T[V] saying
> A docu[mentary]—of the most evil city in our country
> > A friend was telling in laughter that the reason there were so many of us in
> > "New" was the 30–40 hegira we were[26]

Here the streets run "into the arms" of the others, each turning back to look at what Spencer terms "the atrocity ghetto": the poet places Lincoln in the context of new violence, a "topical news route" yet one with "urgent pressure." We see Spencer referencing the Great Migration as the 1930–40 "hegira" and characterizing both New York and Newark as ironic destinations for migrants fleeing discrimination and economic hardship in the South.

In a draft linking the Lincoln and Jones, Spencer toys with making them "a composite":

> Leroi Jones meets Abraham Lincoln a composite
> When Abraham Lincoln met Leroi Jones
> Don't let the cliché people fool you
> What we do not know / hurts:
> The white marble
> Court House is the
> Only handsome building[27]

To her 1959 poem about Lincoln and his belief in "the sanctity of human aspiration," Spencer adds a new entry in 1972 that assumes a different moral perspective—one of judgment. Both entries inhabit the same pages in her notebook but are written in markedly different handwriting and in distinct voices as well. These different but paired decades of composition show Spencer's move from an investment in "ephemeral" "salvation," which must "continually be restored" to "a truth I perceive" and a "just judge," who is the speaker herself.[28] What is striking about this manuscript, besides its explicit dialogue with Spencer's earlier composition—one "past and present" of 1959 and 1972—is the introduction of the speaker's voice. The "I" of the poet, who by the time of the second entry's writing has witnessed two centuries and ninety years of America, makes its entrance.

In the 1972 entry, Spencer offers a rough version of the witnessed images, the statue and the poet leaving the courthouse:

> Leroy + Abe
> This is today the all; This I could not see the shadow of so that I could tremble in hope
> The dark boy on my knee
> 2 boys white and dirty as the balled snow
> They pelt us with
> The little slave-[illegible] on the dock his wife
> Their tiny babe in arms
> If the Christians leaving sparing this courthouse, Newark, New Jersey, today (you see there is a Newark New York) would look back—
> (it is the season of crèche and Christians, commercial and the like)
> Their if an illusion hanging in the air behind them of Ethiope father mother and child emerging from the Creche—hands stretched—or a knotted fish—
> These two: when the judge (no doubt as just judge must my mind for your mind, why? Of Past and present) said no jail + a fine.
> Each knew *all* about the gun—
> And of a truth I perceive . . .

her afric sari much too thin
for winter was swirled by
snow as Lro's lady stept down
clutching their child
the small father seemed even smaller
but he walked tall
(keep my forever memory one gone who was tall and walked and worked and
    gently strong, in the evening/ twice in a long life could trust my agony to
    share his own)
so it might be tonight with[29]

The "I" is a "we" and an "us." The interior reflection, "These two: when the judge
(no doubt as just judge must my mind for your mind, why? Of Past and present) said no jail + a fine. / Each knew *all* about the gun— / And of a truth I perceive..." conveys the poet's awareness of a long history of injustice, and her use
of the word "judge" as both noun and verb, the cleaving of "just judge" and the
"judge must," makes space for her evaluation. (In an earlier draft Spencer considers having the judge spoken to by a voice, possibly Lincoln's, that dictates
the sentence he hands down: "And the judge being spoken to hears a voice saying, 'Lincoln is sitting out there: under advancement of all conditions no sentence. Two dollars fine!'"[30])

The poet's voice of judgment provides her with space to personally reflect
on loss in the midst of this witnessed scene of sentencing: in this unfinished
fragment, we see the author connecting her active memory of her husband, Edward, with "Leroy." As the poet witnesses Baraka with his family in the swirling,
cold wind, babe in arms and protectively wrapped, she is compelled both to
marvel and to remember. "Keep my forever memory one gone who was tall and
walked and worked and gently strong, in the evening / could twice in a long life
could trust my agony to share his own" refers to Edward, and to the "personal
agony" each shared with the other.[31]

Baraka reminded Spencer of her husband, who was remembered as "gentle,
generous, kindly, honorable and with a sensitive intelligence" and described as
"one of Lynchburg's most respected, exemplary citizens" in the obituary published in the *Lynchburg News*. He was ambitious and innovative as well. "One of
the accomplishments characterizing him was his acquisition and approval of
rental property so that the area was called Spencer Place in official recognition
and was sometimes referred to as an initiatory, private, housing development
in the city." The Spencers earned "respect for their contribution to the better
life of the community."[32] Yet this obituary is striking for its lack of reference to
civil rights and Edward's advancement of a *Black* private housing development.
Edward, like Anne, was acutely aware of the importance land ownership and
habitation and how incarceration impacted the ability of Black ex-prisoners

to purchase or rent homes. In an autobiographical piece from well before Edward's death, "Sunday at the Prison," Spencer recollects that one Sunday, he took the children to prison rather than to church. Spencer observes that most of the incarcerated were Black, that the guards tried to ask why they were there, and that Edward said the Spencers worked to pay their salary. The family ate lunch there and then left.[33] Edward's gentle and kindly nature was balanced by his desire to raise politically conscious children and assert his—and their— place in the world.

Edward was the subject of the final version of a poem that she revised over the course of a decade. "O Man," presumably about Lincoln, finally becomes a poem titled "Black Man O' Mine," about Edward. The poem records the evolution of Spencer's Black aesthetics, developing prior to and in tandem with the Black Arts Movement, and traces the development of an autonomous voice that remained attached to an idea of national identity and belonging but also explored the meaning of a Black self-determinacy that did not need to be explained to or translated for mainstream America. Transforming the bastion of her poem about Lincoln into countercultural activism, Spencer embraces the revolutionary culture, pride, and self-determination she witnessed and cautions, "I would pray, no labor with the young to keep pride without be[ing] proud such difference has humility—a contact with every man alive."[34] This beautiful portrait of Black love and a Black man is accompanied by the poet's voice, the "I" who is physically there, witnessing, guiding, willing, and judging.

In the sequence of the three draft poems, "O Man," "Dark Man," and "Black Man O' Mine," "O Man" specifically references the circle of Lincoln and the angles of the courthouse creating the bastion:

> The angles—so many
> Angles if we are wise
> Enough to fit them together
> Never let man's Life in
> They make
> Time, his first circle
> His first verso circle:
> It spells love—that
> Thing above them
> The beast[35]

In this draft poem, time is represented in the image of a circle moving right, and then left—"verso." Love is found in the circular site of Lincoln; the courthouse is "the beast," its "angles . . . Never let man's Life in."

In her next draft poem, Spencer explores depth-driven vertical and turning images representing the cycle of nature itself. "Dark" is a trope for life, vitality, Earth itself:

Dark man o' mine
Earth were your pleasure
It could not give what
I give to you

Or the ocean would yield
And you could discover
The ages of treasure
To have and to view

Dark man o' mine
Now I turn[36]

Darkness becomes blackness in a later draft, the embrace of a beautiful man
and his "massing dark" that, in demanding authentic emotional response,
draws the speaker's depth of feeling, her "darkest part":

Black Man o' mine,
And I hush and caress you, close, close to my heart,
All your loving is just your needing what's true
Then with your massing dark comes my darkest part,
For living without your loving is only rue.
Black man o' mine, if the world were your lover
It could not give what I give to you.[37]

The final version adds a new verse and new lines:

Black man o' mine,
If the world were your lover,
It could not give what I give to you,
Or the ocean would yield and you could discover
Its ages of treasure to hold and to view;
Could it fill half the measure of my heart's portion . . .
Just for you living, just for you giving all this devotion,
Black man o' mine.

Black man o' mine,
As I hush and caress you, close to my heart,
All your loving is just your needing what's true;
Then with your passing dark comes my darkest part,
For living without your loving is only rue.
Black man o' mine, if the world were your lover
It could not give what I give to you.[38]

The Black man and the "I" speaker, the poet herself, "half the measure," are
the portrait of an infinite love the depth of which creates a powerful Black aes-

thetic. While Spencer's anthologizers from the 1960s and 1970s, such as Hayden and Davis, characterized Spencer's poetry as embodying a raceless aesthetic, we see, as they could not, that in her unpublished works from 1960 to 1975 Spencer both created and developed her poetics through a Black aesthetic. The "I" of Spencer's works in this period marks a distinctive turn to the poet as speaker, as a poet-warrior setting the terms of love and beauty and also exposing hatred and ugly truths. It is in this context that Spencer acquiesced to her poem "White Things," which had not been reprinted since 1923, appearing in Davis's 1975 anthology *The New Negro Renaissance*. This decision reflects Spencer's embrace of a new, more powerful role as a poet in the last years of her life. While she did not publish later poems such as "Black Man O' Mine" and "Bastion at Newark," she placed her antilynching poem of 1923 in the context of Leroi Jones's conviction and the general atmosphere of enforced terror that African Americans had to endure, as she recognized that Black people, as well as Jones and his poem "Black People," were on trial.

Just as the bastion became the meeting point of Lincoln and Leroi in her draft poems over the decades, so did Spencer herself become the point of convergence: she emerges among these men as poet and just judge. Baraka advocated for Black control of "their own institutions—in this case, housing," stated a 1972 press release announcing the groundbreaking for the Newark housing development named Kawaida Towers.[39] The release noted that "Baraka refers to Newark as 'New Ark,' which reflects his conviction that the city can be made to lead the rebirth of all the nation's cities."[40] Spencer stayed abreast of these events, evidenced by her echo of Baraka's "New Ark" in one of her manuscripts. She advances Baraka's idea of rebirth through Black self-determination by introducing the image of children playing on Lincoln's lap outside the courthouse. In this image there is both continuity and contrast: the "babe" in his wife's arms is mirrored by the children who sit with Lincoln.

Spencer recognizes that the failure of modern cities to provide a sustaining environment for Black people in places like Newark and New York has been wrongfully blamed on Black families. Noting that "Lincoln is still at New[ark]," Spencer invokes his authority and his ideal of freedom, as her speaker views the children before him in this "sinful city":

> He was still at Newark no roistrous bone in his beautiful angular soul, none now
>   here before This mélange of Court House here where four uncertain roads
>   almost converge by accident—and because he is so still two fluid & nine or
>   ten boy—smaller yet, beside this
> He parlyed with himself—about chattledom I said to me! Not about keeping
>   men down but sending them up as he went up with them—the only way—[41]

Spencer here returns to the "out and up" motif of her "John Brown" poem but rather than turning to the stars for resolution, she turns to the children, their convergence with the roads in this place. As she draws these images of encounter together, her poems, too, converge. Under the title "Newark Junction: Milam & Till," she unites her Lincoln and these children:

> There sits in bronze Mr. Lincoln intertia itself which does not himself move! Stand high look across from this high Court House window People, hurried passing slacken look and hurtle on—why? Time only can answer. Two little boys who are not yet people: one sits in his great lap & lays a small patting hand on this, quiescent brown finger the other boy—how Abe would laugh an[d] love and[42]

Spencer moved from her experimentation with the nationally oriented epic form of "John Brown" to a folk, or better yet people's poetry, the ballad. The ballad with its verse narrative form and orientation toward everyday people takes on a special significance in this manuscript as a means of giving expression to Black Arts and situating "Leroi" in the longer history of "Lincoln" while recognizing the revolutionary nature of this moment. The ballad imparts a knowledge that is passed down the generations through the practice of living memory. It is powerfully significant to Spencer's aesthetic, especially as the poet enters into her poems as witness, practicing living memory and positioning herself to pass these memories on to her "heirs." At the same time, through the ballad form, Spencer acknowledges her mortality and demonstrates her attentive understanding of Baraka as a defiant folk hero of a world that will continue after she returns to the earth.

An early experimentation with the ballad form's invocation of folk personae yielded this version titled "Leroi Meets Lincoln":

> A. Lincoln, Lincoln, the only
> Man in the world named Lincoln
> And the only man in the
> World named Jones,
> Jones, Leroi Jones—born
> Far apart in Time, and space
> And manners
> They met and wedded—no—
> Melded—they call this pro-
> Pinquity unavoidable: no place
> to travel but the Circle—that
> is the Law.
> For us the doom.
> Whatever happens must happen here

Lincoln, Lincoln, Jones, Jones, as the "only [men]" in the world, are introduced as opposites "born / Far apart in Time, and space / And manners," as in the ballad's formal contrasts of personae, but in Spencer's complication of the ballad's action, they "meld" in "the Circle."

Considering the day of judgment and its resolution, Spencer writes:

> coming thru the CH door:
> for Leroy, by Whittier: All around the desert
> circles underneath a brazen sky
> only one green spot remaining
> where the grass is never dry
> From the horror of that desert
> From its—[*sic*] fire of hell
> Turns the fainting spirit, thither
> As a diver seeks the / its bell[43]

Spencer's allusion is to John Greenleaf Whittier's 1848 poem "The Slaves of Martinique": "O blessed hope of freedom," declares the male speaker, referencing Haiti's revolution. "Hate of Slavery, hope of Freedom, Love is mightier than all." Perhaps the most significant image that Spencer reuses by recalling Whittier, recontextualizing his lines from a natural surrounding to the urban one of Newark, is that of the circle. This is the relevant stanza from "The Slaves of Martinique":

> All around the desert circles, underneath a brazen sky,
> Only one green spot remaining where the dew is never dry!
> From the horror of that desert, from its atmosphere of hell,
> Turns the fainting spirit thither, as the diver seeks his bell.[44]

"Contrite" souls dedicated the "copper" Lincoln statue in 1902, Spencer's speaker writes. Addressing "people," the speaker, who identifies herself as "from Africa," warns them that the "cliché" (what one doesn't know doesn't hurt) is a deception: "What we do not know hurts":

> When Abraham Lincoln met Leroy Jones
> Don't let the cliché
> people fool you
> What we do not know hurts:
> The white marble
> Court House is the
> only handsome building
> There (maybe) I
> Know a lot of things, most of them wrong
> The *staff* had their
> Dinner and because of it
> I was—it was snowing

Like an angry one
Broom sweeps a room
Flakes hadn't yet
decided where they
wanted to go—I'm
from Africa, cold
weather gets me down, usually and
out
But I'm not often
In normal situation
Of a court
As in a Great Court
Dominated by a
Copper great statue
Of our Lincoln what
Is it doing in
This place here
Where 3 roads
Meet—I was for
Once think of shiver
Two episodes happened
As I stood and gazed dedicated I was
Told in 1902 by
Some contrite souls
And now being gazed at
by me—another
such soul.[45]

And finally, in one of her last drafts, Spencer experiments with parataxis, synes-
thesia, and interpolation: as one idea leaves off, another begins, linked without
conjunction. These linkings are significant because they redirect the speaker's
ideas into the language of Black Arts, even quite literally, the Bantu-based language of Kiswahili—from which Baraka adopted his new name:

This is short for the day is cold
Of [illegible] huh day in . . . her no [illegible] yet—just its arrow heads / striking in
to kill what's left of summer / inside their white marble elegant Edifice of Justice
/ on side the gavel too striked like winter—inside too there are two people / of
[illegible] innocent—using Bant[u] language of a looming Big Man—whatever /
we of avg. size the judge what ever / and a small culprit seize the man / The great
doors open / The arrows of snow make images / indistinct/ and his parl is over
/ the small man. Smaller woman / and tiny babe stand in cold silhouette/ Leroy
[sic] has now met Lincoln. / He is free / Lincoln is free for the aro[gant] / kids to

shake fist at him / for my / the great grandson / To set on his earth color leaf +
grain / The carpet is red / Halls are white / Judge in Black is white / Man in dark
is Black / Book is / Book is Holy read and black / I [illegible] out, stomach queasy
/ outside-no better or is it / yes. There is Abe Lincoln / in bronze / He was what
I am / Like me and you—whoever you are / he had great hopeless pains of his
spirit / and pain in all his body from recognition/ he was murdered—the land of
his spirit and / taken apart-captured + killed

Having acknowledged the snow that kills summer, the speaker directs her
eyes into the "Edifice of Justice," its whiteness mirrored by the white judge,
while "Book is / Book is Holy read and black" plays on red as color and as a
homonym for a "read" holy book to which, one presumes, humankind would
adhere. The irony that destabilizes the colors white, red, and "Black" recalls
Spencer's "White Things," where the supremacist imperative replaces the
"blood in a ruby rose" with a "poor white poppy-flower," and the speaker records the murderous deeds of whites, burning the color of Earth's landscape
and "a race of black, black men" to the whiteness of ash: "Man-maker, make
white!" Lincoln here stands as a contrasting image; he is "in bronze," "his earth
color" representing likeness and humanity: "He was what I am / Like me and
you—whoever you are." The lynch victim of Spencer's "White Things" is here
replaced by Lincoln, who "had great hopeless pains of his spirit / and pain all
in his body from recognition/ he was murdered—the land of his spirit and /
taken apart—captured + killed." The "leaf + grain" of Lincoln's countenance in
bronze, situated outside, is almost organic in its elements and contrasts with
the smooth marble whiteness of the courthouse; the speaker's "great grandson" sits on Lincoln's lap while Leroi, his wife, and baby in arms exit the cold,
white courthouse. The Black Arts provides a sustaining language of possibility
that is interspersed with images of contrasting violence. Freedom exists outside the courthouse, but it is an ephemeral state that, if pursued, can result in
pain, death, dismemberment. Lincoln is like a lynch victim; he is like Emmett
Till, whose lynching in Mississippi in 1955 was a contemporary example of the
same terror and brutality. In her manuscript drafts, Spencer writes about Lincoln, Leroi, and Till on the same page and titles her fragmentary ballad of Emmett Till "Lincoln is Still at Newark."

Perhaps the most moving aspect of this manuscript version of "Leroi Jones
meets Lincoln," written in Spencer's advanced years in barely legible letters,
is the way it is composed in between the typed, mimeographed lines of a legal brief about New York City's unfair housing practices. It is most likely from
the office of her son in-law Francis E. Rivers. The brief begins with the date
on which the complaint was filed: July 24, 1964, but Spencer, ever the recycler, writes her lines sometime after February 1968. I believe this manuscript
is from 1972. The claimant in the brief is named "Leroy." The dialogue between

media that Spencer's manuscript introduces—the legal brief and the poetry, the courts and the poet, Leroy of New York and Leroi of Newark—foregrounds her preoccupation with the urban housing crisis of Newark and New York, emblems of segregation and struggle.

Spencer connects the experience of forced movement and the struggle for home and homeland to a larger global struggle for decolonization and land rights, as in her reflection on South African apartheid:

> what I hear about
>
> sounds home like home at its worst
>
> Mrs. Oyerenda sent me a list of
>
> Apartheid flowers[46]

The phrase "sounds home like home" offers a stuttering caesura, effectively emphasizing homeliness within the self and unhomeliness without—"like home at its worst."

"Man must adjudicate—," Spencer observes, "whether it be more sin [to burn a tree or to worship one]."[47] In these lines, she returns to her poem "Substitution," in which she advances the idea, as she had explained to James Weldon Johnson, that "no living thing can escape suffering." In a different manuscript, she sees the reflection of God in nature, rather than in human beings' institutions of worship: "Genesis first chap 2nd verse—and the spirit of God Moved upon the face of the waters + so the vast and all the rest of God *a moving living God*."[48] "Was there ever a time when the Jew Jehovah God was not in the Vatican and the Saint Peters and Saint Pauls and the first.... When we were heathen were still worshipping ... the bees + the trees the sun and the moon the Hebrew patriarchs gave their God a soul—And the spirit of God moved."[49]

Spencer voices her support of Black diplomacy on the world stage in a post–World War II world, taking up "Ralph [Bunche]" ("Tracks a new breed of men not boys a new breed"), Eva Jefferson, and Shirley Chisholm in the same reflection: "John Brown and his body Harriet Tubman and her guns—(speaking [illegible] of Just Man [illegible] and the whites all dead ones are great or is it greedy—and speaking of Tubman why don't they send a woman or 2 or 3/ Women ove[r] to a / minister [administer]—that fine mausoleum of potentates and show us Natives over USA it can be done send Eva Jefferson maybe her Ma + Pa would go, send Shirley Chisolm to touch +go, and her husband/ No ballroom + beaded ribbons are needed on any of us for my grandfather."[50] Jefferson, known as the "peaceful warrior," was a Black student at Northwestern University who agitated for civil rights on campus, and Chisholm, the first Black woman elected to U.S. Congress (1968), was in 1972 the first Black woman candidate for a major party ticket in the run for president.

Spencer's "we" is often nationally inclusive, but she also specifically references the "we-ness" of Black people. "Negroes are just people," she notes:

The Amenities of being a Negro

... We black people are being bombarded by the subversive phonetics of those who call us angels and those who call us devils are the same soft enemy, and like a maiden of great wealth, we want to be loved—or hated for ourselves. We are just people. In all the American human potpourri we are the easiest people to be loved.

Negroes don't mind fighting a losing battle but we hate furiously having to even win a war![51]

This loving and loveable state does not guarantee life or livelihood in place, but it does generate a legacy of friendship and a reminder of everything left to treasure in this world, of which love is a part: "This one thing that is truth we can believe: when a friend, as one says, dies it can truly be said, I have a friend—everything left to treasure is still here of which love is just a part—Lincoln left himself to the world."[52] She summons forth her previously authored poems such as "I Have a Friend," merging them into her new experiences and perceptions of the world.

Hope is also a part of this world. In a February 1967 letter to Grace Nail Johnson, of whom she "daily recall[ed] your lovely image as among the last so close ties of this so strange world," she sent a newspaper clipping that mentioned Jim and stated that "I have been too hopeful: I would write an article (Good Reading for illiterates by one of them) reminded that Mencken, and Jim both spoke encouragingly of my prose but I'll not settle for the kind of stuff I find my mind cannot do, now, if ever—."[53]

Yet she was as certain that her hopes for the younger generation—its poetry, diplomacy, love, and revolutionary example—were not misplaced as she was of her final return to Earth's soil. In a brief entry titled "On Swahili," she remarks, "And I do hope that *we* have enough ... to hang on to this strap of now civilization we have sought, agglutenates (pardon) civilization—it must be, until we get chance + time to sit down, catch breath + even giggle!"[54] Spencer regarded her poems as living, moving, soul-practicing entities. Through them, she sought the continuity provided by Earth, by living things that feel and have soul, as suggested by her 1927 poem "Substitution," which she revised in 1973. "Is Life itself but many ways of thought ...,?" the speaker asks. "God thinks ... and being comes to ardent things." As God thinks or dreams, so too are poems made: "Or dreams a little, while creation swings / The circle of His mind and Time's full girth." The mind of God and the mind of the poet assume a shared, intimate space of thought: "As here within this noisy peopled room / My thought leans forward ... quick! you're lifted clear / Of brick and frame to moonlit garden bloom,— / Absurdly easy, now, our walking, dear, / Talking, my leaning close to touch your face ... / His All-Mind bids us keep this sacred place!"[55] The reader too is drawn into this "sacred place," which is the poem itself, its meditation on poetry revealing truth through its very form. Unfinished and fragmentary, "Leroi Meets Lincoln" expresses "the countercultural hopes" of the 1960s and beyond.[56] Spencer did not live to see this projected future. Spencer and her son-in-law, defenders of expressive and legal rights to home, died in the same year—1975—just one day apart: Spencer on July 27 and Rivers on July 28.

"Till"

Soil and Civil Rights in
Anne Spencer's Manuscript Poetry

> The poet looks beyond the book he has made,
> Or else he had not made it.
>
> —ELIZABETH BARRETT BROWNING, *Aurora Leigh*

In this epilogue, I use a specific example from Spencer's archive of unpublished writing to illuminate her developing aesthetic view and practice during the latter part of her life. Spencer described herself as a "scrap scribbler"; she spent a lifetime jotting down notes and lyrics, most of which were never completed. In one of these fragments, she writes about Emmett Till, whose lynching in 1955 at the age of fourteen drew national attention to the brutal reign of terror in the Jim Crow South, the South in which Spencer continued to live. Spencer's fragment exemplifies the importance of her manuscripts to the developing critical conversation about her, demonstrating the breadth of her engagements and aspirations as a poet in the civil rights era and beyond and revealing that she sought to live "beyond the book" she desired to produce for the public.

In a close reading of the manuscript draft of the poem, I offer a line-by-line scansion, categorize its form, date its composition, and link it to another literary representation of Emmett Till, the aim being to lay the critical groundwork for a consideration of Spencer's poetics in this period. By considering her writing over the range of nearly her lifetime with an emphasis on the latter half of her life, I expand the limited perspective of her writing by both period and aesthetic and show the profound social and political shaping of African American life at midcentury on her unpublished work. The collective experience of de jure segregation, continued poverty and substandard education, failed promises to America's African American servicemen of World War II, and ongoing housing and employment discrimination all inform Spencer's midcentury writing.

Far too often Spencer's significance as a poet has been limited to the simplistic idea that in a segregated world that would not admit her as an equal, she isolated herself from it, metaphorically retreating to her garden to write poetry. This idea can be attributed in part to her male anthologizers, who granted little space and roles to women authors of the New Negro Renaissance. Although she often was distinguished from other women writers of the period, Spencer shares their diminished status. The effect of placing Spencer alone in her garden enclosure is a powerful dispossession, and she perhaps suffers more from this relegation to a static natural world than from the hefty burdens posed by her gender and race. Contextualizing Spencer's writing in national culture and among other writers, we find that she is of a moment and a milieu, engaging with others even if she is not publishing. She was immersed in her sociopolitical world and took a deep interest in the ideas, aesthetic choices, ideologies, and political affiliations of other writers. By acknowledging the broader context of her work, we facilitate exploration of her varied experimentations in writing—and in so doing may shed light on the larger concerns of African American writing at midcentury and beyond.

Among American writers, the collective outlook in the post–World War II period was defined by an increasingly global and ecological perspective of Earth.[1] In Spencer's writing the garden more specifically is an expansive rhetorical space in which to discuss the environmental experience of African Americans in the nation. In Spencer's poetry, the garden, more generally Earth itself, is the site of scenes of encounter, a threshold between irrevocable states of humanity: life and death, peace and war, union and division. Properly nuanced and contextualized, the garden metaphor in Spencer's manuscript writing delivers an embodied exploration of African American citizenship in the midst of the civil rights era through to 1975.

Spencer's "Milam & Till" fragment from this era demonstrates this emphasis, although she does not so much seek to document the historical event as to feel through its meaning:[2]

> The boy's name was Till (Till then I worked with Word Books and pictured ones but had not seen this word as a personal noun till Till[)]—a lame fourteen year-old made his miracle trip from there to here. I can prove it miraculous only if you read, say, Dante

> I've told you. He was lame ill—grown and fourteen with doubtless some small pocket money bribe to show off before his kin but Big City—up-North unfare, mishaply had his mouth to the woman now—I know forever grieved she did have her tradition

> Death for Tiny Till first, then a grave, in the great river meant to be permanent— can anything meant have meaning till we seek truth for its own sake—up to then we were reluctant to leave our tradition—[3]

The speaker who frames the telling describes living through and understanding anew the meaning of "Till." She has encountered "Till" in "Word Books" and references an arc of learning propelled by her encounter with Till's story. But a more significant meaning reveals itself: the word "till" creates a before and an after, whether as preposition (as in the dictionary definition) or as "personal noun" referring to the family name of mother and son. The word ("till") and name ("Till") conveys the idea that time is not as continuous and unbroken but punctuated by births and deaths. Spencer's use of the family name "Till" rather than the given name "Emmett" establishes a formal, almost impersonal distance from him. Till has died, but so too has the "tradition" of conforming to the law of segregation. "Up to then we were reluctant to leave our tradition," the speaker states, drawing attention to of the fact that both imposition and acquiescence are factors in the "custom" of segregation.

The fragment moves from describing the learning acquired through word and picture books to making a larger claim for national truth, the national story of Till and of civil rights. The speaker makes Till a hero while referencing the suffering and difficulty that led to this acclaimed status. Spencer is more interested in a larger humanity than in specifics here, suggesting his body was dumped in a river rather than a tributary and referencing the "mouth" of Till rather than the whistle that had purportedly provoked his lynching, whose mishap and "misshape" in the form of Till's stutter evokes the river's mouth. The reference to the "great river" that is Till's impermanent grave alludes to the Mississippi, which runs nearly the length of the United States, from north to south, from northern Minnesota to the Gulf of Mexico.[4] "Death for Tiny Till first, then a grave, in the great river meant to be permanent" conveys the importance of the river as both archetype and a geographical feature that embodies continuity and mutability. The topographical element represents both elevation and depth: the depth of the grave brings Till to the surface; he cannot be kept below. So too with the truth. The obscuring of it, "meant to be permanent," cannot hold. "Can anything meant have meaning until we seek truth for its own sake," the speaker ponders, searching for the source and pathways of a truth that defies "tradition." This fragment manuscript pairs the topographical feature of the river with the archetypal death and life of truth, insisting on the edification of all who observe this sequence of events, which are tied to the larger history of racialized oppression in the United States. "I've told you," the speaker states. The present perfect "have told" references a past history that is still relevant, a history that has already been told, if not yet acknowledged.

Spencer employs her distinctive diction and syntax to enhance this message in the fragment. The national story of his death is confirmed by several elements, particularly the shifting repetitions of the "proper noun": "Till ("Till," "till Till," "Tiny Till . . . till"). These repetitions are paired with the in-line rhyme of "ill" and the repetition of "lame" and "fourteen" in "a lame fourteen year-old" and "He was lame ill—grown and fourteen." As a preposition, "till" references "to": time, before and after, applied to the fate of the fourteen-year-old boy "till" evokes the boy, not man, lynched by Milam. Truth is likened to a child, suppressed by the murderous man who cannot be mentioned within its lines. And yet it exists and will emerge. "Till" advances an ultimatum tied to time not past and time not future but now: the time of living and of demanding equality.

The manuscript fragment relies on inversion and a wordplay that links elements that would otherwise be divided into distinct units of thought, with phrases like "up-North unfare" and "mishaply." "Fare" for travel resounds with "fair" as in justice, while the North is also implicated in the practice of Jim Crow. "Mishaply" suggests accident and intention, although whose is left ambiguous. These inventive terms contribute to the complex sequencing of words and phrases in the manuscript's syntax, which often obscures—sometimes partially, sometimes completely—place, the agents of action, and the encounter leading to Till's death. "Mishaply had his mouth to the woman now" and "forever grieved" are phrases that whose subject is unclear: "mishaply" could be a sort of adjective ("the misshapen one") posing as a subject or else "his mouth" could be the subject, while either the speaker of "I know" or the woman who "had her tradition" could be subject of "forever grieved." The "miracle trip from here to there" could be North to South or from life to death. It is a trip likened to that undertaken in Dante's *Divine Comedy*, but it's not clear whether the journey is to the inferno, purgatory, or paradise. What does emerge clearly from the obscure movements and actions within the fragment is the function of "tradition" as untruth, as invalid oppression.

The varied repetitions, obscuring subjects and places through complex syntax and wordplay, and the dashes separating and punctuating the meaning, contribute to the fragment's overall effort to plumb the depths of truth as concealed and revealed through human practice. "Milam & Till" is a moving example of Spencer's frequent use of parataxis. Her technique was possibly drawn from her heavy reading of the classics, particularly Caesar. She applied it to everyday life in Lynchburg; in one such example, she described a pair of beagles that roamed Pierce Street as "Tweedle" and "Dum"—indicating simultaneously her humor and her laser-sharp poetic revision and daring improvement of Lewis Carroll's own "Carrollisms."

As Constance Hale has observed, parataxis holds "disparate ideas in diffident equilibrium."[5] It produces the effect of compression—evident here and in much of Spencer's poetry and prose—and also an arresting rhythm that results from the placement of words in ambiguous relation to one another. Whether that rhythm is a regular beat or a stuttering sequence, it is experienced both visually and aurally, as it combines the temporal and existential experience of the ideas through the placement of the words themselves. The reader encounters words that inhabit highly unstable space: they might be separated or linked, even made a single word; some ideas "might use punctuation—commas, semicolons, full stops—to force the juxtaposition." But parataxis "might also run one idea into another by using *ands* to smooth the jump from one autonomous thought to the next." The ideas and words may jostle one another, create a brief space from one another, or create an approximate and uncertain interdependence, as in Spencer's poem "Creed." In the "Milam & Till" fragment, parataxis produces all of these effects at once. Thus, "the method is not as simple as it appears, resulting in a complex texture and tone that can be both lyric and ironic."[6]

Parataxis creates the effect of a lack coordination and subordination: phrases possess an *equal* status. It creates an immediacy, a suddenness, and vivid arrangement. The style is found in both prose and poetry, and it yields discursive patterns that establish a space and connection between the author and the reader. It "makes prose less narratively precise, more discursive"; "especially in poetry, parataxis allows a writer to array fragments that work off each other in ways *the reader* is left to figure out."[7] It makes for a distinct reading experience that works against a developmental narrative, as the reader is thrust into the role of evaluating the uncertain relations presented by the author. Parataxis can be seen as a form of refusal, in which the elimination of causal sequence is replaced by the challenge of relation. Given the subject of Spencer's fragment, its parataxis challenges the reader to make space for Spencer's writing, the representation of Till and the subject of civil rights.

The fragment's use of parataxis dramatizes the impossibility of a ballad telling of Till's story, which would rely on a developmental narrative. Instead, the uncertain relations of the fragment's parts reveal the challenge of representing experience outside of a causal sequence affirming "tradition" and heroic agency. Spencer uses parataxis in the "Milam & Till" fragment to interrogate the ballad form, an early and important form of American literature that delivers stories of work or protest, experiences of common person's plight mixed with heroic action. The ballad is simple in its formal construction, organized by stanzas and characterized by a straightforward beat. It "tells a plain story as simply as a song or a nursery rhyme. But it is never an exercise in innocence, for it is almost always a tale of violence ending in death."[8] As a literary tradition, the ballad is, as Spencer shows through "Milam and Till," an eerie mode, one that conveys a haunting of America's idealistic soul.

While the form of Spencer's fragment appears to be prose, it is still organized into visual stanzas. The obscure speaker of Spencer's "Till" is unknown but repeats truths already told, whether by other balladeers or by the speaker herself. Ballads themselves exist in variations that obscure the original author; this speaker acknowledges her repetitions in telling the tale of "Tiny Till," already "grown." The contradiction of "tiny" and "grown" is important to the delivery of the ballad, to the extreme states it speaks to: violence and peace, guilt and innocence, good and evil, and, at last, living and dead. These extreme qualities run throughout Spencer's fragment, but they reference less the lynching itself and its purported justification than the responses to these events by "she" and "we": "her" tradition and "ours." Without reference to herself, without appeal to emotions or delineation of personal attitudes, the speaker still conveys the crucial importance of "seek[ing]" "truth" "for its own sake" rather than mistakenly attributing truth to a "meaning" that is simply intended—"meant"—without basis ("tradition," its possessives).

Although incomplete, Spencer's manuscript draws attention to the central issue of civil rights, always present ("I've told you") but made into a spectacle by the brutal murder of Till, a child. "Till" relates a current event that was heavily covered by the press, and therefore it resembles a specific type of ballad—the broadside, a printed form of the ballad that was mass circulated and that focused on a current event, person, or issue. At the time of Till's lynching, newspapers functioned as a type of broadside in their coverage the trial, some of them printing the physical evidence of his brutal death in the mass circulation of photographs of his maimed corpse.

An attentive reader of African American poetry at this point might be reminded of another, more well-known poem about Emmett Till that experiments with the ballad form. Gwendolyn Brooks's "A Bronzeville Mother Loiters in Mississippi. Meanwhile, a Mississippi Mother Burns Bacon," which, together with her "The Last Quatrain of the Ballad of Emmett Till," depicts the aftermath of the trial of Emmett Till's murderers, drawing on the perspectives of two mothers. One was white, the wife of Roy Bryant, one of Till's murderers, who claimed Emmett had whistled at her, the mother of two children; the other was Black, Mamie Till, the mother of Emmett. The two mothers inhabit two separate but interconnected poems, parts of the same ballad. The ballad has a profound and irrevocable effect on both women as an exercise of the power of "Southern patriarchy," as a recent critic describes it.[9] This directly bears on Spencer's manuscript draft, as the "tradition" of Southern patriarchy rests on a controlling narrative of white womanhood.

These two poems by Brooks, first published in 1960, reached a broad audience, and it is highly likely that Spencer, who read the foremost literary journals and books of the day, read Brooks's poetry.[10] It is not my task in this chapter to provide an in-depth reading of Brooks's poems. Rather, I intend to show that both authors draw on the ballad form as a means of engaging the national narrative. Their formal engagements are indicative of a collective witnessing, but Spencer's unfinished manuscript functions as a specific "shadow archive" of the poems by Brooks, who occupied a public role as a celebrated author.[11]

Spencer's "Till" is her own ballad telling. Its engagement with "tradition" references the stasis of segregation, the orientation to roles already formed, a stasis that can describe the ballad form itself. In Spencer's and in Brooks's work the ballad is treated ironically, the simple contrasts inverted to reveal the manipulation of the heroic form and the murder and terror enacted by the "fine prince" and the "maid mild" who reside at the heart of the ballad's narrative. They are shown to be simultaneously murderous and utterly compromised, all-dominating and impotent, definitive and impossible. Yet the ballad form itself holds the power to expose these truths, to intervene in the narrative, and to make a case against the tyranny of the world that it seems to represent—demonstrating the potential for both the form's and the world's transformation.

This formal transformation, which Spencer facilitates through parataxis, not only produces a better ballad but opens up a more expansive existence for African Americans, in their transformed relation to land and the nation. Till, that transient state of before and after, references not just time and a person but the preparation of soil for a future use. It is the one meaning of the word that is not present in Spencer's fragment, as if to say that there is no home, no land for this child to belong to—not yet. Just as gardeners and farmers work the earth, digging, stirring, overturning it, so also does the poet work her manuscripts, overturning and replanting them, demonstrating the ways in which land is tied to nature and to humans.[12] Till, the family name, represents this threshold existence of soil as earth and estate. The silent call to till the land, made through its very absence from Spencer's manuscript, is an invocation to uproot, prepare, and plant a better future use. Although the manuscript references a "proper noun," "Till" is an action word, a verb that will effect these changes to minds and nations and to literary forms. One "Tiny Till" brought the matter of cultivation before the nation as it was entering a global discourse.

The story of Earth's cultivation is also the history of humankind. To till the earth is to care for it. This deep and considered care of the soil bears on the human enterprise of democracy. Both soil and civil rights require care and cultivation; both are part of the process of affirming humanity, a process that entails planting seeds and nurturing them to maturity. Spencer's investment in soil was an investment in its future state of use, a use that would yield rights and equality. Deeply devoted to the truths of her nation and to guiding its actions so that they would match its ideals, Spencer recognized that literature, culture, and politics grow out of this soil. While such care as Spencer's cannot fully ensure the yield of the soil, the very act of tending it is one of humanization. Spencer's manuscript "Till" encourages her readers to witness anew the poem's truth telling and to see the poet and her form anew.

The Meeting Point

John Brown, Lincoln, and Till inhabited Spencer's imagination all at once, crossing the porous boundaries of her works in an extended and unending composition that reflected her life itself—life beyond "the book"—and that is captured in the line "'Newark Junction' Milam & Till" that begins the "Milam & Till" fragment. This single line unites Spencer's earlier and concurrent draft poems about heroes in a single experiment, serving as a junction in her manuscript poetry. The setting off of "Newark Junction" in quotation marks allows the parataxis to convey a heightened awareness of historical and imaginative meeting points in truth or in tradition. The manuscripts about Till, John

Brown, Lincoln, and Leroi are themselves the witnesses of historical and poetic junctions. Parataxis creates discursive space for Spencer's distinct and interconnected manuscript writings, her relations with other poets, and the potential coherence of American and African American literary projects.

This heightened awareness of junctions is enhanced by the fragment's "end," which invokes John Brown, his "home": "Death for Tiny Till first, then a grave, in the great river meant to be permanent—can anything meant have meaning till we seek truth for its own sake—up to then we were reluctant to leave our tradition—we are told, truly, that Jno never had a home sweet home his was held by a tradition."[13] "Tradition" is revealed to be a powerful agent that can deny homeland. Yet that which is buried is birthed again. Spencer references the family's unsuccessful struggle to have Brown's body retrieved for burial after his execution. Like Till's body, which was meant to be concealed in a watery grave, its mutilation denied, Brown's body is denied its "home sweet home," is "*held* by *a* tradition."[14] Both Brown and Till's bodies bring forth what they are denied: truth, home, and soil.

"Lock your heart, then, quietly," advises the speaker of Spencer's poem "Sybil Warns Her Sister." Spencer no longer had James Weldon Johnson as advisor and confidante, but she had memory as her practice and the abiding presence of her poetic personae to guide her lines and living. She "crave[d] . . . the literal communicating word":

> In our land I deeply crave the beauty + comfort of the literal communicating
> > word
> rightly sought
> they are
> with wings that we face its fact
>
> Or when we run, as harried sap must and take each hurdle high or low move the
> > barrier or bridge the gap.[15]

The "literal communicating word" conveys beauty, offers comfort, and has energy; likened to plant or tree sap, the word is a living and sustaining thing.

In her unpublished works from 1940 to her death, Spencer reflects on the continuity of words beyond human mortality: "If you find tiresome my going into a refrain about words, I crave mercy. I'm just on the eve of their complete disclosure and dying—youth, take up the story where its devotees (language, word, human communication) leave off and go away on determined terminal affairs—understood + perfected war will stop love + freedom cover the earth."[16] The protective mode of Sybil's locked heart and cultivated language can protect Earth as well. "Complete disclosure and dying" marks the inevitable end of one human life. But the next generation may honor the story of those devoted to "language, word, human communication" by bearing in mind life's finite nature, its "terminal affairs" and "determined" project of human understanding and connection. The reader stands together in the same line with Spencer without mediation and so is able see what is at stake: which will be perfected, war or human communication? The author's wish for posterity is not "perfected war" or to "stop love + freedom" but "perfected" language that will stop war and enable "love + freedom" to cover Earth. Through parataxis, Spencer underscores the extreme nature of the possible outcomes, even while acknowledging the individual's finite project in the larger, contingent world.

Here we may recall Spencer's poem "For Jim, Easter Eve," its garden of profound grief and separation, and the continuity—"comfort"—of memory. It was the last poem she published. After Johnson's death, Spencer began directly engaging a rich intellectual history of historical and contemporary writers as well as focusing on the inward processes of memory. Spencer acknowledged her refusal to complete her works even while assuring interested editors like Roy Basler and John Ferrone at Harpers that a book of her collected writings was forthcoming. Spencer lived and wrote past *that* book to *her* book in an unexpected interpretation of the lines of Elizabeth Barrett Browning's *Aurora Leigh* that she marked. She wrote past her book without ever producing it, bypassing the necessity of manuscript completion: "The poet looks beyond the book [she] has made / Or else [she] had not made it."

While bypassing "the book," Spencer affirmed the poem and language itself as the channel between physical and metaphysical states of being, acknowledging the poem's tangible qualities and its power to create new space, both imaginative and real. Her manuscripts become the living embodiments of poetry and the author's experiences. Spencer's "letter" written between sisters extends to other addressees, as in this letter written from age to youth, from grandmother to "grandchile":

> Dear perfectly great grandchile,
>
> I hope for the moment when from what has been given you will say "Dranny what is a poem?"
>
> I will reply that I've been trying a time to find the big thing a real poem is: up to now I reached a part of its parts:
>
> Yes, you can even look at a poem with your eyes, like it was a cup + saucer, or a floor mop or a chair
>
> You can look down at the earth with your eye eyes, one morning where day before yesterday you planted a pint of swollen beans in a pint spot and stand a little scared, at the trembling noiseless struggle of life taking over in so impossible an area[17]

Spencer's wonderful, intimate wordplay here is a window into conversations taking place in the Spencer family home: the "great" "grandchile," the "eye eyes," the "pint" as factual measure and the connotative "pint" of the small, humble space in the earth. It is a letter that engages the notion of time itself, the contemporary moment as well as the idea of the poem over time, between decades of humankind's finite living. She plays with ideas of time, underscoring the impermanence of human experience. Poems are tangible things; they are life itself, expanding into "so impossible an area." Spencer is not yet a great grandmother, but she has a "great" grandchild. The little plant must "struggle" to live in seemingly impossible circumstances. The gardener is a little uncertain, "scared"; the struggle is in motion, "trembling noiseless." These experiences taken together form the poet; a letter becomes letters, letters become a living archive; and Spencer and her "grandchile" are the curators of these letters.[18]

Through Spencer's reflection on the poem, we learn that the struggle of "between" is not necessarily tragic, unfulfilling, or disappointing. We discover that Spencer is curator of a living, transforming archive that, like gardens themselves, may teach humans to "relearn the art of seeing and reaccess the deep time folded within their forms."[19] Her unpublished manuscripts point to these arts of perception and the potential power of the visionary artist in the world. Spencer's manuscripts explore radical concepts of time and place and demand new ways of seeing and ample space in which to be considered. Her poems depict encounters on the threshold of a before and an after; her manuscripts, written across decades of experience, formally enact a process of the between, transitory and layered states of being and consciousness in which the poet is a curator of living memory. The manuscripts themselves are ways of seeing "beyond the book," to the permanent contingency of human experience.

Spencer's 1974 manuscript poem "Earth, I thank you," originally titled "Earthly Earth" demonstrates this wisdom of the soil: a recognition of the living garden as one that creates and sustains happiness such as that which she references in her autobiographical draft of the "taboo" of "being a Negro woman."[20] It is an abiding process of self-humanization through time and being—present, past, and future—that affirms "life's intrinsic value to flourish."[21] The poem itself affirms this value, transfiguring the self through its resistance to tyranny and false sovereignty. Till as a "personal noun" is transfigured from Earth itself to "grunt through," verb and preposition—to action and a place—creating consciousness and understanding. Spencer's garden is *not* a space of maintenance but rather the grounds for transformation, indeed revolution. One of her last authored manuscript poems, it embraces a transitive relationship between the imagination and the world at large, the "real world" that can be so transformed.

> Earth, I thank you
> for the pleasure of your language
> You've had a hard time
> bringing it to me
> from the ground

to grunt thru the noun
To all the way
Feeling seeing smelling touching
—awareness
I am here![22]

Spencer's manuscripts cultivate new forms of representation, placing the garden, its soil, and its caretakers in national and global conversations about a world ecology. As caretakers and attentive readers of her manuscripts, we are prompted to recognize their defiant practice of manuscript as archive as an act of love, not just of "self-love" but of "ethical grounding": an "ethics of care" guiding our twenty-first-century considerations of African American women's archives and Spencer's lifelong endeavors to bring into being a garden of humankind.[23]

Introduction. Anne Spencer between Worlds

1. State and city notables were in attendance, including Joan S. Jones (Virginia House of Delegates), Elliot S. Schewel (Virginia Senate), Caldwell Butler (U.S. Congress), C. W. Seay (former vice mayor of Lynchburg; senior board member, Friends of Anne Spencer Memorial Foundation), Junius R. Fishburne Jr. (executive director, Virginia Historic Landmarks Commission), Frederick Herman (chair, Virginia Historical Landmarks Commission), Joseph Freeman (mayor of Lynchburg), Beatrice Poole (president, Federation of Garden Clubs), Haywood Robinson Jr. (executive board member, Friends of Anne Spencer Memorial Foundation), Donald W. Johnson, John H. Hughes III, L. Garnell Stamps, and Cynthia Granger.

2. Chauncey E. Spencer to Sterling A. Brown, March 14, 1977, box 16, folder S, Sterling A. Brown Papers, Moorland-Spingarn Research Center, Howard University ("Our dear Daisy and Sterling—your letter and statement concerning mother was not only timely but it fit perfectly within the dedication program. We thank you both very very much for being a great part of the official dedication. Always with our warmest wishes and love—Anne + Chauncey"). Chauncey's wife also was named Anne; he often called her "Anne junior" to distinguish between the two.

3. Brooks and Hawkins, "Conversation," 278.

4. Program for February 26, 1977, landmark dedication of 1313 Pierce St., Lynchburg, Va., box 16, folder S, Sterling A. Brown Papers, Moorland-Spingarn Research Center, Howard University.

5. Greene, *Time's Unfading Garden*, 78.

6. I discuss the Johnson Memorial Committee and the founding of the James Weldon Johnson and Grace Nail Johnson Papers at Yale University in chapter 2. Spencer was instrumental in the establishment of this archive of his writings. Spencer stopped writing for almost three years after his death.

7. Cloutier, *Shadow Archives*, 211. Petry regarded her journals "'as sacred space where she recorded her private thoughts' and where she would revisit events and experiences from her own life—as she did in earlier drafts of her fiction" (210). She later "deliberately 'embarked on a shred and burn campaign' of her archive in the 1980s" (210). For Cloutier, Petry is "a representative example of the many reasons the papers of black female authors are so few in number and remain neglected even by the repositories who own them" (13).

8. Cloutier, *Shadow Archives*, 1–2.

9. Cloutier, *Shadow Archives*, 13.

10. Honey, *Aphrodite's Daughters*, 27.

11. As Mia Bay, Farah J. Griffin, Martha S. Jones, and Barbara D. Savage collec-

tively observe, "Far from finished, this work of recuperation remains vital and necessary to restoring and expanding the record of black women's lives throughout the diaspora. Alongside this attention to the contours of lived experience, literary scholars have brought to light the corpus of black women's writings, from poetry and essays to the short story and the novel. Feminist scholars have explained the centrality of black women to the construction of freedom, democracy, and citizenship through particular attention to the intersectional quality of black women's activism and thought" ("Toward an Intellectual History of Black Women," 3–4).

12. As the lifetime of work by Darlene Clark Hine, Ula Taylor, and Deborah Gray White attests, there are both historical and institutional challenges to charting Black women's lives in and through archives. See Hine, *Hine Sight*, Taylor, *Veiled Garvey*, and White, *Telling Histories*.

13. Newsome visited Spencer's home, and the two women had a warm correspondence, some of which can be found in series 1, correspondence, box 5, folder 4, Papers of Anne Spencer and the Spencer, Albert and Shirley Small Special Collections, University of Virginia. Newsome's *Gladiola Garden* was composed and published in the years of their friendship.

Meredith painted Spencer's poem "Lines to a Nasturtium" on the wall of Spencer's kitchen and may have had a role in the design of Ed-an-kraal, Spencer's garden house where she wrote. See Gooden, *Dark Space*, especially his chapter on Meredith. While I acknowledge both Newsome and Meredith as part of Spencer's networks here, more recuperative work on both women is needed.

14. Spencer's poem was published in the 1927 anthology *Ebony and Topaz*, alongside Barrett Browning's well-known poem "The Runaway Slave at Pilgrim's Point." *Ebony and Topaz*, an interracial collection that followed the 1925 anthology *The New Negro*, edited by Alain Locke, contained a broader spectrum of authors, time periods, and art forms. A large number of white authors, such as Paul Green, Julia Peterkin, and Barrett Browning were included. The anthology also featured many of the who's who of African American literati, including Charles S. Johnson, Mae Cowdery, Sterling A. Brown, Langston Hughes, Georgia Douglas Johnson, Alice Dunbar Nelson, Countee Cullen, Zora Neale Hurston, Arna Bontemps, Angelina Weld Grimké, Arthur Schomburg, Phillis Wheatley, Paul Dunbar, Alain Locke, Gwendolyn Bennett, and Helene Johnson. The collection also contains translations of Spanish-language poems.

15. In Ovid's *Metamorphoses*, Sybil guides Aeneas to the underworld and back so that he may consult with his father about war strategies. Sybil explains that was she offered "eternal life, life without end, if I / Lost my virginity to Phoebus's love" (ll. 136–37). In requesting "birthdays as many as those dusty grains" she points to when Phoebus asks what she wants (ll. 141–43), she forgets to specify that those years be passed in a state "for ever young" (l. 145). And so I years are granted but without youth; she tells Aeneas she has passed seven hundred and must yet endure another three hundred. "The time shall come when length of days will shrivel / This frame of mine, and my age-wasted limbs / Shrink to a feather's weight; none will believe/ That I was loved and pleased a god. Perhaps/ Phoebus himself won't know me or deny / He loved me. To such changes I shall pass. / No eye shall see me then: my voice alone / The Fates will leave, my voice by which I'm known" (ll. 146–53).

16. The revisions from the 1927 "Sybil Warns Her Sister" to the 1947 "A Letter to My Sister," which was published in Hughes and Bontemps's *Poetry of the Negro* (1949)

largely take the form of deletions of ellipses, commas, and prepositions and the imposition of a clearly marked two-stanza structure. The deletions of commas make the poem more immediate, as its content is thereby less mediated by explanation through traditional grammatical structure, while the deletion of ellipses removes the intimated quality of the speaker's wisdom and renders it more directly. The stanzaic structure makes clear the three main movements in thought of the poem: from danger to useless fear to survival. One major word is removed in line 1: "plainness": "If you have beauty or plainness, if celibate / Or vowed" is altered to "If you have beauty or not, if celibate / Or vowed." This change emphasizes the elusive nature of the defined category of beauty.

17. Honey, *Aphrodite's Daughters*, 21. While Honey focuses on female erotic poetry of the era, it may also be said that female lyric poetry as a whole, particularly from the New Negro Renaissance, has suffered from this critical neglect.

18. "A woman cannot do the thing she ought, / Which means whatever perfect thing she can, / In life, in art, in science, but she fears / To let the perfect action take her part, / And rest there: she must prove what she can do / Before she does it, prate of woman's rights, / Of woman's mission, woman's function, till / The men (who are prating too on their side) cry, / 'A woman's function plainly is . . . to talk'" (Barrett Browning, *Aurora Leigh*, ll. 8.814–22).

19. In *Aurora Leigh*, the issue of commodification divides poetic from material achievements: "Being but poor, I was constrained, for life, / To work with one hand for the booksellers, / While working with the other for myself / And art" (3.302–5).

20. Reynolds, introduction, 24.

21. As Honey aptly observes, "community awareness and personal awareness were not separate spheres" in the lyrical verse of the African American women authors who were Spencer's contemporaries during the New Negro Renaissance. They "were attracted to the lyric in a racist era that denied them personhood" (*Aphrodite's Daughters*, 17, 20).

22. This invocation of female personhood, referencing both classical and modern, twentieth-century worlds, calls up the more specific field of reference of African American women and the legacy of bondage through the example of the female prophet Sojourner Truth, whom Harriet Beecher Stowe and other abolitionists referred to as the "Libyan Sybil." While this allusion to Truth is not explicit in Spencer's three poems, in her post-1940 writings, Spencer discusses Truth's defiance of slavery and her heroic journey as a truth seeker and visionary. She contemplates Truth's enduring faith, which caused her to challenge to Douglass in the midst of a speech delivered 1860, just eight months prior to the Civil War: "Frederick, is God dead?" (series 5, manuscripts and poems, subseries E, notebook H, box 21 folder 8, Papers of Anne Spencer and the Spencer Family, Albert and Shirley Small Special Collections, University of Virginia). Truth died the year Spencer was born, in 1883. The Truth-Douglass confrontation is also recounted in Redding, *The Lonesome Road* and is excerpted in Berry, *A Scholar's Conscience*, 98–111. Spencer knew Redding's essays well and met him in 1943.

23. See Greene, *Time's Unfading Garden*, 181.

24. Notebook, Anne Spencer Papers, Anne Spencer House and Garden Museum, Lynchburg, Va.

25. See Greene, *Time's Unfading Garden*, 24–26. Spencer told Greene that "when I went to the Seminary [at age eleven] I could call all the words but I couldn't understand them all" (24).

26. Posmentier, *Cultivation and Catastrophe*, 4.

27. As Posmentier observes, "Nature and culture do not have a transparent relationship" (*Cultivation and Catastrophe*, 9).

28. Spencer characterized the experience of Jim Crow in Lynchburg to James Weldon Johnson in an October 20, 1921 letter: "Lynching the body is as final as it is undesirable, but the jim crow car lynches ones soul over and over again" (series 1, correspondence, box 19, folder 447, James Weldon Johnson and Grace Nail Johnson Papers, Beinecke Rare Book and Manuscript Library, Yale University). Her living, tended garden is a space of resistance from this daily death, as Shockley, in *Renegade Poetics*, also notes.

29. Spencer's papers are in two different locations—at the University of Virginia, which is the main repository, and at the Anne Spencer House and Garden Museum in Lynchburg, Virginia. After her death in 1975, Spencer's manuscripts remained in boxes and were inaccessible to scholars. The University of Virginia only purchased the papers now its possession in 2008 and catalogued them in 2011. While I was a Lillian Gary Taylor fellow at the University of Virginia, Anne Spencer's granddaughter, Shaun Spencer-Hester, shared with me some of Spencer's papers located in Lynchburg, Virginia, at the author's home that is now the Anne Spencer House and Garden Museum, located at 1313 Pierce Street. The manuscripts achieve coherence through these two archival sources, which I have pieced together over several years of research.

30. The term "expressive manuscript" comes from Werner and Bervin's *Gorgeous Nothings*, which approaches Emily Dickinson's letter poems from a material and visual standpoint. Just as more scholarship is needed on African American women's libraries and archives, so too more consideration must be given to their intellectual history.

31. I am indebted to Cameron's work on Emily Dickinson in *Choosing Not Choosing*, particularly her assertion that refusal elicits an interrogation of relation.

32. See McHenry, *Forgotten Readers*.

33. Program for February 26, 1977, landmark dedication of 1313 Pierce St., Lynchburg, Va., box 16, folder S, Sterling A. Brown Papers, Moorland-Spingarn Research Center, Howard University.

34. Daphne Brooks, *Liner Notes for the Revolution*, 369.

35. Daphne Brooks, *Liner Notes for the Revolution*, 4.

Chapter 1. Anne Spencer's Creed

1. The Albert and Shirley Small Special Collections at the University of Virginia holds Spencer's inscribed copy of this book.

2. Greene, *Time's Unfading Garden*, 10, 16.

3. Greene, *Time's Unfading Garden*, 17.

4. Greene, *Time's Unfading Garden*, 31.

5. Here I only reference books that were clearly owned by Spencer or the Spencer family. I am grateful to Valerie Kelco, my research assistant, whose work has made this discussion of Spencer's library books held by the University of Virginia possible.

6. Greene, *Time's Unfading Garden*, 24.

7. Greene, *Time's Unfading Garden*, 25.

8. Greene, *Time's Unfading Garden*, 29.

9. Posmentier, *Cultivation and Catastrophe*, 9. This chapter and the following one reference the gardens of James Weldon and Grace Nail Johnson, Spencer, and Georgia Douglas Johnson.

10. Harrison, *Gardens*, 7.

11. Posmentier, *Cultivation and Catastrophe*, 4. Spencer's poetry, Shockley contends, "invites her readers to enter a space in which they are not hailed immediately or insistently as raced subjects; a space that therefore *looks* 'raceless' but is *for* black people (especially black women) [and] . . . where readers are able to contemplate and analyze moral and metaphysical ideas that can inform the struggle for equality in which they are engaged" (*Renegade Poetics*, 129).

12. The poem is reprinted in Greene, *Time's Unfading Garden*, 190–91.

13. 'A common vacationing spot for well-to-do African Americans from 1900 onward, Harpers Ferry "attracted many of Washington's [black] elites" during the hot summer months (Taylor, *The Original Black Elite*, 88).

14. Spencer underlined the line in her ten-volume *Complete Works of Thomas Carlyle*, the set of which is housed in the University of Virginia's special collections.

15. Series 5, manuscripts and poems, subseries A, "Why Read Books," box 17, folder 60, Papers of Anne Spencer and the Spencer Family, Albert and Shirley Small Special Collections, University of Virginia. These notes are undated, but evidence suggests Spencer composed them in the late 1960s.

16. Upon her graduation Spencer received *The Holman New Self-Pronouncing Sunday-School Teacher's Bible: Containing the Old and New Testaments*, her personal copy of which the Albert and Shirley Small Special Collections at University of Virginia holds. The inscription to this volume reads "Rev. R. H. Boyd, May 8th, 1899, to Anne B. Spencer née Scales, upon her graduation." Spencer recognized the unique value of her education at Virginia Seminary and while her Christian belief distinguished her from her adamantly secular friends such as the Johnsons (who nevertheless were formally affiliated with the Episcopal Church), her view of faith was nevertheless unconventional in that she acknowledged the existence of many branches of worship while recognizing each's limitations.

17. If author libraries provide a "glimpse" of a writer's "entire intellectual life at once," reveal the writer's "intellectual curiosity" and "pride in [her] own work," and demonstrate the writer's "need to read voraciously and to collect books," they also clearly represent political choices in the case of African American writers (Oram and Nicholson, *Collecting, Curating, and Researching Writers' Libraries*, 1–2). McHenry's *Forgotten Readers* and Williams's *Self-Taught* offer invaluable studies of autodidacticism, literacy, and communal reading practices.

18. In her pathbreaking work on three women writers of the Harlem Renaissance, Gloria Hull characterizes Lynchburg, Virginia, as an "unlikely place" for such a literary gathering as Spencer's, which took place over the decade of the 1920s and into the mid-1930s. For Hull, Georgia Douglas Johnson's Washington, D.C., home on S Street was a far more likely "nexus for the intercity connections that helped make the movement a truly national one" (*Color, Sex, and Poetry*, 6).

19. Virginia Seminary was incorporated in 1888 by agreement with the American Baptist Home Mission Society; its first class was held January 1890. Rev. Phillip Fisher Morris was its first president; in 1891, Rev. Gregory W. Hayes, a Presbyterian, assumed

the position, which he occupied for sixteen years (Newkirk, *Spectacle*, 219–20). Spencer arrived in 1893 and developed a warm relationship with President Hayes and his wife, Mary, that lasted beyond her graduation in 1899.

20. My account of Ota Benga is indebted to Newkirk's *Spectacle*. While there are other books that describe this tragic exploitation of an African man, Newkirk's treatment humanizes Ota Benga rather than rendering him an object of spectacle.

21. Adams, *Sideshow, U.S.A.*, 26.

22. See Adams, *Sideshow, U.S.A.*, 40–41.

23. Newkirk, *Spectacle*, 65.

24. Newkirk, *Spectacle*, 75.

25. Newkirk, *Spectacle*, 225.

26. See Adams, *Sideshow, U.S.A.*, 42, as well as Newkirk's *Spectacle* in its entirety.

27. Because of this legislation, Virginia's Native population was not permitted a category on birth certificates and was not permitted Native American names; these policies led to mass extermination by way of "documentary genocide": state-enforced categories of black or white identity. See Hardin, "Documentary Genocide," and Heim, "How a Long-Dead White Supremacist Still Threatens the Future of Virginia's Indian Tribes." Spencer had both black and Native American ancestors. More research needs to be done on her genealogy and lifetime of identification with indigenous Virginian culture and people in relation to her choosing to identify as Black.

28. Greene places Johnson's arrival in Lynchburg in "1917 or 18" (*Time's Unfading Garden*, 49), but it can be pieced together that Johnson arrived in April 1918.

29. Spencer to James Weldon Johnson, May 8, 1924 , series 1, correspondence, box 19, folder 447, James Weldon Johnson and Grace Nail Johnson Papers, Beinecke Rare Book and Manuscript Library, Yale University.

30. Greene, *Time's Unfading Garden*, 49; James Weldon Johnson to Spencer, 1918, and November 1920, series 1, correspondence, box 19, folder 447.

31. Greene, *Time's Unfading Garden*, 50.

32. The Spencer-Johnson correspondence is found in series 1, correspondence, box 19, folders 447 (1919–30), 448 (1931–38), and 449 (undated), in the James Weldon Johnson and Grace Nail Johnson Papers, Beinecke Rare Book and Manuscript Library, Yale University.

33. McHenry, *To Make Negro Literature*, 79–80.

34. McHenry, *To Make Negro Literature*, 80.

35. Holloway, *BookMarks*, 42.

36. The story of Spencer's employment at Dunbar Library is provided in Greene, *Time's Unfading Garden*, 47–48.

37. "Dunbar" was the second poem Spencer published, just months after "Before the Feast at Shushan," both in the *Crisis*. Her short-form poetry can also be found in her unpublished manuscript poems "1975" and "Earth, I thank you."

38. The Albert and Shirley Small Special Collections at University of Virginia holds the copy of this book.

39. Spencer recalled receiving a multivolume set of Emerson's complete writings as a graduation present from Dr. Bolling when she completed her studies at Virginia Seminary (series 5, manuscripts and poems, subseries D, notebook, box 20, folder 11, Papers of Anne Spencer and the Spencer Family, Albert and Shirley Small Special Collections, University of Virginia). Dr. Bolling's son was an accomplished artisan woodworker who

may have designed the original pergola in the Spencers' garden. See Brown and Lewis, *The Negro in Virginia*, 284.

Spencer noted what writers had to say about America. She read Dickens's "American Notes," Tocqueville's *Democracy in America*, and Thackeray's *The Virginians* alongside Whitman, Emerson, Thomas Paine, James Fenimore Cooper, Edgar Allen Poe, O. Henry, and Flannery O'Connor. Emily Dickinson's poems for young people round out the collection. Other, older texts, such as Tasso's *Jerusalem Delivered* and Cicero's *Ten Orations with the Letter to His Wife*, also gave Spencer ways to understand the peculiar American condition of slavery and segregation. Cicero's text along with Barrett Browning's *Aurora Leigh* form the backdrop to her "A Letter to My Sister." She also had a lifelong interest in juvenilia. The Spencer library that is now housed at the University of Virginia Library contains four volumes of Rudyard Kipling's poetry.

40. Series 5, manuscripts and poems, subseries A, "Why Read Books," box 17, folder 60, Papers of Anne Spencer and the Spencer Family, Albert and Shirley Small Special Collections, University of Virginia. As Richard Oram observes, a writer's library can be "broadly defined to include all of the books an author collected during the course of a creative lifetime, as well as the proximate books accumulated by spouses, partners, and others" (*Collecting, Curating, and Researching Writers' Libraries*, 1). Some of Spencer's most treasured books remain at the Anne Spencer House and Garden Museum, including a signed copy of Johnson's original 1912 edition of *The Autobiography of an Ex-Colored Man*, which is inscribed to Edward Spencer.

41. Manguel evocatively refers to the library as a "nest" (*The Library at Night*, 178).

42. However, a complementary global digital library of Spencer's interactions and correspondences could serve to complement her physical library. Such a project would be in line with and realize Spencer's poetics of relation, merging her physical and imaginative worlds. As Oram observes, "the Internet makes real-time updatable catalogs and worldwide collaborative efforts possible" (*Collecting, Curating, and Researching Writers' Libraries*, 3). Andrew M. Stauffer's crowdsourced project, Book Traces (http://www.booktraces.org), calls attention to the challenge of reading books in a digital age in a project that links the physical and material history of books with our contemporary era of digital access and that aims to avoid erasing readers' histories'. It is an endeavor that seeks to merge print and digital encounters with texts without supplanting the older, irreplaceable forms—those books held in the hand, bearing inscriptions demonstrating occasions and personal connections and yielding the occasional seed catalogue or receipt as a bookmark. See also http://www.nines.org, the Networked Infrastructure for Nineteenth-Century Electronic Scholarship, based at the University of Virginia and directed by Stauffer.

43. Recalling a community meeting with a local politician that he and his mother attended, Spencer's son Chauncey notes that if Spencer found herself in a tense situation that required profanity in order for her to expose deception, she would deliver (*Who Is Chauncey Spencer?*, 15).

44. Popular spreads in 2018 issues of *Home and Garden*, *Southern Cultures*, and *World of Interiors* advance this narrative, whereas Frischkorn and Rainey, *Half My World*, and White, *Lessons Learned*, introduce more productive contexts specific to Spencer's writing life.

45. Shockley, *Renegade Poetics*, 128. I am indebted to Shockley's innovative work on Spencer's poetics, which effectively demonstrates that the author's published works

amount to a practice of lyrical and politicized engagement with black womanhood. I extend her interpretation of the garden as a real and metaphoric space to Spencer's manuscript works, which function as an alternative space for the expression of black women's experience and imagination.

46. Contemporary scholarship on Spencer has focused almost exclusively on her published poems and by and large essentializes her writing as either black *or* feminist, almost enforcing their opposition, thereby isolating her. I agree with Shockley, who notes that "we must be willing to look beyond the 'recognizably black' in search of black aesthetics" (*Renegade Poetics*, 130). See Karapetkova, "'Chatterton, Shelley, Keats, and I,'" Hyest, "Anne Spencer's Feminist Modernist Poetics," and Wheeler, "Anne Spencer's Epistolary Activism."

47. Shockley, *Renegade Poetics*, 129.

48. Series 5, manuscripts and poems, subseries C, manuscript fragments, box 20, folder 1, Papers of Anne Spencer and the Spencer Family, Albert and Shirley Small Special Collections, University of Virginia. Throughout this book I allow Spencer's unique spelling, abbreviation, syntax, and diction to stand as is, intervening only where clarification is needed.

49. I agree with Shockley that Spencer's poems "participate in, rather than simply offer refuge from, the struggle for racial and gender equality she carried out in her nonliterary life" (*Renegade Poetics*, 23).

50. Shockley, *Renegade Poetics*, 9. Shockley defines Black aesthetics as "a multifarious, contingent, non-delimited complex of strategies that African American writers may use to negotiate gaps or conflicts between their artistic goals and the operation of race in the production, dissemination, and reception of their writing" (9). Several works point to the archive as an evolving and dynamic concept. See Taylor, *The Archive and the Repertoire*, Brown, *Babylon Girls*, Honey, *Aphrodite's Daughters*, Hine, *Hine Sight*, and Taylor, *The Veiled Garvey*.

51. James Weldon Johnson to Spencer, September 24, [1930], series 1, correspondence, box 19, folder 447, James Weldon Johnson and Grace Nail Johnson Papers, Beinecke Rare Book and Manuscript Library, Yale University. This letter confirms Spencer's "Translation" as the title of the new poem to be included in the revised edition.

52. Greene's *Time's Unfading Garden* offers useful information about Spencer's family background, and his interviews with the author prior to her death in 1975 importantly document her attitudes toward other writers and poetry in general. One unannotated volume of Spencer's published poems, Nina Salmon's *Anne Spencer*, reprints what Greene compiled in his appendix with a few short manuscript poems added.

53. Green, "The Life of a Poet Allergic to Endings."

54. Johnson, *The Book of American Negro Poetry*, 213.

55. I discuss Spencer's contemporaries and friends James Weldon Johnson, Sterling Brown, Langston Hughes, and Georgia Douglas Johnson more fully in chapter 2.

56. Hayden, *Kaleidoscope*, 34; Cullen, *Caroling Dusk*, xiii; Lewis, *The Portable Harlem Renaissance Reader*, 299.

57. However, male poets such as Melvin Tolson made careers out of "the art of being difficult." See Woodson, "Melvin Tolson and the Art of Being Difficult."

58. Davis and Redding, *Cavalcade*, 269.

59. Yet the author of her biographical gloss recognized Spencer's expansive intellectual engagement: "Age has not dimmed the brilliance of Anne Spencer's mind. At

ninety she is still writing poetry, still commenting wisely—and, on occasion, ironically—on contemporary life" (Davis and Redding, *Cavalcade*, 269).

60. Untermeyer, *American Poetry since 1900*, 374. In their 1941 anthology *The Negro
Caravan*, editors Sterling Brown, Arthur P. Davis, and Ulysses Lee locate Untermeyer
among the influential critics that included Amy Lowell and Harriet Monroe who "spon-
sored" the "New Poetry Movement," which "repudiated sentimentality, didacticism, optimism, romantic escape, and 'poetic' diction." They further note that this movement
produced "such important poets as Edwin Arlington Robinson, Robert Frost, Vachel
Lindsay, Edgar Lee Masters, and Carl Sandburg" and that "the lessons it taught were
beneficial to Negro poets" (280).

61. Kerlin, *Negro Poets and Their Poems*, 156–58. "Under the conditions of American
life the Negro woman's heart offers difficulties peculiar to itself," Kerlin notes, presenting Spencer's poem "At the Carnival" alongside works by Alice Dunbar-Nelson, Georgia Douglas Johnson, Angelina Weld Grimké, and Jessie Fauset as "a fruitful train of reflections, tending toward profound ethical truth" (158). When Kerlin invited Spencer to
contribute poems to his anthology, Johnson had encouraged her to accept: "There is
no reason why you should not be in two anthologies" (series 1, correspondence, box 4,
folder 7, Papers of Anne Spencer and the Spencer Family, Albert and Shirley Small Special Collections, University of Virginia). Kerlin enjoyed a warm correspondence with
Spencer.

62. Brown, *The Negro in American Fiction and Negro Poetry and Drama*, 65–66.
Brown compares Spencer to Dickinson, noting her "deceptively simple manner" in the
poems "Neighbors," "I Have a Friend," and "Innocence," and finds "Before the Feast of
Shushan'" to be "a poem of vivid sensuous beauty, telling an old story in modern terms."

63. Cullen, *Caroling Dusk*, xiii.

64. Cullen, *Caroling Dusk*, 47. The beginning of the autobiography reads: "From
Lynchburg, Virginia, where she lives, Anne Spencer writes, "'Mother Nature, February, forty-five years ago forced me on the stage that I, in turn, might assume the role of
lonely child, happy wife, perplexed mother—and, so far, a twice resentful grandmother.
I have no academic honors, nor lodge regalia. I am Christian by intention, a Methodist
by inheritance, and a Baptist by marriage. I write about some of the things I love. But I
have no civilized articulation for the things I hate."

65. Hayden, *Kaleidoscope*, 34.

66. Lewis, *The Harlem Renaissance Reader*, 299. Lewis's selection is "Lady, Lady," the
same selection as appears in Locke's 1925 *The New Negro*.

67. Kuenz, "Modernism, Mass Culture, and the Harlem Renaissance," 508.

68. Kuenz, "Modernism, Mass Culture, and the Harlem Renaissance," 511.

69. Johnson, "Double Audience Makes Road Hard for Negro Authors"; Johnson, "Negro Authors and White Publishers."

70. Redding, "The Negro Author," 142.

71. Redding, "The Negro Author," 145.

72. Redding, "The Negro Author," 146.

73. Redding believed that Richard Wright had succeeded in writing an American
book for an American audience with his portrayal of Bigger Thomas in his 1940 novel
Native Son. Bigger is "a symbolic figure of American life, a figure who would hold within
him the prophecy of the American future" ("The Negro Author," 146). The prophetic element of such a character as Bigger to which Redding refers also makes him problem-

atic, as his plight is framed through a protest that appeals to a white audience. In my view, such a character presents the profound enactments of segregation on his existence but also addresses the process by which the reading public would determine an American future of its own choosing. In other words, the power was still placed squarely in the hands of an American reading public.

74. Hughes and Bontemps, *The Poetry of the Negro*, 622. A November 1, 1948, typed letter from Hughes to Spencer states that an *Ebony* magazine review of his 1949 anthology *The Poetry of the Negro* requests a photo of Spencer. "A nice letter from Coleman Rosenberger had this to say about your work: 'I feel that it is a shame—as I have said in the forthcoming *Virginia Reader*—that Mrs. Spencer has never published a volume of her work. Do you suppose that there is any chance that Knopf might be interested in a collection? The examples of her work that I have seen certainly deserve publication. It seems to me that a volume of her work would be a good thing for both literary and non-literary reasons.' There is 100% agreement on my part. I think you have written some of the loveliest poems of our time" (Langston Hughes Papers, JWJ MSS 26, series 1, box 149, folder 2766, James Weldon Johnson and Grace Nail Johnson Papers, Beinecke Rare Book and Manuscript Library, Yale University).

75. As Kuenz observes, "As editors like [James Weldon] Johnson announced their projects in terms of their designs on the good opinion of readers, the proliferation of books as commodities colored the discourse of modernist writers[,] who increasingly positioned 'authentic' literary works [such as single-author volumes of poetry] in opposition to this mass market" ("Modernism, Mass Culture, and the Harlem Renaissance," 510–11). Georgia Douglas Johnson, a rare example of an African American woman poet who published more than one volume of poetry, self-published, using Boston publishers Cornhill and B. J. Brimmer, which were, in succession, poet and magazine verse anthologizer William Stanley Braithwaite's vanity presses. Despite the fact that she decided to self-publish, her poetry was subjected to an editorial "weeding out" by W. E. B. Du Bois and Alain Locke, who influenced which ones she published, according to Alice Dunbar-Nelson. See Hull, *Give Us Each Day*, 88. Honey makes a similar observation about other women poets subjected to "aesthetic accusations" (*Aphrodite's Daughters*, 15–16).

76. Kuenz, "Modernism, Mass Culture, and the Harlem Renaissance," 509.

77. More than one biographical note in the anthologies containing her poetry describe her poems in terms of her relationship to her city, her education, her vocation, and her care for her garden and horticulture (Hughes and Bontemps, *The Poetry of the Negro*, 622). See also her 1948 letter to Arna Bontemps in the Langston Hughes Papers, series 1, correspondence, box 35, folder 211, James Weldon Johnson and Grace Nail Johnson Papers, Beinecke Rare Book and Manuscript Library, Yale University.

Chapter 2. Routes of the Renaissance

1. Lewis, *The Harlem Renaissance Reader*, 299.

2. See McHenry, *Forgotten Readers*, and Krasner, "Dark Tower and the Saturday Nighters," for discussions of Douglas Johnson's Saturday Nighters.

3. Lamothe, *Inventing the New Negro*.

4. Harrison, *Gardens*, 49.

5. McHenry, *Forgotten Readers*, 17–18. The African American literary societies that

convened during the Harlem Renaissance have presented an interpretative challenge to scholars. As David Krasner observes, "Magazines have enjoyed scholarly attention because they endure as written archives. By contrast salons, like theatre, have been undervalued largely because they belong to ephemera and oral history. Nevertheless, salons facilitated a forum for artists to evaluate each other's work. They played a critical role in the clustering of ideas, in linking people across genres, and in influencing themes germane to African American drama" ("Dark Tower," 81).

6. As Shockley observes, "Spencer used both her poetry and her garden as spaces where she could *think* about and *experiment* with ways of conceptualizing and articulating the power dynamics among the people of her society in light of those she observed among nonhuman creatures" (*Renegade Poetics*, 23).

7. Redding, *To Make a Poet Black*, 118–19.

8. Redding, *To Make a Poet Black*, 124.

9. I am indebted to Posmentier, *Cultivation and Catastrophe*, 5, for the idea of poetry as an alternative space of existence, similar to the garden.

10. Harrison, *Gardens*, 68.

11. Gardens inspire imaginative and human expressions and allow us to explore a way of being in the world through the very idea of home. I am indebted to Robert Pogue Harrison for this idea. See his *Gardens*, 81.

12. Series 5, manuscripts and poems, subseries A, "Why Read Books," box 17, folder 60, Papers of Anne Spencer and the Spencer Family, Albert and Shirley Small Special Collections, University of Virginia.

13. Anne Spencer to Langston Hughes, n.d., Langston Hughes Papers, JWJ MSS 26, series 1, box 149, folder 2766, Beinecke Rare Book Library, Yale University. Based on the context, it was likely written in 1942.

14. Brown received his bachelor of arts in 1922 and his master's in 1923. He had a varied and distinguished teaching career at Virginia Seminary and College (1923–26), Lincoln University in Missouri (1926–28), Fisk University (1928–29), and Howard (1929 until he retired). Beginning in 1932 he had a literary book review column in *Opportunity* called Literary Scene: Chronicle and Comment. In 1936 he was appointed directing editor of Negro materials at the Federal Writers Project at the Washington headquarters. He received a Guggenheim Fellowship in 1937 to work on a narrative poem called "When Ham Laughed" (Sterling A. Brown to Anne Spencer, undated, series 1, correspondence, box 1, folder 3, Papers of Anne Spencer and the Spencer family, Albert and Shirley Small Special Collections, University of Virginia).

15. Sterling A. Brown to Anne Spencer, undated, series 1, correspondence, box 1, folder 3, Papers of Anne Spencer and the Spencer family, Albert and Shirley Small Special Collections, University of Virginia.

16. Sterling A. Brown to Anne Spencer, undated, series 1, correspondence, box 1, folder 3 Papers of Anne Spencer and the Spencer Family, Albert and Shirley Small Special Collections, University of Virginia.

17. Sterling A. Brown to Chauncey Spencer, February 23, 1977, series 1, correspondence, box 1, folder 3, Papers of Anne Spencer and the Spencer Family, Albert and Shirley Small Special Collections, University of Virginia.

18. Sterling A. Brown to Anne Spencer, undated, series 1, correspondence, box 1, folder 3 Papers of Anne Spencer and the Spencer Family, Albert and Shirley Small Special Collections, University of Virginia.

19. This copy of Edmunds's book is in the library at the Anne Spencer House and Garden Museum, Lynchburg, Va.

20. James Weldon Johnson to Spencer, March 12, 1927, series 1, correspondence, box 19, folder 447, James Weldon Johnson and Grace Nail Johnson Papers, Beinecke Rare Book and Manuscript Library, Yale University.

21. Spencer to Sterling A. Brown, July 9–18 [1927], box 19, folder 2, Sterling A. Brown Papers, Moorland-Spingarn Research Center, Howard University.

22. Anne Spencer to James Weldon Johnson, n.d. series 1, correspondence, box 19, folder 449, James Weldon Johnson and Grace Nail Johnson Papers, Beinecke Rare Book and Manuscript Library, Yale University.

23. Countee Cullen to Sterling A. Brown, box 6, folder C, Sterling A. Brown Papers, Moorland Spingarn Research Center, Howard University.

24. Countee Cullen to Sterling A. Brown, May 2, 1927, box 6, folder C, Sterling A. Brown Papers, Moorland-Spingarn, Howard University.

25. Countee Cullen to Spencer, May 26, 1927, series 1, correspondence, box 1, folder 5, Papers of Anne Spencer and the Spencer Family, Albert and Shirley Small Special Collections, University of Virginia.

26. Countee Cullen to Spencer, November 17, 1927, series 1, correspondence, box 1, folder 5, Papers of Anne Spencer and the Spencer Family, Albert and Shirley Small Special Collections, University of Virginia. Dunbar is referring to "At the Carnival."

27. Sterling A. Brown to Anne Spencer, undated, series 1, correspondence, box 1, folder 3 Papers of Anne Spencer and the Spencer Family, Albert and Shirley Small Special Collections, University of Virginia.

28. Brown, *The Negro in American Fiction and Negro Poetry and Drama*, n.p.

29. Spencer to James Weldon Johnson, undated, series 1, correspondence box 19, folder 449, James Weldon Johnson and Grace Nail Johnson Papers, Beinecke Rare Book and Manuscript Library, Yale University.

30. Greene, *Time's Unfading Garden*, 73.

31. Spencer's son Chauncey recalled, "Langston Hughes visited our home in 1927" (*Who Is Chauncey Spencer?*, 15).

32. Spencer to Langston Hughes, April 9 [1942], Langston Hughes Papers, JWJ MSS 26, series 1 box 149, folder 2766, James Weldon Johnson and Grace Nail Johnson Papers, Beinecke Rare Book and Manuscript Library, Yale University. While the date on the letter is missing the year, the reference to Hughes's *Shakespeare in Harlem* suggests it was written in 1942.

33. Hughes, *The Collected Poems of Langston Hughes*, 128.

34. Spencer to Langston Hughes, n.d., Langston Hughes Papers, JWJ MSS 26, series 1, box 149, folder 2766, James Weldon Johnson and Grace Nail Johnson Papers, Beinecke Rare Book and Manuscript Library, Yale University.

35. Spencer to James Weldon Johnson, "Saturday," series 1, box 19, folder 448, James Weldon Johnson and Grace Nail Johnson Papers, Beinecke Rare Book and Manuscript Library, Yale University.

36. Spencer to Langston Hughes, April 9, [1942], Langston Hughes Papers, JWJ MSS 26, series 1, box 149, folder 2766, James Weldon Johnson and Grace Nail Johnson Papers, Beinecke Rare Book and Manuscript Library, Yale University; Spencer to Carl Van Vechten, June 24, 1943, Carl Van Vechten Papers, "Letters from Blacks," box SO-TE, James Weldon Johnson and Grace Nail Johnson Papers, Beinecke Rare Book and Man-

uscript Library, Yale University. The Van Vechten papers have been recently reordered and cataloged; the information provided here pertains to the papers as they were when I did my research and may no longer reflect current cataloging.

37. Spencer to Langston Hughes, April 9 [1942], Langston Hughes Papers, JWJ MSS 26, series 1, box 149, folder 2766, James Weldon Johnson and Grace Nail Johnson Papers, Beinecke Rare Book and Manuscript Library, Yale University; Spencer to Langston Hughes, undated, Langston Hughes Papers, JWJ MSS 26, series 1, box 149, folder 2766, James Weldon Johnson and Grace Nail Johnson Memorial Papers, Beinecke Rare Book and Manuscript Library, Yale University. Although the second letter is undated, because she mentions she has turned seventy-six, it can be deduced that the year is 1958.

38. See Hull, *Color, Sex, and Poetry*, 165.

39. Spencer, interview with J. Lee Greene, 1972. I am grateful to Shaun Spencer-Hester for sharing this recorded interview with me.

40. Hull, *Color, Sex, and Poetry*, 165–66; McHenry, *Forgotten Readers*, 274.

41. It is likely that Douglas Johnson asked her good friend Spencer to write this review, demonstrating a bond of trust between the two poets, however different their approaches to the writing of poetry. On Mencken encouraging Spencer to write prose commentary, see Spencer to James Weldon Johnson, series 1, correspondence box 19, folder 449, James Weldon Johnson and Grace Nail Johnson Papers, Beinecke Rare Book and Manuscript Library, Yale University. Although the letter is undated, it can be inferred it is from 1925–26, as she mentions that Mencken has just reviewed Alain Locke's 1925 anthology *The New Negro*.

42. I agree with Shockley, who argues for the significance of Spencer's review in her *Renegade Poetics*, 142.

43. Series 5, manuscripts and poems, subseries C, manuscript fragments, box 20, folder 1, Papers of Anne Spencer and the Spencer Family, Albert and Shirley Small Special Collections, University of Virginia.

44. Douglas Johnson's *The Heart of a Woman* (1918), her first volume of poetry, was characterized by reviewers as exhibiting a simple, gendered lyricism and was also criticized for lacking overtly racial content. *Bronze* (1922), Douglas Johnson's second collection provided, in the words of Hull, the "obligatory race poetry" that was seen to be missing from her first collection. Hull describes it as "her weakest book" (*Color, Sex, and Poetry*, 19). Douglas Johnson's first two volumes of poetry were reviewed by leading men of the Harlem Renaissance period with blunt condescension or tepid acknowledgment. Du Bois, who was later and briefly Douglas Johnson's lover after her husband's death, call her verse in *Bronze* "sometimes trite, but . . . singularly sincere and true, and as a revelation of the soul-struggle of the women of a race it is invaluable" (foreword to *Bronze*, 7). William Stanley Braithwaite, the publisher of the presses that had published *Heart of a Woman* and *Bronze*, characterizes her work as "intensely feminine" (introduction, vii). Douglas Johnson's male colleagues diminished and marginalized her by gender, presenting her verse as an almost childishly "sincere," significant not for its craft but for its ethnographic contribution. Margaret Walker, in a late interview, recalled the popularity of Douglas Johnson's verse and drama. But that popularity, which did not translate to financial success, was the result of tremendous effort on the author's part. Not only had she self-published all of her volumes of poetry, at great personal expense, but she also took every opportunity she could to market volumes of her poetry, all the while still writing. She used her skill of making connections between

authors as a means of validating her own work. Her popular reputation, or "celebrity status," in the words of Hull, was the result of her writing skills as an artist and a correspondent (*Color, Sex, and Poetry*, 168). In her diary, Alice Dunbar-Nelson suggests that Douglas Johnson submitted her verse to Alain Locke and William Stanley Braithwaite to be "cleaned up," making way for its publication (*Give Us Each Day*, 84).

45. In an undated latter from 1927 to Johnson, Spencer tells him that W. E. B. Du Bois has solicited her poems and a photo of her garden for the *Crisis*. Spencer makes it clear to Johnson that she does not want to be entered into the magazine's contest, offering this partial reason: "I react to life more as a human being than as a Negro being but I admit the latter is 1927 model. The Tom-Tom forced into poetry seems a sad state to me." By this Spencer meant that she was a thoroughly modern, independent "Negro being," not an agent of a performative black identity belonging to a prior century (series 1, box 19, folder 449, James Weldon Johnson and Grace Nail Johnson Papers, Beinecke Rare Book and Manuscript Library, Yale University).

46. Series 5, manuscripts and poems, subseries A, "Sunday at the Prison," box 17, folder 52, Papers of Anne Spencer and the Spencer Family, Albert and Shirley Small Special Collections, University of Virginia.

47. "Taboo," Anne Spencer Papers, Anne Spencer House and Garden, Museum, Lynchburg, Va.

48. Mencken, *In Defense of Women*, ix–x. Spencer's copy of this edition is held at the University of Virginia library (HQ1221 M5 1922b).

49. Mencken, *In Defense of Women*, xi.

50. Mencken, *In Defense of Women*, 196.

51. Mencken, *In Defense of Women*, 197.

52. Series 5, manuscripts and poems, subseries A, "In the Thicket," box 17, folder 27, Papers of Anne Spencer and the Spencer Family Papers, Albert and Shirley Small Special Collections, University of Virginia. Johnson, White, and Mencken put so much emphasis on Spencer's review that Greene concluded the short story was authored by Johnson, an assumption based on the belief that she would be most inclined to review the work of her fellow writer and friend. Spencer never thought so.

53. See my discussion of these unpublished editorials in chapter 3.

54. Spencer to James Weldon Johnson, May 7, 1934, series 1, correspondence, box 19, folder 448, James Weldon Johnson and Grace Nail Johnson Papers, Beinecke Rare Book and Manuscript Library, Yale University.

55. Spencer to James Weldon Johnson, undated, series 1, correspondence, box 4, folder 7, Papers of Anne Spencer and the Spencer Family, Albert and Shirley Small Special Collections, University of Virginia. Spencer mentions a letter she had received from Mencken, likely dating her letter to Johnson to 1921–22, as that is around the time she had received a letter from Mencken; if so, this means she was thinking about her Main Street novel long before she began discussing it with Johnson and White.

56. Series 5, manuscripts and poems, subseries D, notebook, box 20, folder 3, Papers of Anne Spencer and the Spencer Family, Albert and Shirley Small Special Collections, University of Virginia.

57. Brown, *The Negro in Virginia*, 350.

58. Brown, *The Negro in Virginia*, 351.

59. Quoted in Carey, *Anita Loos*, 108.

60. Series 5, manuscripts and poems, subseries C, manuscript fragments, box 20,

folder 1, Papers of Anne Spencer and the Spencer Family, Albert and Shirley Small Special Collections, University of Virginia.

61. Spencer to James Weldon Johnson, May 10, 1934, series 1, correspondence, box 19, folder 448, James Weldon Johnson and Grace Nail Johnson Papers, Beinecke Rare Book and Manuscript Library, Yale University.

62. Alroy Spencer to Anne and Edward Spencer, 1935, series 1, correspondence, box 4, folder 7, Papers of Anne Spencer and the Spencer Family, Albert and Shirley Small Special Collections, University of Virginia.

63. James Weldon Johnson to Spencer, undated , series 1, correspondence, box 19, folder 449, James Weldon Johnson and Grace Nail Johnson Papers, Beinecke Rare Book and Manuscript Library, Yale University.

64. James Weldon Johnson to Spencer, March 19, 1919, series 1, correspondence, box 19, folder 447, James Weldon Johnson and Grace Nail Johnson Papers, Beinecke Rare Book and Manuscript Library, Yale University. In the same letter, Johnson tells her he is sending her poem "Before the Feast at Shushan," which she had recently sent him, "to Mencken, editor of Smart Set." "It has a mystic beauty," Johnson observes, "which one would find difficulty to analyze or define, but it is there, nevertheless," although in another letter he quibbled over the preposition of her poem's title, proposing "The Feast of Shushan" instead (James Weldon Johnson to Spencer, January 1, 1920, series 1, correspondence, box 19, folder 447 James Weldon Johnson and Grace Nail Johnson Papers, Beinecke Rare Book and Manuscript Library, Yale University). Spencer did not agree: she shot back "I do not like the title 'The Feast of Shushan.' How can you see it so?" Spencer to James Weldon Johnson, January 6, 1920, series 1, correspondence, box 19, folder 447, James Weldon Johnson and Grace Nail Johnson Papers, Beinecke Rare Book and Manuscript Library, Yale University). Mencken did not accept it for publication, but it was finally published in February 1920 in the pages of the *Crisis*. In a letter sent one month later, Johnson writes he is "glad you took Mr. Mencken's criticism like a good fellow. So many beginners are unable to take frank criticism unless that criticism is praise. I wish you would work the poem over. I hope, also, that you will send some shorter things that I may forward to Mr. Mencken" (James Weldon Johnson to Spencer, April 16, 1919, series 1, correspondence, box 19, folder 447, James Weldon Johnson and Grace Nail Johnson Papers, Beinecke Rare Book and Manuscript Library, Yale University).

65. James Weldon Johnson to Spencer, April 12, 1922, series 1, correspondence, box 19, folder 447, James Weldon Johnson and Grace Nail Johnson Papers, Beinecke Rare Book and Manuscript Library, Yale University; Spencer to James Weldon Johnson, April 12, 1922, JWJ MSS 49, series 1, correspondence, box 19, folder 448, James Weldon Johnson and Grace Nail Johnson Papers, Beinecke Rare Book and Manuscript Library.

66. James Weldon Johnson to Spencer, July 10, 1924, series 1, correspondence, box 19, folder 447, James Weldon Johnson and Grace Nail Johnson Papers, Beinecke Rare Book and Manuscript Library, Yale University.

67. James Weldon Johnson to Spencer, undated [ca. 1924], series 1, correspondence, box 19, folder 449, James Weldon Johnson and Grace Nail Johnson Papers, Beinecke Rare Book and Manuscript Library, Yale University.

68. Spencer to James Weldon Johnson, undated, series 1, correspondence, box 19, folder 449, James Weldon Johnson and Grace Nail Johnson Papers, Beinecke Rare Book and Manuscript Library, Yale University. This undated letter references Mencken's re-

view of the *New Negro* anthology (edited by Alain Locke) in the *American Mercury*, dating it to 1925.

69. Spencer to James Weldon Johnson, undated (ca. 1927), series 1, correspondence, box 19, folder 449, James Weldon Johnson and Grace Nail Johnson Papers, Beinecke Rare Book and Manuscript Library, Yale University.

70. Spencer to James Weldon Johnson, November 1 [1937], series 1, correspondence, box 19, folder 448, James Weldon Johnson and Grace Nail Johnson Papers, Beinecke Rare Book and Manuscript Library, Yale University. Spencer's manuscript papers contain indications of notes and starting points for short stories and articles; for example, there are notes for a "Zilla" story in a notebook that is presumed by the archive to date to 1936 (Zilla was a common pen name for nineteenth-century newspaper stories authored by African American women), but there is no evidence she ever wrote such a story (series 5, manuscripts and poems, subseries D, notebook, box 20, folder 5 Papers of Anne Spencer and the Spencer Family, Albert and Shirley Small Special Collections, University of Virginia; McHenry, *Forgotten Readers*, 64–65). Spencer wrote to Brown that she'd like him to meet Zilla Warren. "Zilla" may be one of the pseudonymous personae that Spencer hoped would help her create prose.

71. Spencer to James Weldon Johnson, January 29, 1930, series 1, correspondence, box 19, folder 447, James Weldon Johnson and Grace Nail Johnson Papers, Beinecke Rare Book and Manuscript Library, Yale University. Mencken's writing also influenced Spencer.

72. Spencer to Carl Van Vechten, June 16, 1943, Carl Van Vechten Papers, "Letters from Blacks," box SO-TE, James Weldon Johnson and Grace Nail Johnson Papers, Beinecke Rare Book and Manuscript Library, Yale University.

73. Spencer to Carl Van Vechten, June 24, 1943, Carl Van Vechten Papers, "Letters from Blacks," box SO-TE, James Weldon Johnson and Grace Nail Johnson Papers, Beinecke Rare Book and Manuscript Library, Yale University.

74. Spencer to Grace Nail Johnson, undated letter [ca. 1939], series 1, correspondence, box 35, folder 211, James Weldon Johnson and Grace Nail Johnson Papers, Beinecke Rare Book and Manuscript Library, Yale University. Spencer wrote this letter after the tragic accident and during the time in which Grace was convalescing under the care of Lucille Miller. Spencer acknowledged that she had read all the obituaries and appreciations. "We are all happier that you are getting well fast, and of your gallant response to such a challenge. Gem, I believe now, as ever, passes on to you the many things you alone can do for him. Your love, and inner knowledge will tell you what they are. This belief has helped me these last few days, given me a new and I think right perspective. (—and I've has such doubts about writing the wrong expressions to you, from so far away, that I'm asking Miss Miller to censor this letter for me first) . . ." She continued: "*I wrote Walter about a matter for your attention when you are well.*" The matter was the memorial archive. Spencer also forwarded materials directly to Grace, evidenced by her remark that "we found these notes of Gem's + took the liberty of making a copy. You will like the original—being from his broadcast here they are historic now."

75. Hull, *Color, Sex, and Poetry*, 186. On May 16, 1942, Harold Jackman wrote Brown: "I am helping Carl Van Vechten gather manuscripts of Negro writers for the James Weldon Johnson Memorial Collection at Yale. Mrs. Georgia Johnson told me she called you about it and that you promised to look up something for me. I shall be so pleased if you will send me one of yours—with all the corrections, etc. And I shall expect to hear

from you soon. We would like to have it as soon as possible" (box 10, folder J, Sterling A. Brown Papers, Moorland-Spingarn Research Center, Howard University).

76. Spencer to Carl Van Vechten, June 16, 1943, Carl Van Vechten Papers, "Letters from Blacks," box SO-TE, James Weldon Johnson and Grace Nail Johnson Papers, Beinecke Rare Book and Manuscript Library, Yale University. Yale University Library's acknowledgment of materials received for the James Weldon Johnson collection specified "forty-seven letters, signed, from James Weldon Johnson to Anne Spencer, dated March 19, 1919 to May 31, 1938. Typewritten letter, signed, from Ollie J. Sims to Mrs. Spencer, dated June 16, 1938. Typewritten word of endorsement to Miss Pearson from James Weldon Johnson, undated. Typewritten letter, signed, from Harold Jackman to Carl Van Vechten, dated July 8, 1942. Autograph letter, signed, from Anne Spencer to Harold Jackman, dated July 1, 1942. In a Thicket laid in. (For the James Weldon Johnson memorial Collection). Bernhard Knollenberg, Librarian." Knollenberg sent a letter of thanks to Spencer on August 13, 1942, stating that he was "particularly pleased with the forty-seven letters, covering the period 1919 to 1938, from James Weldon Johnson to you. . . . I have also read with interest your letter of July 1, 1942, to Mr. Jackman concerning your gift. I was particularly struck by your remark that when a letter is answered one cherishes it less than when it remains unanswered, and that one should therefore 'treat it as a child cautiously might a piece of candy, look, lick, but don't eat'" (Records of the Librarian, RU 120, folder 1320, Beinecke Rare Book and Manuscript Library, Yale University). I am grateful to Nancy Kuhl, curator of the American collection at the Beinecke Rare Book and Manuscript Library for access to this information.

77. Spencer to Harold Jackman, July 1, 1942, Records of the Librarian, RU 120, folder 1320, Beinecke Rare Book and Manuscript Library, Yale University.

78. McHenry, *Forgotten Readers*, 7. Despite Douglas Johnson's endeavor to amass her manuscripts and correspondence, the main record of her works was thrown away after her death, leaving sparse documentation of her active life of reading and writing at the center of her literary circle. Spencer's archive suffered losses of her work as well, although Spencer herself concealed some of her works from Greene.

79. Greene, *Time's Unfading Garden*, 164.

80. Greene, *Time's Unfading Garden*, 164.

81. Greene, *Time's Unfading Garden*, 164.

82. McHenry, *Forgotten Readers*, 14.

83. McHenry, *Forgotten Readers*, 297.

84. Daphne Brooks, *Liner Notes for the Revolution*, 4.

85. Cloutier, *Shadow Archives*, 2; Daphne Brooks, *Liner Notes for the Revolution*, 373.

86. Cloutier, *Shadow Archives*, 9–10.

87. Both Spencer and Petry attended the dedication of the James Weldon Johnson Memorial Collection at Yale University in 1950. On Petry's attendance, see Cloutier, *Shadow Archives*, 236.

88. Redding, "Black Art, White Audience," 149. The editorial was written in 1950 on the occasion of the dedication of the James Weldon Johnson Memorial Papers at Yale University's Sterling Memorial Library, Archives Division.

89. Kuenz, "Modernism, Mass Culture, and the Harlem Renaissance," 513. The prolific author of novels, histories, biographies, editorials, and a memoir discovered "the Southern-based African-American middle class . . . proved more economic in its tastes than its white counterpart," Lawrence Jackson notes. As a consequence, this middle

class denied Redding his authorial quest for "respect from a black audience" ("Irredeemable Promise," 718).

90. Spencer invited Grace to stay at 1313 Pierce Street once she was well enough to travel. "Ed and I thought too, that after you are well enough it might be good for you here with us. If you wish to do so, please come. Miss Miller, as well. Or anything ever that we can do. Chauncey sent us an impressionistic story he wrote about you that's quite good for the average writer and surprising from him. I'll save it for you. Ed sends his devotion, and even threatens to write to you later. And forever to Gem and to you mine also" (Spencer to Grace Nail Johnson, undated letter [ca. 1939], series 1, correspondence, box 35 folder 211, James Weldon Johnson and Grace Nail Johnson Papers, Beinecke Rare Book and Manuscript Library, Yale University).

91. Series 5, manuscripts and poems, subseries C, manuscript fragments, box 20, folder 1, Papers of Anne Spencer and the Spencer Family, Albert and Shirley Small Special Collections, University of Virginia. Of the poetry collections listed on the pamphlet, Spencer marked off Edwin Robinson, *Collected Poems*, William Stanley Braithwaite, *Book of Modern English Verse*, and Louis Untermeyer, *Modern American Poetry*. These lines "The days of grief have left me / I have no tears to shed" seem to anticipate Georgia Douglas Johnson's 1943 poem "I Have No Tears to Shed," which, although ostensibly about a World War II soldier, may be applied to any hero: "But now at length I bend above / My gallant soldier, dead / I have no tears to shed upon / A hero's sacred bed" (Hull, *Color, Sex, and Poetry*, 192). Just as in the case of the solider, James Weldon Johnson's sacred duty demands a reconfiguration of the expression of personal grief.

92. A typographical error by the publisher printed the word "quiet" (l. 9) as "quite."

93. Spencer she claimed she sent "A Mood for Memory" to Carl Van Vechten for inclusion in the James Weldon Johnson Memorial Collection with her prose drafts of short stories. But there is no record of such a contribution, as indicated by letters from Spencer to Jackman and the university librarian. Cloutier notes Van Vechten's "meticulous records" of the memorial collection's inventory, shared with the university librarian Babb (*Shadow Archives*, 232–33). Spencer did, however, send Johnson's autograph manuscript notes for a radio broadcast in Lynchburg to Grace Nail Johnson (Spencer to Grace Nail Johnson, undated letter [ca. 1939], series 1, correspondence, box 35, folder 211, James Weldon Johnson and Grace Nail Johnson Papers, Beinecke Rare Book and Manuscript Library, Yale University).

94. Spencer to Carl Van Vechten, June 24, 1943, Carl Van Vechten Papers, "Letters from Blacks," box SO-TE, James Weldon Johnson and Grace Nail Johnson Papers, Beinecke Rare Book and Manuscript Library, Yale University.

95. Spencer also more clearly organized the stanzas and saw to the correction of the typographical error when it the poems was reprinted in Hughes and Bontemps' anthology. One of Spencer's most often-republished poems, it has born variant titles, including "For Jim, Easter Eve," the abbreviated "For Jim," and "1938–1948."

96. It is reprinted in Greene's appendix, where he states in error that it was first published in the Hughes and Bontemps 1949 anthology (*Time's Unfading Garden*, 187).

97. In this draft letter, she explains to a "darling critic" who solicits the poem that she was "trying to memorialize memory itself the possession of memory beyond the material" (series 1, correspondence, box 5, folder 13, Papers of Anne Spencer and the Spencer Family Papers, Albert and Shirley Small Special Collections, University of Virginia). The letter was probably drafted to one of her later anthologizers.

98. Cullen first published this poem in his 1927 collection *Caroling Dusk*.

99. Series 1, correspondence, box 5, folder 13, Papers of Anne Spencer Family Papers, Albert and Shirley Special Collections, University of Virginia.

100. Greene, *Time's Unfading Garden*, 124.

101. For a full discussion of this archive's creation, see my afterword, "Remembering Johnson," in *James Weldon Johnson's Modern Soundscapes*.

102. On November 15, 1947, Grace wrote, "Anne Spencer mailed to me—Nov. 4–1947 to Gt. Barrington, Mass.—mailed back to me to N.Y.C. Nov. 6—and received Nov. 7— '47" (series 1, correspondence, box 35, folder 211, James Weldon Johnson and Grace Nail Johnson Papers, Beinecke Rare Book and Manuscript Library, Yale University). Spencer's letter exists only in Grace's autograph copy, which is what I have provided here.

103. Grace Nail Johnson to Spencer, November 15, 1947, series 1, correspondence, box 35 folder 211, James Weldon Johnson and Grace Nail Johnson Papers, Beinecke Rare Book and Manuscript Library, Yale University.

104. Grace Nail Johnson to Spencer, November 15, 1947, series 1, correspondence, box 35, folder 211, James Weldon Johnson and Grace Nail Johnson Papers, Beinecke Rare Book and Manuscript Library, Yale University.

105. Grace Nail Johnson to Spencer, November 15, 1947, series 1, correspondence, box 35, folder 211, James Weldon Johnson and Grace Nail Johnson Papers, Beinecke Rare Book Library, Yale University.

106. Crawford, *Blackness Post-Blackness*, 2.

107. Harrison, *Gardens*, 108.

Chapter 3. "Virginia as Narcissus"

1. Hull, *Color, Sex, and Poetry*, 192. Hull is specifically referring to Spencer's friend Georgia Douglas Johnson.

2. Spencer, *Who Is Chauncey Spencer?*, 13.

3. Series 5, manuscripts and poems, subseries C, manuscript fragments, box 20, folder 1, Papers of Anne Spencer and the Spencer Family Papers, Albert and Shirley Small Special Collections, University of Virginia.

4. Entries from the day journal describe trips to hot springs throughout the United States and trips abroad to warmer climes. Handwriting in ink provides brief notes on each day of 1927.

5. I discuss Francis Rivers in chapter five.

6. Greene, *Time's Unfading Garden*, 165. Spencer did not share the manuscript notes for "Virginia as Narcissus" with Greene.

7. Interview recording courtesy of the Anne Spencer House and Garden Museum, Lynchburg, Va., transcription mine. Of the Harriet Beecher Stowe reference, Greene writes, "Spencer was under the impression that in *Uncle Tom's Cabin* Stowe had drawn on Virginia history" (*Time's Unfading Garden*, 165).

8. Tate's contradictory claims conveniently protect him from criticism in the contemporary political landscape in which he wrote this essay. As Hammer observes, "Tate's 'proprietary ideal' . . . insisted upon the morally uplifting effects of owning property, including slaves as well as land. . . . Trivially for Eliot, urgently for Tate, the Southern rebel dramatized the contradictions of modernist reaction" (*Hart Crane and Allen Tate*, 104).

9. Spencer's emphasis on labor aligns "Virginia as Narcissus" with the work of her contemporaries, including Richard Wright's *Black Boy* and Gwendolyn Brooks's *Maude Martha*.

10. Brown and Lewis, *The Negro in Virginia*, 346–47. The petition for equal pay for African American teachers was filed by the NAACP on June 12, 1938, just weeks before James Weldon Johnson's last visit to Lynchburg and his fatal accident in Maine, on behalf of Aline Elizabeth Black with the Norfolk Board of Education. The petition was reproduced in the November 5, 1938, *Afro-American*, a magazine Spencer read.

11. Hammer, *Hart Crane and Allen Tate*, 102.

12. Rubin, *A Gallery of Southerners*, 108.

13. Hammer, *Hart Crane and Allen Tate*, 103.

14. Series 5, manuscripts and poems, subseries D, notebook, box 20, folder 3, Papers of Anne Spencer and the Spencer Family, Albert and Shirley Small Special Collections, University of Virginia.

15. Series 5, manuscripts and poems, subseries A, "Modern Poetry," box 17, folder 34, Papers of Anne Spencer and the Spencer Family, Albert and Shirley Small Special Collections, University of Virginia.

16. Posmentier, *Cultivation and Catastrophe*, 15. I apply this idea to Spencer's manuscripts, including her prose.

17. Cloutier, *Shadow Archives*, 20.

18. On nonalignment, see Dunbar's chapter on Richard Wright in *Black Regions of the Imagination*, 58–90.

19. Dunbar, *Black Regions of the Imagination*, 5.

20. Series 5, manuscripts and poems, subseries D, notebook, box 20, folder 3, Papers of Anne Spencer and the Spencer Family, Albert and Shirley Small Special Collections, University of Virginia.

21. I concur with Dungy's observation that "there are any number of explanations for the exclusion of black nature poetry from the dominant canon to date, but in its origins and in each of its major renaissances, black poetry in America has recorded perspectives on the natural world as various as black perspectives on the nation. A broader understanding of this country and its poetry is occluded when we overlook or refuse to look carefully at black poets' varied use of landscape, animal life, and ecological poetics" (*Black Nature*, xxviii).

22. Dunbar writes, "*The region* is a way to make sense of the antinational narrative concerns of these black writers as they set about both documenting and reimagining a set of 'homegrown" experiences within a more worldly framework" (*Black Regions of the Imagination*, 6–7). Posmentier discusses the "antimimetic properties" of the work of reterritorialized African American urban writers such as Gwendolyn Brooks, who, she argues, "abstracts and metaphorizes the material history of the plantation, writing new forms of black social consciousness in urban spaces" precisely by creating distance from land, nation, and region (*Cultivation and Catastrophe*, 69).

23. Black people under segregation and in the midst of desegregation were, as Robert Reid-Pharr notes, "engaged in a constant process of choosing blackness, choosing a relationship to American history that privileges critique without insisting upon the destruction of either state or society" (*Once You Go Black*, 14).

24. Posmentier evocatively uses the idea of "provision ground," the occasional practice of allotting small parcels of land to the enslaved in Caribbean colonies, as a means

of understanding the way in which geographic and landed location and alienation informs black poetic expression. She suggests that in reading the poetry, we "understand 'provision' as a verb," one that creates "black diasporic futurity" by rejecting certain treatments of subject and literary form (*Cultivation and Catastrophe*, 69).

25. Series 5, manuscripts and poems, subseries D, notebooks, box 20, folder 3, Papers of Anne Spencer and the Spencer Family, Albert and Shirley Small Special Collections, University of Virginia.

26. Series 5, manuscripts and poems, subseries D, notebook, box 20, folder 3, box 20, folder 3, 23, Papers of Anne Spencer and the Spencer Family, Albert and Shirley Small Special Collections, University of Virginia.

27. Series 5, manuscripts and poems, subseries D, notebook, box 20, folder 3, 25, Papers of Anne Spencer and the Spencer Family, Albert and Shirley Small Special Collections, University of Virginia.

28. Series 5, manuscripts and poems, subseries D, notebook, box 20, folder 3, 26, Papers of Anne Spencer and the Spencer Family, Albert and Shirley Small Special Collections, University of Virginia.

29. Series 5, manuscripts and poems, subseries D, notebook, box 20, folder 3, 32, Papers of Anne Spencer and the Spencer Family, Albert and Shirley Small Special Collections, University of Virginia.

30. Series 5, manuscripts and poems, subseries D, notebook, box 20, folder 3, 32, Papers of Anne Spencer and the Spencer Family, Albert and Shirley Small Special Collections, University of Virginia. Spencer continues, "In our street we were so young conditioned that we were appalled to see Jeb Scott lying under the "white man's" truck with the car's entrails lying beside him. And almost as shocked to see him move the thing later gaily down the street again with no part of it left behind!"

31. Series 5, manuscripts and poems, subseries A, "Some Literary People and the Negro," box 17, folder 49, Papers of Anne Spencer and the Spencer Family, Albert and Shirley Small Special Collections, University of Virginia.

32. Series 5, manuscripts and poems, subseries A, "Some Literary People and the Negro," box 17, folder 49, Papers of Anne Spencer and the Spencer Family, Albert and Shirley Small Special Collections, University of Virginia; Faulkner, *Faulkner at Nagano*, 85. Faulkner traveled to Japan in 1955 for two weeks, where he lectured and toured temples, doing the bidding of the U.S. State Department.

33. Faulkner, *Essays, Speeches, and Public Letters*, 79.

34. Faulkner, *Faulkner at Nagano*, 141.

35. Series 5, manuscripts and poems, subseries D, notebook, box 20, folder 3, Papers of Anne Spencer and the Spencer Family, Albert and Shirley Small Special Collections, University of Virginia.

36. Series 5, manuscripts and poems, subseries D, notebook, box 19, folder 2, Papers of Anne Spencer and the Spencer Family, Albert and Shirley Small Special Collections, University of Virginia.

37. Series 5, manuscripts and poems, subseries D, notebook, box 20, folder 3, Papers of Anne Spencer and the Spencer Family, Albert and Shirley Small Special Collections, University of Virginia.

38. Harrison, *Gardens*, 73–74.

39. Harrison, *Gardens*, 19.

40. As Dungy writes, "African American literary engagement with the natural

world," especially through nature poetry, "cycles through the spectrum of alignment with worlds beyond the human" (*Black Nature*, xi).

41. Harrison, *Gardens*, 161. "No one embodies the care-dominated nature of human beings more than a gardener," he observes (25).

42. Series 5, manuscripts and poems, subseries D, notebook, box 20, folder 3, 8, Papers of Anne Spencer and the Spencer Family, Albert and Shirley Small Special Collections, University of Virginia. Spencer annotates these observations, remarking "good points."

43. Clarke, *Anti-Slavery Days*, 11. Published one year after Spencer's birth, this heavily annotated book is part of Anne Spencer's personal library at the Anne Spencer House and Garden Museum, Lynchburg, Va.

44. Brown and Lewis, *The Negro in Virginia*, 347.

45. "Migration, high during Underground Railroad days," Brown and Lewis explain, "has reached serious proportions since emancipation. According to census statistics, the proportion of Virginia-born Negroes to migrate was 28.8 per cent in 1900, 28.9 per cent in 1910, 31 per cent in 1920, and 36.5 per cent in 1930—a higher ratio of out-of-State Negro migration than is shown in any other state except Kentucky" (*The Negro in Virginia*, 349).

46. Brown and Lewis, *The Negro in Virginia*, v.

47. Brown and Lewis, *The Negro in Virginia*, 352.

48. Gabbin, *Sterling A. Brown*, 67–85.

49. Gabbin, *Sterling A. Brown*, 68. "In a period in which economic woes had turned ethnic and racial groups against each other and in which the knowledge of the past and present cultural and sociological situation of Blacks was still very much in the dark ages of myth and propaganda," she notes, "Brown's energy and talents would be sorely tested" (67).

50. Gabbin, *Sterling A. Brown*, 68.

51. Gabbin, *Sterling A. Brown*, 69.

52. "A number of FWP workers, feeling obligated to present their states as important nationally, engaged in 'some local chest thumping' at the government's expense. It was just such chest-thumping that too frequently deteriorated into attitudes of prejudice, masking as sovereign attitudes, which plagued Brown and unfortunately found their way into the copy of guidebooks" (Gabbin, *Sterling A. Brown*, 69–70).

53. Brown, "The Negro in Washington," 90.

54. Gabbin, *Sterling A. Brown*, 68.

55. Gabbin, *Sterling A. Brown*, 72.

56. Brown's son attended Hampton, and Spencer called on him there, as evidenced by her correspondence with Brown (box 6, folder S, Sterling A. Brown Papers, Moorland-Spingarn Research Center, Howard University).

57. William H. Moses was acknowledged as author and illustrator of the map in the preface to Brown and Lewis, *The Negro in Virginia*, v.

58. Spencer to Sterling A. Brown, June 20, 1936, box 6, folder S, Sterling A. Brown Papers, Moorland-Spingarn Research Center, Howard University.

59. This book is part of the library at the Anne Spencer House and Garden Museum, Lynchburg, Va.

60. Gabbin, *Sterling A. Brown*, 77.

61. Gabbin, *Sterling A. Brown*, 78.

62. See Gabbin's discussion of how *The Negro in New York* differed from to its Virginia counterpart in *Sterling A. Brown*, 78–79.

63. Brown, Davis, and Lee published "Life-Long, Poor Browning," "At the Carnival," "Before the Feast of Shushan," and "Lines to a Nasturtium (A lover muses)" in *The Negro Caravan*. Davis and Redding published "Before the Feast of Shushan," "Letter to My Sister," "At the Carnival," and "Lines to a Nasturtium" in *Cavalcade*. And Davis and Peplow published "White Things" "The Wife-Woman," "At the Carnival," and the newly retitled "Of Shushan" in *The New Negro Renaissance*.

64. See Brown and Lewis, *The Negro in Virginia*, 278–91, 283.

65. James Weldon Johnson, *The Book of American Negro Poetry*, 45.

66. "Certainly none of the Blues, no matter how full of misery, and none of the Shouts, no matter how full of religion, ever get beyond a certain scope of feeling. He can catch up the dark messages of Negro feeling and express them in what he calls 'racial rhythms,' but it is as the iteration of the drum rather than the exposition of the piano. He feels in them, but he does not think. And this is the source of his naïvete" (Redding, *To Make a Poet Black*, 116).

67. Redding, *To Make a Poet Black*, 122.

68. Hutchinson, *Facing the Abyss*, 325.

69. This manuscript poem is published in Greene, *Time's Unfading Garden*, 182.

70. Series 5, manuscripts and poems, subseries D, notebook, box 20, folder 3, 19, Papers of Anne Spencer and the Spencer Family, Albert and Shirley Small Special Collections, University of Virginia. She continues: "And it is of course Mark Twain who points out in a letter to his daughter Jean that white folk were unknown at that time." The manuscript poem appears in Greene, *Time's Unfading Garden*,182.

71. Brown and Lewis, *The Negro in Virginia*, 283.

72. Brown and Lewis, *The Negro in Virginia*, 284.

73. Hughes began writing a column for the *Chicago Defender* in 1942. Douglas Johnson had a syndicated column called Homely Philosophy starting in 1926, while J. Saunders Redding had one called A Second Look in the *Afro-American* magazine. Sterling Brown had a column in *Opportunity* magazine. Tolson, whom Spencer read but did not meet, had a column called Caviar and Cabbage in the *Washington Tribune*.

74. Spencer, *Who Is Chauncey Spencer?*, 48–49.

75. Cited in Spencer, *Who Is Chauncey Spencer?*, 51.

76. Spencer, *Who Is Chauncey Spencer?*, 51.

77. Spencer, *Who Is Chauncey Spencer?*, 54.

78. Spencer, *Who Is Chauncey Spencer?* 52.

79. Spencer, *Who Is Chauncey Spencer?*, 54.

80. Chauncey E. Spencer to J. Lee Greene, June 25, 1972, series 1, correspondence, box 3, folder 2, Papers of Anne Spencer and the Spencer Family, Albert and Shirley Small Special Collections, University of Virginia.

81. Spencer, *Who Is Chauncey Spencer?*, 52–53. Spencer states that the letter was published January 20, 1945.

82. Series 5, manuscripts and poems, subseries A, manuscripts with a title, manuscript articles, box 17, folder 7, Papers of Anne Spencer and the Spencer Family, Albert and Shirley Small Special Collections, University of Virginia.

83. Series 5, manuscripts and poems, subseries A, "Some Literary People and the

Negro," box 17, folder 49, Papers of Anne Spencer and the Spencer Family, Albert and Shirley Small Special Collections, University of Virginia.

84. Series 5, manuscripts and poems, subseries D, notebook, box 20, folder 3, 364, Papers of Anne Spencer and the Spencer Family, Albert and Shirley Small Special Collections, the University of Virginia.

85. Series 5, manuscripts and poems, subseries D, notebook, box 20, folder 3, Papers of Anne Spencer and the Spencer Family, Albert and Shirley Small Special Collections, University of Virginia. Notebooks.

86. A copy of this poem can be found in the Anne Spencer Papers, Anne Spencer House and Garden Museum, Lynchburg, Va.

87. The Spencers' copy of the original, anonymously authored 1912 edition of Johnson's *The Autobiography of an Ex-Colored Man* is inscribed to Edward Spencer, dated May 17, 1913, and signed "James Johnson," indicating, I believe, that he signed it in 1912, before he changed his name to James Weldon Johnson. It is unclear whether Johnson met Edward at this time or provided the Spencers with a previously signed edition of the book, which was hard to come by prior to its 1927 reissue.

88. Series 5, manuscripts and poems, subseries C, manuscripts concerning politics, box 19, folder 7, Papers of Anne Spencer and the Spencer Family, Albert and Shirley Small Special Collections, University of Virginia.

89. Series 5, manuscripts and poems, subseries D, notebook, box 20, folder 3, Papers of Anne Spencer and the Spencer Family, Albert and Shirley Small Special Collections, University of Virginia.

90. As Baptist writes, "Four of the first five presidents would be Virginia slaveholders. Eight of the first dozen owned people" (*The Half Has Never Been Told*, 9).

91. Spencer, *Who Is Chauncey Spencer?*, 13.

92. Carlyle, *Complete Works*, 3:67–78. Spencer's copy of the 1882 edition the *Complete Works*, published by the John Lovell Company, is held in the University of Virginia's special collections (PR4420 1882). Volume 9 is missing from the collection.

93. Series 5, manuscripts and poems, subseries A, "Virginia as Narcissus," box 17, folder 58, Papers of Anne Spencer and the Spencer Family, Albert and Shirley Small Special Collections, University of Virginia.

94. Tocqueville, *Democracy in America*, 364. Spencer's "prophecy" margin notes appear on page 364, while "1831–1781=50" appears on page v. This volume is held in the University of Virginia library (JK216.T7 1899 v. 1).

95. Tocqueville, *Democracy in America*, v.

96. Tocqueville visited America in 1831, ostensibly to study prison reform in the country. He produced a study coauthored with Gustav de Beaumont in 1833 titled *On the Penitentiary System in the United States and Its Application to France*. By the time of his visit, it had been fifty years since the battle of Yorktown, Va., which ended the fighting in the War of Independence; the Treaty of Paris (1783) recognized the United States as independent.

97. Series 5, manuscripts and poems, subseries A, "For Narcissus," box 17, folder 18, Papers of Anne Spencer and the Spencer Family, Albert and Shirley Small Special Collections, University of Virginia.

98. Thackeray, *The Virginians*, 234. Spencer's note appears on 235–36 of the International Book Company's 1859 edition. Spencer's personal copy of the novel is held in the

Albert and Shirley Small Special Collections at the University of Virginia (PR 5620 A1 1959).

99. Thackeray, *The Virginians*, 236, 235.

100. Spencer to James Weldon Johnson, undated, series 1, correspondence, box 19, folder 449, James Weldon Johnson and Grace Nail Johnson Papers, Beinecke Rare Book and Manuscript Library, Yale University. In this same letter she mentions "White Man," another unwritten idea for a prose manuscript—"started off on the mythical b-o-o-k, arrived at the axiomatic 'childhood is a secret thing in a public place'—admired it so very much haven't been able to stir from that point yet!"—the ideas for which she folded into "Virginia as Narcissus."

101. Darwin, *On the Origin of Species by Means of Natural Selection*, 10–11. The edition is held in the library at the University of Virginia (QH365.O2 1890) and bears the inscription "Anne Bethel Spencer 1905." Spencer wrote "Hybrids and Mongrels compared" on pages 287–89.

102. Clarke, *Anti-Slavery Days*, 130. Spencer's annotated copy is held at the Anne Spencer House and Garden Museum, Lynchburg, Va.

103. Series 5, manuscripts and poems, subseries D, notebook, box 20, folder 3, 21–22, Papers of Anne Spencer and the Spencer Family, Albert and Shirley Small Special Collections, University of Virginia.

104. Darwin, *On the Origin of Species by Means of Natural Selection*, 480.

105. Darwin, *On the Origin of Species by Means of Natural Selection*, 10–11.

106. As Harrison observes, absolute monarchy and absolute reason are not so far apart: absolute monarchy assumes a new form in "the fiercely humanistic pride that began in the so-called age of reason and that triumphalistically proclaimed humankind the 'master and possessor of nature' (Descartes, *Discourse on Method*, 1637), calling on men to pursue that mastery and possession through a scientifically enhanced exercise of power and will, or will-to-power for short" (*Gardens*, 113).

107. Series 5, manuscripts and poems, subseries A, "Virginia as Narcissus, " box 17, folder 58, Papers of Anne Spencer and the Spencer Family, Albert and Shirley Small Special Collections, University of Virginia. "Virginia as Narcissist" is, of course, a play on "Virginia as Narcissus."

108. Series 5, manuscripts and poems, subseries D, notebook, box 20, folder 3, Papers of Anne Spencer and the Spencer Family, Albert and Shirley Small Special Collections, University of Virginia; series 5, manuscripts and poems, subseries A, "Some Literary People and the Negro," box 17, folder 49, Papers of Anne Spencer and the Spencer Family, Albert and Shirley Small Special Collections, University of Virginia. Spencer acknowledges "U. S. senator Jacob Javits, R. N. Y.," who, in his "integration from the top down," is a truth seeker trying by testimonial evidence to rescue the character of Reconstruction true and the Carpetbaggers" (series 5, manuscripts and poems, subseries D, notebook, box 20, folder 3, Papers of Anne Spencer and the Spencer Family, Albert and Shirley Small Special Collections, University of Virginia).

109. Series 5, manuscripts and poems, subseries A, "Some Literary People and the Negro," box 17, folder 49, Papers of Anne Spencer and the Spencer Family Papers, Albert and Shirley Small Special Collections, University of Virginia.

110. Series 5, manuscripts and poems, subseries D, notebook, box 20, folder 3, Papers of Anne Spencer and the Spencer Family, Albert and Shirley Small Special Collections,

University of Virginia. "A plea of an ardent sect in axiomatic form comes to mind," she continues: "Let God be true—we sat and listen to official lying and knew they were lying—only some come lying / We must *overbear* these taxes for equal schools."

111. Spencer's "cure" echoes the works of her favorite poet of the classical era, Ovid's *Ars Amatoria* and *Remedia Amoris*. The former satirizes the moral reforms of Augustus in an age of greed, while the latter represents a poet's futile endeavor to free those trapped by love (Martin, introduction, xix–xx).

112. Series 5, manuscripts and poems, subseries A, "Virginia as Narcissus," box 17, folder 58, Papers of Anne Spencer and the Spencer Family, Albert and Shirley Small Special Collections, University of Virginia.

113. Series 5, manuscripts and poems, subseries A, "Virginia as Narcissus," box 17, folder 58, Papers of Anne Spencer and the Spencer Family, Albert and Shirley Small Special Collections, University of Virginia.

114. James Weldon Johnson to Spencer, March 2, 1923, series 1, correspondence, box 19, folder 447, James Weldon Johnson and Grace Nail Johnson Papers, Beinecke Rare Book and Manuscript Library, Yale University.

115. The poem is reprinted in Greene, *Time's Unfading Garden*, 191–92.

116. Series 5, manuscripts and poems, subseries D, notebook, box 20, folder 3, 31, Papers of Anne Spencer and the Spencer Family, Albert and Shirley Small Special Collections, University of Virginia. With "Macaulay: 'don't confuse myth with Claudius Narcissus,'" Spencer is referring to Macaulay's criticism of William Temple: "The manner in which Temple mixes the historical and the fabulous reminds us of those classical dictionaries, intended for the use of schools, in which Narcissus the lover of himself and Narcissus the freedman of Claudius, Pollux the son of Jupiter and Leda and Pollux the author of the Onomasticon, are ranged under the same headings, and treated as personages equally real" (*Critical and Historical Essays*, 243). Spencer directly engages Macauley in her notebook (series 5, manuscripts and poems, subseries E, undated notebooks, box 21, folder 9, Papers of Anne Spencer and the Spencer Family, Albert and Shirley Small Special Collections, University of Virginia). Her copy of the complete works of Macaulay is not in the library at the University of Virginia, but her copies of Macaulay's *Lays of Ancient Rome* and *Life and Writings of Addison* (PR4963 A7; PR3306. M3 1896) are.

117. Series 5, manuscripts and poems, subseries D, notebook, box 20, folder 3, Papers of Anne Spencer and the Spencer Family, Albert and Shirley Small Special Collections, University of Virginia.

118. Series 5, manuscripts and poems, subseries D, notebook, box 20, folder 3, 362, Papers of Anne Spencer and the Spencer Family, Albert and Shirley Small Special Collections, University of Virginia.

119. Series 5, manuscripts and poems, subseries D, notebook, box 20, folder 3, Papers of Anne Spencer and the Spencer Family, Albert and Shirley Small Special Collections, University of Virginia.

120. Series 5, manuscripts and poems, subseries D, notebook, box 20, folder 3, 34, Papers of Anne Spencer and the Spencer Family, Albert and Shirley Small Special Collections, University of Virginia. Notebooks.

121. Series 5, manuscripts and poems, subseries D, notebook, box 20, folder 3, 35, Papers of Anne Spencer and the Spencer Family, Albert and Shirley Small Special Collections, University of Virginia.

122. Series 5, manuscripts and poems, subseries D, notebook, box 20, folder 3, 42, Papers of Anne Spencer and the Spencer Family, Albert and Shirley Small Special Collections, University of Virginia.

123. Series 5, manuscripts and poems, subseries D, notebook, box 20, folder 3, 42, Papers of Anne Spencer and the Spencer Family, Albert and Shirley Small Special Collections, University of Virginia.

124. Series 5, manuscripts and poems, subseries D, notebook, box 20, folder 3, 368, Papers of Anne Spencer and the Spencer Family, Albert and Shirley Small Special Collections, University of Virginia.

125. Series 5, manuscripts and poems, subseries D, notebook, box 20, folder 3, 356–57, Papers of Anne Spencer and the Spencer Family, Albert and Shirley Small Special Collections, University of Virginia.

126. Series 5, manuscripts and poems, subseries D, notebook, box 20, folder 3, 356–57, Papers of Anne Spencer and the Spencer Family, Albert and Shirley Small Special Collections, University of Virginia.

127. Series 5, manuscripts and poems, subseries D, notebook, box 20, folder 3, Papers of Anne Spencer and the Spencer Family, Albert and Shirley Small Special Collections, University of Virginia.

128. Spencer to Roy Basler, undated, series 1, correspondence, box 5, folder 13, Papers of Anne Spencer and the Spencer Family, Albert and Shirley Small Special Collections, University of Virginia.

129. Spencer to John Ferrone, March 1970, series 1, correspondence, box 5, folder 13, Papers of Anne Spencer and the Spencer Family, Albert and Shirley Small Special Collections, University of Virginia.

130. On a scrap of paper, Spencer wrote: "Sterling after 30 minim[um] [years], maybe, at D.C.'s Howard Univ—had, on retirement this fall a *Wshing Post* page, also headed the 3-man team of *Negro Caravan*—" (series 5, manuscripts and poems, subseries C, manuscripts concerning literature and libraries, box 19, folder 2, Papers of Anne Spencer and the Spencer Family, Albert and Shirley Small Special Collections, University of Virginia). In her correspondence with Ferrone, Spencer wrote, "Your Sterling A. Brown, whose poems Southern Road you'all published—would do a just preface" (March 1970, series 1, correspondence, box 5, folder 13, Papers of Anne Spencer and the Spencer Family, Albert and Shirley Small Special Collections, University of Virginia).

131. Spencer to John Ferrone, March 1970, series 1, correspondence, box 5, folder 13, Papers of Anne Spencer and the Spencer Family, Albert and Shirley Small Special Collections, University of Virginia.

Chapter 4. "John Brown"

1. Keller, *Forms of Expansion*, 4.

2. Hovenden's painting is housed in the American wing, gallery 762, at the Metropolitan Museum of Art. Spencer likely viewed it there on one of her many trips to New York.

3. The reproduction of the painting appears between pages 52–53.

4. Clarke, *Anti-Slavery Days*, 157.

5. Villard, *John Brown*, 554. But in a letter to Mrs. George L. Stearns dated November 29, 1859, republished in Villard's book, Brown declares: " I have asked to be *spared* any *mock*; or *hypocritical prayers made over me*, when I am publicly *murdered*: & that my only *religious attendants* be poor *little, dirty, ragged, bare headed & barefooted Slave boys ; & Girls*; led by some old *grey headed Slave Mother*" (551).

6. Nudelman, *John Brown's Body*, 34.

7. Stauffer remarks, "John Brown is almost never associated with the women's rights movement. He is too often viewed as a warrior-patriarch, which seems a far cry from feminism. But according to his daughter Annie, 'John Brown was strong for women's rights and women's suffrage'" (*Black Hearts of Men*, 232).

8. Stauffer expands the definition of religious modernism, including not only transcendentalism but also radical abolitionism as important precursors to it. "Religious modernists," he explains, "sought to minimize the distinctions between the sacred and secular, this world and the next, the ideal and the real, and religion and science" (*Black Hearts of Men*, 38).

9. Stauffer notes that "by contrast, most other abolitionists achieved only sympathy (*Black Hearts of Men*, 39). The term "empathy," he explains, was "first used in 1872 to describe abstraction and internal subjectivity in theories of art, whereby the subject (or viewer) identifies so closely with the feelings evoked by the object (or image) that the subject and object are fused—the viewer becomes one with the image" (39).

10. Series 5, manuscripts and poems, subseries F, "A Dream of John Brown," box 22, folder 11 Papers of Anne Spencer and the Spencer Family, Albert and Shirley Small Special Collections, University of Virginia, emphasis mine.

11. Series 5, manuscripts and poems, subseries C, manuscript fragments, box 20, folder 1, Papers of Anne Spencer and the Spencer Family, Albert and Shirley Small Special Collections, University of Virginia.

12. Cullen, *Caroling Dusk*, 47.

13. Series 5, manuscripts and poems, subseries C, manuscript fragments, box 20, folder 1, Papers of Anne Spencer and the Spencer Family, Albert and Shirley Small Special Collections, University of Virginia.

14. Series 5, manuscripts and poems, subseries D, notebook J, box 20, folder 10, Papers of Anne Spencer and the Spencer Family, Albert and Shirley Small Special Collections, University of Virginia. Spencer later revised line 7; in in "Po' Little Lib," the line reads "ridden blades are severed as by a lance" (series 5, manuscripts and poems, subseries A, box 22, folder 37, Papers of Anne Spencer and the Spencer Family, Albert and Shirley Small Special Collections, University of Virginia).

15. Series 5, manuscripts and poems, subseries D, notebook J, box 21, folder 10, Papers of Anne Spencer and the Spencer Family, Albert and Shirley Small Special Collections, University of Virginia, emphasis mine. One page between "John Brown" and "Tragedy" is torn out. The "prescient Friend" could be Greene himself.

16. Series 5, manuscripts and poems, subseries D, notebook, box 20, folder 1, Papers of Anne Spencer and the Spencer Family, Albert and Shirley Small Special Collections, University of Virginia .

17. Spencer's "ligouary"—also referenced in "Virginia as Narcissus"—refers to the crescent-shaped region in northwest Italy that was ruled by various nations, overtaken by Napoleon Bonaparte, and then made part of Italy in the 1860s.

18. Murrell Edmunds to Greene, July 13, 1972, series 1, correspondence, box 3, folder 6, Papers of Anne Spencer and the Spencer Family, Albert and Shirley Small Special Collections, University of Virginia. In an August 24, 1972, letter (series 1, correspondence, box 3, folder 6), Edmunds describes himself as another Virginia writer and "refugee," repeating again the "absurd custom": "It was socially unacceptable to address Negroes except by their first names."

19. Posmentier, *Cultivation and Catastrophe*, 9.

20. I agree with Posmentier that poetry can be one response to this crisis, functioning as a lyric archive of social and environmental history. Attempts to theorize black environmental experience likewise constitute such an archive, produced in the ephemeral contexts of lecture halls, classrooms and out-of-print periodicals and marking "an aesthetics of rupture and connection"(*Cultivation and Catastrophe*, 9–10). Spencer's reading circle in Lynchburg offered a forum for such theorization.

21. Toi Derricotte has reflected that the ambiguity of poetry that reads like prose or of prose in a long poem is potentially subversive: it can "undermine consciousness, ... get beneath consciousness, kind of subvert the idea of form, and put the reader in a very different place, a more natural place." Using the paragraph as a way to provide contrast in the structure of a poem, she says, relates to "timing. I mean, that's one of the things that a poet does, ... controlling the way images and information come to you in time." For Derricotte, the paragraph embodies "this sense of ... opening up into this space." "In revision, I think you can decide when the long line is appropriate and when the paragraph gives that sense to the reader that they're immersed in it, that things are piling up on top of each other, the images, the material, thoughts, ideas, and it's messy. You know, they feel like they're in the mess of it. Whereas, with the poem, you know, you're in this very controlled way of moving through information and [it] gives a very entirely different effect" ("Reading and Writing Long Poems")

22. Miller, *Black American Poets between Worlds*, 2.

23. I am grateful to Robert Stepto for our conversation in 2016 that led to these observations.

24. As Phillips observes, "Epic often ends up resisting the nation, as much as the form has been enlisted to celebrate the identity and history of many nations over the course of its history" (*Epic in American Culture*, 5).

25. Johnson, *The Book of American Negro Poetry*, 26–27.

26. Johnson, *The Book of American Negro Poetry*, 47. Johnson contrasts the "obviousness" of Harper's nineteenth-century verse with the "complexness" of Spencer's twentieth-century lyric verse in his anthology, highlighting his friend's modernism.

27. Miller, *Black American Poets between Worlds*, 2.

28. Keller, *Forms of Expansion*, 3–4. Clarifying her use of the term "long poem," Keller writes, "for those troubled by the infrequency with which works by women figure in discussions not only of the long poem but of contemporary poetry more generally ... a broad application of the term long poem has strategic advantages: then the respect and status accorded to effective long poems is not reserved for a single type, such as the epic or the lyric sequence" (4). While I am sensitive to this evaluation, I believe it is most appropriate to read Spencer's "John Brown" poem as an epic. The deprecation of epic in the second half of the twentieth century that the New Criticism embraced undermined the very idea of American poetry, according to Christopher Phillips. While

the New Critical approach had, he argues "rhetorical power in justifying the study of literature as an independent field of inquiry," studying poetry as lyric and the lyric as literary "sequestered poetry to such an extent that ... American poetry was no longer American literature" (*Epic in American Culture*, 7).

29. Noting the similarity between epic and elegy, Phillips notes that "epic, by far the more elite of the two genres, was historically reserved for learned men as authors, and only men and women of a certain level of cultural attainment as readers" (*Epic in American Culture*, 9).

30. Benét, *John Brown's Body*, 308. More than one writer responded to this call.

31. Series 5, manuscripts and poems, subseries D, notebook, box 19, folder 6, Papers of Anne Spencer and the Spencer Family, Albert and Shirley Small Special Collections, University of Virginia. At the time he was cast in *John Brown's Body*, Massey was best known for his role as Lincoln in the film *Abe Lincoln in Illinois*.

32. "Most of the young writers among American Negroes had made first publication in the columns of the *Crisis*. In the next few years we published work from Claude McKay, Langston Hughes, Jean Toomer, Countee Cullen, Anne Spencer, Abram Harris and Jessie Fauset." Du Bois, *Dusk of Dawn*, 270–71.

33. See "A 'Romantic Realist,'" 122–23, and "A Poet and His Art," 162–63.

34. Lavelle Porter discusses this in "Life Upon These Shores."

35. Series 5, manuscripts and poems, subseries D, notebook, box 20, folder 9, Papers of Anne Spencer and the Spencer Family, Albert and Shirley Small Special Collections, University of Virginia. Spencer writes off the page, so part of the word is missing.

36. Blight, *Frederick Douglass*, 305.

37. Du Bois, *John Brown*, 5. *John Brown* was reissued on its fiftieth anniversary of publication, on the hundredth anniversary of Harpers Ferry. Du Bois added notes to the original work that are marked by italics; this comment is one such addition.

38. See, for example, the exchange between David S. Reynolds and Christopher Benfey about the ethics of violent rebellion in "An Exchange on John Brown" in the May 9, 2013, issue of *New York Review of Books*.

39. Posmentier evocatively explores "catastrophe" by referencing its definition in the *OED* as a dénouement—the change or revolution that produces the conclusion or final event of a dramatic piece (*Cultivation and Catastrophe*, 23).

40. Cloutier, *Shadow Archives*, 17–18.

41. Greene, *Time's Unfading Garden*, 44.

42. Spencer, *Who Is Chauncey Spencer?*, provides the dates of birth for himself and his sisters Bethel and Alroy.

43. Series 5, manuscripts and poems, subseries D, notebook, box 20, folder 3, and subseries A, "A Dedication," box 17, folder 15, Papers of Anne Spencer and the Spencer Family. Albert and Shirley Small Special Collections, University of Virginia.

44. Greene, *Time's Unfading Garden*, 43–44.

45. Red notebook, Anne Spencer Papers, Anne Spencer House and Garden Museum, Lynchburg, Va. This thought appears on the back of a mimeographed deposition, most likely a scrap from the office of Francis E. Rivers, Spencer's son in-law, who worked for the city court.

46. Series 5, manuscripts and poems, subseries D, notebook, box 20, folder 3, 63, Papers of Anne Spencer and the Spencer Family, Albert and Shirley Small Special Collections, University of Virginia. The entry is marked by Spencer: "Jy '72."

47. Series 5, manuscripts and poems, subseries D, notebook, box 20, folder 3, 61, Papers of Anne Spencer and the Spencer Family, Albert and Shirley Small Special Collections, University of Virginia.

48. This poem is reprinted in Greene, *Time's Unfading Garden*, 186.

49. The phrase "a shadowy third" directly references Ellen Glasgow's 1923 short story of the same name. Spencer read Glasgow's works, including her 1913 novel *Virginia*.

50. Greene notes "—Pop took her to Harper's Ferry" (series 5, manuscripts and poems, subseries E, notebook J, box 21, folder 10, Papers of Anne Spencer and the Spencer Family, Albert and Shirley Small Special Collections, University of Virginia). Spencer recalled that she wrote a poem about John Brown that she submitted for consideration to *Opportunity Magazine* with "The Wife Woman." She told Greene that the latter but not the former was accepted for publication: "Opportunity accepted Wife-Woman but rejected John Brown poem" Greene's notes record (series 5, manuscripts and poems, subseries D, box 20, folder 11, 8–9, Papers of Anne Spencer and the Spencer Family, Albert and Shirley Small Special Collections, University of Virginia). But "Wife-Woman" was published in Johnson's *Book of American Negro Poetry* (1922), so it is possible that Spencer misremembered the details surrounding these poems.

51. Series 5, manuscripts and poems, subseries A, "Harper's Ferry," box 17, folder 25, Papers of Anne Spencer and the Spencer Family, Albert and Shirley Small Special Collections, University of Virginia.

52. Of course, Spencer refers to the gospel of John to contextualize John Brown's defiant stance against slavery at Harpers Ferry. "In my father's house there are many rooms; if that were not so, I would have told you, because I am going there to prepare a place for you." (John 14:2 NASB).

53. Cottle, *Early Recollections*, 192.

54. Keller, *Forms of Expansion*, 17.

55. "Partly because the recovery of earlier long poems by women is so recent a development . . . women attempting to write long poems have been conscious of entering a territory previously mapped by male poets and traditions. Consequently, these women have tended not so much to 'think back through [their] mothers' (Virginia Woolf's phrase) as to work with, struggle against, and revise the approaches of their fathers" (Keller, *Forms of Expansion*, 16).

56. Such betweenness, Canadian poet Smaro Kamboureli notes, "is not a matter of simple deviation from previously established generic conventions; rather, it is a matter of multiple encodings and decodings, of shifting value systems, of infraction" (Keller, *Forms of Expansion*, 13). The texts Keller chooses to study as long poems (rather than "*the* long poem" [4] as she emphasizes in her introduction) is more expansive, not so preoccupied with rule-breaking "transgression."

57. Spencer's attempt to write "John Brown" resembles Whitman's endeavor to write an "epic of democracy" to counterbalance the emphasis of *Leaves of Grass* on the individual. As Phillips explains, Whitman "realized that his attempt to sing the great national poem had morphed into a celebration of 'the great composite *Democratic Individual*,' of himself and/ as the cosmos. The purpose of *As a Strong Bird* was to announce that while the 'epic of Democracy,' Leaves of Grass, was now complete (in its fifth edition in 1872), he still intended to write the other half of his original project, *Democratic Nationality*' (L, 651). In writing of himself as a representative and a comrade of all, Whit-

man decided that he had lost sight of the nation somewhere along the line" (*Epic in American Culture*, 156–57).

58. Keller, *Forms of Expansion*, 17.

59. Series 5, manuscripts and poems, subseries E, notebook, box 21, folder 2, Papers of Anne Spencer and the Spencer Family, Albert and Shirley Small Special Collections, University of Virginia. These notes are written on Blue Horse writing tablet, as is much of the "John Brown" manuscript at the Anne Spencer House and Garden Museum, Lynchburg, Va.

60. As Phillips emphasizes, "Writers of epic choose their traditions" (*Epic in American Culture*, 14).

61. Johnson, "Guide to the Classics.'"

62. "All writing of epic begins with reading epic," remarks Phillips, observing the phase of "apprenticeship" in reading epic that is succeeded by the "self-assertion" of, at last, epic writing. (*Epic in American Culture*, 20).

63. Spencer's references to Carlyle in "John Brown" are implicit.

64. Carlyle, *Complete Works*, 10:68.

65. Carlyle, *Complete Works*, 10:66–67.

66. Carlyle, *Complete Works*, 10:67.

67. Carlyle, *Complete Works*, 10:76.

68. Phillips points out that Carlyle's *The French Revolution* was called an "epic" by reviewers (*Epic in American Culture*, 147).

69. As Phillips notes, Carlyle develops this expanded concept of epic in his consideration of Shakespeare; the *Oxford English Dictionary*, he adds, refers to Carlyle's remarks about Shakespeare as where the word "epic" is first used in this way (*Epic in American Culture*, 148).

70. Carlyle, *Complete Works*, 10:65.

71. Carlyle, *Complete Works*, 7:190.

72. Phillips, *Epic in American Culture*, 148.

73. Carlyle, Carlyle, *Complete Works,* 7:208. Spencer dog-eared and marked this page.

74. Series 5, manuscripts and poems, subseries A, "Mortal Sin is Not Unbelief," box 17, folder 25, Papers of Anne Spencer and the Spencer Family, Albert and Shirley Small Special Collections, University of Virginia. Spencer wrote this poem written on the program for 1960 South Carolina State College Christmas tree lighting ceremony.

75. Series 5, manuscripts and poems, subseries D, notebook J, box 21, folder 10, Papers of Anne Spencer and the Spencer Family, Albert and Shirley Small Special Collections, University of Virginia, 24. The last phrase was left unfinished.

76. In 1964, as Spencer convalesced with her daughter Bethel Stevenson in Newark, her garden fell into disrepair; a young girl was raped there. In the variant mythologies of Orion is his rape of an Ethiopian princess; I believe Spencer's Orion references this deeply upsetting experience, a violation of a girl and also of Spencer's garden space.

77. Series 5, manuscripts and poems, subseries D, notebook J, box 20, folder 10, 60–61 Papers of Anne Spencer and the Spencer Family, Albert and Shirley Small Special Collections, University of Virginia.

78. Spencer read these lines in a 1958 issue of the *Second Century* magazine, the copy of which is held at the Anne Spencer House and Garden Museum, Lynchburg, Va.

79. Series 5, manuscripts and poems, subseries D, notebook, box 20, folder 1, Papers

of Anne Spencer and the Spencer Family, Albert and Shirley Small Special Collections, University of Virginia.

80. Series 5, manuscripts and poems, subseries C, manuscript fragments, box 20, folder 1, 24, Papers of Anne Spencer and the Spencer Family, Albert and Shirley Small Special Collections, University of Virginia. The last phrase was left incomplete. I discuss the significance of Francis Rivers in chapter 5.

81. Notebook, Anne Spencer Papers, Anne Spencer House and Garden Museum, Lynchburg, Va.

82. In his 1888 essay "A Backward Glance O'er Travel'd Roads," Whitman describes how he wanted to leave epic behind but discovered that it "had somehow been pursuing him." Phillips claims that Whitman does not dismiss the past in the making of his poetry but rather "reveals a fascinating tension in his relationship with his ancestors: the new work is not epic, but must go *through* it."

83. Phillips, *Epic in American Culture*, 152.

84. Series 5, manuscripts and poems, subseries E, notebook J, box 21, folder 10, Anne Spencer Family Papers, Papers of Anne Spencer and the Spencer Family, Albert and Shirley Small Special Collections, University of Virginia.

85. Phillips, *Epic in American Culture*, 136–37.

86. Clarke, *Anti-Slavery Days*, 162.

87. Villard, *John Brown*, 589.

88. Clarke, *Anti-Slavery Days*, 35.

89. Series 5, manuscripts and poems, subseries E, notebook K, box 21, folder 11, Papers of Anne Spencer and the Spencer Family, Albert and Shirley Small Special Collections, University of Virginia.

90. Villard, *John Brown*, 554.

91. Nudelman, *John Brown's Body*, 35.

92. Nudelman, *John Brown's Body*, 35.

93. In the 1959 reprint of his 1909 *John Brown* with addenda, Du Bois's tone is more strident, his solution socialist in outlook. Du Bois changed his original conclusion about revolution as loss, writing, "*But if it is a true revolution it repays all losses and results in the uplift of the human race. One could wish that John Brown could see today the results of the great revolution in Russia; that he could see the new world of Socialism and Communism expanding until it already comprises the majority of mankind; until it has conquered the problem of poverty, made vast inroads on the problem of ignorance and even begun to put to flight the problem of avoidable disease*" (296).

94. This quote and the subsequent ones come from the 1961 issue of the *Second Century* housed at the Anne Spencer House and Garden Museum.

95. The issue of the magazine was anticipatory, looking ahead to 1965.

96. Series 5, manuscripts and poems, subseries D, notebook, box 20, folder 3, Papers of Anne Spencer and the Spencer Family, Albert and Shirley Small Special Collections, University of Virginia.

97. Series 5, undated notebooks, subseries E, notebook J, box 21, folder 10, Papers of Anne Spencer and the Spencer Family, Albert and Shirley Small Special Collections, University of Virginia.

98. Notebook, Anne Spencer Papers, Anne Spencer House and Garden Museum, Lynchburg, Va.

99. Series 5, undated notebooks, subseries E, notebook J, box 21, folder 10, 141, Papers of Anne Spencer and the Spencer Family, Albert and Shirley Small Special Collections, University of Virginia.

100. Series 5, manuscripts and poems, subseries A: Manuscripts with a title, Manuscripts and articles, box 17, folder 7, Papers of Anne Spencer and the Spencer Family, Albert and Shirley Small Special Collections, University of Virginia.

101. Series 5, manuscripts and poems, subseries D, notebook J, box 20, folder 10, 144, Papers of Anne Spencer and the Spencer Family, Albert and Shirley Small Special Collections, University of Virginia.

102. Greene, *Time's Unfading Garden*, 168.

103. Series 5, manuscripts and poems, subseries F, poem fragment concerning Ruth Brown, box 21, folder 26, Papers of Anne Spencer and the Spencer Family, Albert and Shirley Small Special Collections, University of Virginia.

104. Greene confirms this latter reference to the singer in an interview with Spencer (*Time's Unfading Garden*, 171). She did not share the poem.

105. This poem appears in Greene, *Time's Unfading Garden*, 175. Greene's note states that it was "composed in 1974."

106. Series 5, manuscripts and poems, subseries F, poem fragment concerning Ruth Brown, box 21, folder 26, Papers of Anne Spencer and the Spencer Family, Albert and Shirley Small Special Collections, University of Virginia.

107. Slocum, "Newly Discovered Anne Spencer Poem Unveiled to the Public."

108. Slocum, "Newly Discovered Anne Spencer Poem Unveiled to the Public."

109. Greene confirms this (*Time's Unfading Garden*, 168).

110. Series 5, manuscripts and poems, subseries E, notebook, box 20, folder 10, Papers of Anne Spencer and the Spencer Family, Albert and Shirley Small Special Collections, University of Virginia. This statement appears at the end of the notebook.

111. Spencer, "Another April," unpublished manuscript poem. Dungy includes this poem in her *Black Nature* anthology (74).

112. Slocum, "Newly Discovered Anne Spencer Poem Unveiled to the Public."

113. Series 5, manuscripts and poems, subseries E, notebook, box 20, folder 11, Papers of Anne Spencer and the Spencer Family, Albert and Shirley Small Special Collections, University of Virginia.

114. Phillips, *Epic in American Culture*, 17.

115. Series 5, manuscripts and poems, subseries E, notebook, box 20, folder 1, Papers of Anne Spencer and the Spencer Family, Albert and Shirley Small Special Collections, University of Virginia.

116. Series 5, manuscripts and poems, subseries E, notebook, box 20, folder 3, Papers of Anne Spencer and the Spencer Family, Albert and Shirley Small Special Collections, University of Virginia.

117. I am grateful to Anne Waldman's "Reading and Writing Long Poems" For this idea.

118. Phillips, *Epic in American Culture*, 19.

119. Vendler, "I Heard Voices in My Head," 47.

Chapter 5. "Leroi Meets Lincoln" / "Bastion at Newark"

1. Davis, *From the Dark Tower*, 138. For a contemporary discussion of African American literature's periodization and the collective forging of a literary tradition, see Warren's *What Was African American Literature?*

2. Davis, *From the Dark Tower*, 141. Davis argues that Tolson's *Libretto for the Republic of Liberia* and Brooks's *Annie Allen* are technically brilliant works that contrast with their earlier, more politically engaged poetry.

3. Brooks, introduction, xxix.

4. As Gabbin notes, "Brooks succeeded Carl Sandburg as Poet Laureate of Illinois" in 1968, a symbolic shift in a watershed year (introduction, xvii).

5. Cloutier, *Shadow Archives*, 23.

6. Series 5, manuscripts and poems, subseries D, notebook, box 20, folder 3, 67, Papers of Anne Spencer and the Spencer Family, Albert and Shirley Small Special Collections, University of Virginia. Lincoln was born on February 12, 1809.

7. Notebook, Anne Spencer Papers, Anne Spencer House and Garden Museum, Lynchburg, Va.

8. Series 5, manuscripts and poems, subseries D, notebook, box 20, folder 3, 68, Papers of Anne Spencer and the Spencer Family, Albert and Shirley Small Special Collections, University of Virginia.

9. Spencer to J. Lee Greene, undated, series 1, correspondence, Papers of Anne Spencer and the Spencer Family, box 1, folder 8, Albert and Shirley Small Special Collections, University of Virginia.

10. The Lincoln statue was designed by sculptor Daniel Chester French and carved by the Piccirilli brothers of marble from Alabama, Colorado, Georgia, and Tennessee. The Piccirilli brothers were marble carvers from the Bronx.

11. Spencer to Grace Nail Johnson, February 21, 1967, Series 1, correspondence, box 35, folder 11, James Weldon Johnson and Grace Nail Johnson Papers, Beinecke Rare Book and Manuscript Library, Yale University, emphasis mine.

12. For a full account of the city of Newark, see Mumford, *Newark*.

13. See Newark Riots Papers, https://newarkpubliclibrary.libraryhost.com/repositories/3/resources/130.

14. Signed into law on July 15, 1949, the Housing Act of 1949 sought to ensure "a decent home and a suitable living environment for every American family."

15. Dunbar, *Black Regions of the Imagination*, 157.

16. Rivers had to wait until 1944 to apply to the New York Bar Association, as that was when the American Bar Association finally adopted an antidiscrimination policy.

17. Fowle, "Francis E. Rivers Dies."

18. For the most complete account of Baraka's writing and activism, see Woodard, *Nation within a Nation*.

19. Cobb, "Policing the Police in Newark."

20. Barron, "A Poet Looks Back on a Bloody Week in 1967."

21. Baraka's "Black People" was published in the *Evergreen Review* after the Newark rebellion: "We must make our own World, man, our own world, and we cannot do this unless the white man is dead. Let's get together and kill him my man . . . let's make a world we want black children to grow and learn in." It is reprinted in *The LeRoi Jones/Amiri Baraka Reader*, 224.

22. Barron, "A Poet Looks Back on a Bloody Week in 1967."

23. Series 5, manuscripts and poems, subseries D, notebook, box 20, folder 8, Papers of Anne Spencer and the Spencer Family, Albert and Shirley Small Special Collections, University of Virginia. This note is dated February 14, 1968.

24. Series 5, manuscripts and poems, subseries A, "Bastion at Newark," box 17, folder 9, Papers of Anne Spencer and the Spencer Family, Albert and Shirley Small Special Collections, University of Virginia.

25. This draft can be found in the Anne Spencer Papers at the Anne Spencer House and Garden Museum, Lynchburg, Va.

26. Notebook, Anne Spencer Papers, Anne Spencer House and Garden Museum, Lynchburg, Va.

27. Series 5, manuscripts and poems, subseries D, notebook, box 20, folder 3, Papers of Anne Spencer and the Spencer Family, Albert and Shirley Small Special Collections, University of Virginia.

28. Series 5, manuscripts and poems, subseries D, notebook, box 20, folder 3, 67, Papers of Anne Spencer and the Spencer Family, Albert and Shirley Small Special Collections, University of Virginia.

29. "Collaborator" is written in black ink in the margin alongside the title; the last phrase is unfinished (series 5, manuscripts and poems, subseries D, notebook, box 20, folder 3, 68–70, Papers of Anne Spencer and the Spencer Family, Albert and Shirley Small Special Collections, University of Virginia. This entry is dated 1972. The first page of this later manuscript is 69, the second is 68, and the third is 70. As Penelope Green observes in "The Life of a Poet Allergic to Endings," Spencer's manuscripts sometimes have the second page as the first, although she does not discuss specific manuscripts.

30. This draft is in the Anne Spence Papers at the Anne Spencer House and Garden Museum in Lynchburg, Va.

31. Although it is unclear here, we might speculate that the agony includes the loss of the baby John and that Spencer's "twice" perhaps also refers the loss of Johnson.

32. Series 6, topical and miscellaneous files, "Edward Alexander Spencer," *Lynchburg News*, box 16, folder 2, Papers of Anne Spencer and the Spencer Family, Albert and Shirley Small Special Collections, University of Virginia.

33. Series 5, manuscripts and poems, subseries A, "Sunday at the Prison," box 17, folder 52, Papers of Anne Spencer and the Spencer Family, Albert and Shirley Small Special Collections, University of Virginia. "Sunday at the Prison" includes a typed transcript of autograph notes.

34. Series 5, manuscripts and poems, subseries A, "Bastion at Newark," box 17, folder 9, Papers of Anne Spencer and the Spencer Family, Albert and Shirley Small Special Collections, University of Virginia.

35. This draft, titled "Note: O Man," is in the Anne Spencer Papers at the Anne Spencer House and garden Museum, Lynchburg, Va.

36. Series 4, topical and miscellaneous files, box 16, folder 5, Papers of Anne Spencer and the Spencer Family, Albert and Shirley Small Special Collections, University of Virginia. This poem is written on the back of a publication agreement.

37. A partial autograph manuscript of this poem is in the Anne Spencer Papers at the Anne Spencer House and Garden Museum, Lynchburg, Va.

38. "Black Man O' Mine" is published in Greene, *Time's Unfading Garden*, 183.

39. Woodard, *Nation within a Nation*, 230. "Kawaida" means "tradition" in Kiswahili, the Bantu language adopted by Maulana Karenga's Afrocentric movement.

40. Woodard, *Nation within a Nation*, 230. The release concludes by noting that Baraka "views Kawaida Towers as one of the most important steps to be taken towards that rebirth."

41. Series 5, manuscripts and poems, subseries D, notebook, box 20, folder 9, Papers of Anne Spencer and the Spencer Family, Albert and Shirley Small Special Collections, University of Virginia.

42. Series 5, manuscripts and poems, subseries D, notebook, box 20, folder 9, Papers of Anne Spencer and the Spencer Family, Albert and Shirley Small Special Collections, University of Virginia. The line is unfinished. I fully discuss "Newark Junction: Milam & Till" in the epilogue.

43. Series 5, manuscripts and poems, subseries A, "LeRoi Meets Lincoln," box 17, folder 30, Papers of Anne Spencer and the Spencer Family, Albert and Shirley Small Special Collections, University of Virginia. Spencer's "CH" is an abbreviation for "courthouse." Thus, the first line should be read as "coming through the courthouse door."

44. Whittier, *The Poetical Works of John Greenleaf Whittier*, 235.

45. Series 5, manuscripts and poems, subseries A, "LeRoi Meets Lincoln," box 17, folder 30, Papers of Anne Spencer and the Spencer Family, Albert and Shirley Small Special Collections, University of Virginia. On the back of the final page of this manuscript Spencer writes, "Leroi Jones Meets Abraham Lincoln (a composite)."

46. Series 5, manuscripts and poems, subseries D, notebook H, box 21, folder 8, Papers of Anne Spencer and the Spencer Family, Albert and Shirley Small Special Collections, University of Virginia. Series 5, manuscripts and poems, subseries D, notebook E, contains a lengthy list of flower types, including several irises, that possibly are the "apartheid flowers."

47. Series 5, manuscripts and poems, subseries E, manuscript fragments, box 20, folder 1, Papers of Anne Spencer and the Spencer Family, Albert and Shirley Small Special Collections, University of Virginia.

48. Series 4, topical and miscellaneous files, box 16, folder 5, Papers of Anne Spencer and the Spencer Family, Albert and Shirley Small Special Collections, University of Virginia.

49. Series 4, topical and miscellaneous files, box 16, folder 5, Papers of Anne Spencer and the Spencer Family, Albert and Shirley Small Special Collections, University of Virginia.

50. Series 5, manuscripts and poems, subseries D, notebook H, box 21, folder 8, Papers of Anne Spencer and the Spencer Family, Albert and Shirley Small Special Collections, University of Virginia.

51. Notebook, Anne Spencer Papers, Anne Spencer House and Garden Museum, Lynchburg, Va.

52. Series 5, manuscripts and poems, subseries D, notebook E, box 21, folder 5, Papers of Anne Spencer and the Spencer Family, Albert and Shirley Small Special Collections, University of Virginia. Spencer goes on to compare two different portraits of Lincoln offered in biographies by Stephan Lorant and Carl Sandburg. Lorant's portrayal she deems moving, perceptive in its "truth," while Sandburg captures the "physical" man. "Stefan Lorant as alien Moves us most his perception tireless sought truth in es-

sence + he found it—Sandburg the more physical man I belong, for se" (the sentence ends abruptly here). Lorant, born in Hungary, was imprisoned by the Nazis briefly before immigrating to the United States.

53. Spencer to Grace Nail Johnson, February 21, 1967, series 1, correspondence, box 35, folder 211, James Weldon Johnson and Grace Nail Johnson Papers, Beinecke Rare Book and Manuscript Library, Yale University.

54. Series 5, manuscripts and poems, subseries A, "On Swahili," box 17, folder 40, Papers of Anne Spencer and the Spencer Family, Albert and Shirley Small Special Collections, University of Virginia. "Giggle" has one *g*.

55. "Substitution" was first published in Cullen, *Caroling Dusk*. This revised version was completed in 1973 and published in Greene, *Time's Unfading Garden*, 1977.

56. Cloutier, *Shadow Archives*, 23. The archive, he writes, "maps . . . the countercultural hopes of a present to come."

Epilogue. "Till"

1. See Hutchinson's *Facing the Abyss*.

2. Readers seeking a historical discussion of Emmett Till's lynching and the resulting legal miscarriage of justice in holding his murderers accountable should consult Tyson, *The Blood of Emmett Till*, and Anderson, *Emmett Till*.

3. Series 5, manuscripts and poems, subseries D, notebook H, box 21, folder 8, Papers of Anne Spencer and the Spencer Family, Albert and Shirley Small Special Collections, University of Virginia.

4. Till's body was found in the Tallahatchie River, a tributary of the Mississippi River.

5. Hale, "There's Parataxis, and Then There's Hypotaxis."

6. Hale, "There's Parataxis, and Then There's Hypotaxis."

7. Hale, "There's Parataxis, and Then There's Hypotaxis."

8. Milford, *Savage Beauty*, 216.

9. McKibbin, "Southern Patriarchy and the Figure of the White Woman in Gwendolyn Brooks's 'A Bronzeville Mother Loiters in Mississippi. Meanwhile a Mississippi Mother Burns Bacon.'"

10. Brooks republished her Till poems in her 1963 collection *The Bean Eaters*.

11. Brooks authored a brief introduction to the anthology *The Poetry of Black America* that contained Spencer's poems "Letter to My Sister" and "Lady, Lady." Brooks also delivered a reading at the landmark dedication of the Anne Spencer House as a Virginia historic site in 1977, two years after Spencer's death at the age of ninety-three.

12. Harrison, *Gardens*, 39.

13. Series 5, manuscripts and poems, subseries D, notebook H, box 21, folder 8, Papers of Anne Spencer and the Spencer Family, Albert and Shirley Small Special Collections, University of Virginia, emphasis mine.

14. Series 5, manuscripts and poems, subseries D, notebook H, box 21, folder 8, Papers of Anne Spencer and the Spencer Family, Albert and Shirley Small Special Collections, University of Virginia, emphasis mine.

15. Series 5, manuscripts and poems, subseries E, notebook A, box 21, folder 1, Papers of Anne Spencer and the Spencer Family, Albert and Shirley Small Special Collections, University of Virginia.

16. Series 5, manuscripts and poems, subseries D, box 20, folder 12, Papers of Anne

Spencer and the Spencer Family, Albert and Shirley Small Special Collections, University of Virginia.

17. Anne Spencer Papers, Anne Spencer House and Garden Museum. I date this manuscript to the 1950s.

18. Shaun Spencer-Hester is the exemplary "grandchile," who dedicated herself to curating her grandmother's life and works. She has fortified her grandmother's imaginative legacy as executive director and daily curator of the Anne Spencer House and Garden Museum. Shaun's drama "Annie's Pencil" (2010) metonymically presents Spencer's preferred writing instrument as a means of understanding her imagination and the genesis of her writing and relation to others.

19. Harrison, *Gardens*, 124.

20. Series 5, manuscripts and poems, subseries E, notebook A, box 21, folder 1, Papers of Anne Spencer and the Spencer Family, Albert and Shirley Small Special Collections, University of Virginia. I agree with Shockley's observation that the movement of Earth's activities in this poem points to "an organic process of becoming that is (like) the way new ideas take shape in language" (*Renegade Poetics*, 143). I am interested in reading this movement in Spencer's poetics "beyond the book," as physically manifested in the archive of her papers.

21. Harrison, *Gardens*, 78.

22. The poem appears in Greene, *Time's Unfading Garden*, 197. It is one of the few unpublished poems Spencer shared with Greene.

23. Cloutier describes the practice of self-archiving as an act of "self-love," also considering the ethical matters of approaching such personal archives (*Shadow Archives*, 10–11, 211).

Primary Sources

Anne Spencer Papers. Anne Spencer House and Garden Museum, Lynchburg, Va.

James Weldon Johnson and Grace Nail Johnson Papers. Beinecke Rare Book and Manuscript Library, Yale University.

Langston Hughes Papers. Beinecke Rare Book and Manuscript Library, Yale University.

Papers of Anne Spencer and the Spencer Family. Albert and Shirley Small Special Collections, University of Virginia.

Sterling A. Brown Papers. Moorland-Spingarn Research Center, Howard University.

Georgia Douglas Johnson Papers. Moorland-Spingarn Research Center, Howard University.

Chauncey Spencer Papers. Bentley Historical Library, University of Michigan.

Secondary Sources

Adams, Rachel. *Sideshow, U.S.A.: Freaks and the American Cultural Imagination*. Chicago: University of Chicago Press, 2001.

Aiello, Thomas. *The Grapevine of the Black South: The Scott Newspaper Syndicate in the Generation before the Civil Rights Movement*. Athens: University of Georgia Press, 2018.

Alexander, Elizabeth. Introduction to *The Essential Writings of Gwendolyn Brooks*, xiii–xxvi. New York: Library of America, 2013.

Anderson, Devery S. *Emmett Till: The Murder That Shocked the World and Propelled the Civil Rights Movement*. Jackson: University Press of Mississippi, 2017.

Arendt, Hannah. *The Human Condition*. 1958. 2nd ed. Chicago: University of Chicago Press, 1998.

Baldwin, Davarian. *Chicago's New Negroes: Modernity, the Great Migration, and Black Urban Life*. Chapel Hill: University of North Carolina Press, 2007.

Baldwin, Davarian, and Minkah Makalani, eds. *Escape from New York: The New Negro Renaissance beyond Harlem*. Minneapolis: University of Minnesota Press, 2013.

Baptist, Edward E. *The Half Has Never Been Told: Slavery and the Making of American Capitalism*. New York: Basic Books, 2014.

Baraka, Amiri. *S O S: Poems 1961–2013*. Edited by Paul Vangelisti. New York: GrovePress, 2014.

Barron, James. "A Poet Looks Back on a Bloody Week in 1967." *New York Times*, October 10, 2012, http://nyti.ms/SSFCJR.

Bay, Mia, Farah J Griffin, Martha S. Jones, and Barbara D. Savage. "Toward an Intellectual History of Black Women," in *Toward an Intellectual History of Black Women*, edited by Mia Bay, Farah J Griffin, Martha S. Jones, and Barbara D. Savage, 1–14. Chapel Hill: University of North Carolina Press, 2015.

Benét, Steven Vincent. *John Brown's Body*. Chicago: Elephant Paperback, 1990.

Benét, Stephen Vincent. *John Brown's Body*. New York: Dramatists Play Service, 1961.

Bennett, Paula. *My Life a Loaded Gun: Female Creativity and Feminist Poetics*. Boston: BeaconPress, 1987.

Bennett, Paula. *Poets in the Public Sphere: The Emancipatory Project of American Women's Poetry, 1800–1900*. Princeton: Princeton University Press, 2003.

Bernhardt, Peter. *Gods and Goddesses in the Garden: Greco-Roman Mythology and the Scientific Names of Plants*. New Brunswick: Rutgers University Press, 2008.

Blight, David W. *Frederick Douglass: Prophet of Freedom*. New York: Simon and Schuster, 2018.

Bradford, Phillips Verner, and Harvey Blume. *Ota Benga: The Pygmy in the Zoo*. New York: Delta Books, 1992.

Braithwaite, William Stanley. Introduction to *The Heart of a Woman and Other Poems*, by Georgia Douglas Johnson, vii–ix. Boston: Cornhill, 1918.

Brooks, Daphne. *Liner Notes for the Revolution: The Intellectual Life of Black Feminist Sound*. Cambridge, Mass.: Belknap Press of Harvard University Press, 2021.

Brooks, Gwendolyn, and Denise Hawkins. "Conversation." In The *Furious Flowering of African American Poetry*. edited by Joanna V. Gabbin, 274–80. Charlottesville: University Press of Virginia, 1999.

Brooks, Gwendolyn. *Blacks*. Chicago: Third World Press, 1994.

Brooks, Gwendolyn. Introduction to *The Poetry of Black America: Anthology of the 20th Century*, edited by Arnold Adoff, xxix–xxxi. New York: HarperCollins, 1973.

Brown, Carolyn J. *Song of My Life: A Biography of Margaret Walker*. Jackson: University Press of Mississippi, 2014.

Brown, Jayna. *Babylon Girls: Black Women Performers and the Shaping of the Modern*. Durham: Duke University Press, 2008.

Brown, Lois. *Pauline Elizabeth Hopkins: Black Daughter of the Revolution*. Chapel Hill: University of North Carolina Press, 2008.

Brown, Sterling. *The Negro in American Fiction and Negro Poetry and Drama*. New York: Arno Press, 1969.

Brown, Sterling. "The Negro in Washington." In *Washington: City and Capital*, 68–90. Washington, D.C.: United States Government Printing Office, 1937.

Brown, Sterling. *A Son's Return: Selected Essays of Sterling Brown*. Edited by Mark A. Sanders. Boston: Northeastern University Press, 1996.

Brown, Sterling. "Strong Men." In *The Collected Poems of Sterling A. Brown*, edited by Michael S. Harper, 56–58. Chicago: TriQuarterly Books, 1980.

Brown, Sterling, and Roscoe E. Lewis, eds. *The Negro in Virginia*. New York: Hastings House Publishers, 1940.

Brown, Sterling, Arthur P. Davis, and Ulysses Lee. *The Negro Caravan*. New York: Arno Press, 1969.

Browning, Elizabeth Barrett. *Aurora Leigh*. Edited by Margaret Reynolds. Athens: Ohio University Press, 1992.

Browning, Elizabeth Barrett. *Aurora Leigh*. 1884. Anne Spencer's copy. PR4185 A1 1884.

Browning, Elizabeth Barrett. *Elizabeth Barrett Browning: Letters to Her Sister, 1846–1859*. Edited by Leonard Huxley. New York: E. P. Dutton, 1929.

Cameron, Sharon. *Choosing Not Choosing: Dickinson's Fascicles*. Chicago: University of Chicago Press, 1992.

Carey, Gary. *Anita Loos: A Biography*. New York: Knopf, 1988.

Carlyle, Thomas. *Complete Works*. 10 vols. New York: John W. Lovell Company, 1869.

Casper, Scott E. *Constructing American Lives: Biography and Culture in Nineteenth-Century America*. Chapel Hill: University of North Carolina Press, 1999.

Clarke, James Freeman. *Anti-Slavery Days: A Sketch of the Struggle Which Ended in the Abolition of Slavery in the United States*. New York: John W. Lovell Company, 1883.

Cloutier, Jean-Christophe. *Shadow Archives: The Lifecycles of African American Literature*. New York: Columbia University Press, 2019.

Cobb, Jelani. "Policing the Police in Newark." *New Yorker Magazine*, June 28, 2016.

Cottle, Joseph. *Early Recollections, Chiefly Relating to the Late Samuel Taylor Coleridge, during His Long Residence in Bristol*. Vol. 1. London: Longman, Rees, 1837.

Crawford, Margo N. *Blackness Post-Blackness: The Black Arts Movement and Twenty-First Century Aesthetics*. Champaign: University of Illinois Press, 2017.

Cullen, Countee, ed. *Caroling Dusk*. New York: Harper and Brothers, 1927.

Darwin, Charles. *The Origin of Species by Means of Natural Selection; or, The Preservation of the Favored Races in the Struggle for Life*. New York: Hurst, 1890.

Davis, Arthur P. *From the Dark Tower: Afro-American Writers, 1900 to 1960*. Washington, D.C.: Howard University Press, 1974.

Davis, Arthur P., and Michael W. Peplow, eds. *The New Negro Renaissance: An Anthology*. New York: Rinehart and Winston, 1975.

Davis, Arthur P., and J. Saunders Redding, eds. *Cavalcade: Negro Writing from 1760 to the Present*. Boston: Houghton Mifflin, 1971.

Davis, Thadious M. *Southscapes: Geographies of Race, Region, and Literature*. Chapel Hill: University of North Carolina Press, 2011.

Deyle, Steven. *Carry Me Back: The Domestic Slave Trade in American Life*. New York: Oxford University Press, 2005.

Dixon, Melvin. "The Black Writer's Use of Memory." In *History and Memory in African American Culture*, edited by Genevieve Fabre and Robert O'Meally, 18–27. New York: Oxford University Press, 1994.

Douglas, Andrea, ed. *Pride Overcomes Prejudice: A History of Charlottesville's African American School*. Charlottesville: Jefferson School African American Heritage Center, 2013.

Du Bois, W. E. B. *Dusk of Dawn: Toward an Autobiography of a Race*. Piscataway, NJ: Transaction, 1984.

Du Bois, W. E. B. Foreword to *Bronze: A Book of Verse*, by Georgia Douglas Johnson. Boston: B. J. Brimmer, 1922.

Du Bois, W. E. B. *John Brown*. New York: International Publishers, 1959.

Dunbar, Eve. *Black Regions of the Imagination: African American Writers between the Nation and the World*. Philadelphia: Temple University Press, 2013.

Dungy, Camille, ed. *Black Nature: Four Centuries of African American Nature Poetry*. Athens: University of Georgia Press, 2009.

Emerson, Ralph Waldo. *The Portable Emerson*. Edited by Carl Bode and Malcolm Cowley. New York: Penguin, 1981.

Farnsworth, Robert M. *Melvin B. Tolson, 1898–1966: Plain Talk and Poetic Prophecy*. Columbia: University of Missouri Press, 1984.

Faulkner, William. Faulkner, *Essays, Speeches, and Public Letters*. New York: Random House, 1966.

Faulkner, William. *Faulkner at Nagano*. Edited by Robert Archibald Jeliffe. Tokyo: Kenkyusha, 1962.

Fetterley, Judith, and Marjorie Pryse. *Writing Out of Place: Regionalism, Women, and American Literary Culture*. Urbana : University of Illinois Press, 2003.

Ford, Charita M. "Flowering a Feminist Garden: The Writings and Poetry of Anne Spencer." *SAGE* 5, no. 1 (1988): 7–14.

Fowle, Farnsworth. "Francis E. Rivers Dies; Black Judge Was 82." *New York Times*, July 29, 1975, 27.

Fox, Regis M. *Resistance Reimagined: Black Women's Critical Thought as Survival*. Gainesville: University Press of Florida, 2017.

Frischkorn, Rebecca, and Rueben M. Rainey. *Half My World: The Garden of Anne Spencer*. Lynchburg: Anne Spencer House and Garden Museum, Inc., 2003.

Gabbin, Joanne V. Introduction to *Furious Flower: African American Poetry from the Black Arts Movement to the Present*, edited by Joanne V. Gabbin, xvii–xxxii. Charlottesville: University of Virginia Press, 2004.

Gabbin, Joanne V. Introduction to *The Furious Flowering of African American Poetry*, edited by Joanne V. Gabbin, 1–16. Charlottesville: University Press of Virginia, 1999.

Gabbin, Joanne V. *Sterling A. Brown: Building the Black Aesthetic Tradition*. Charlottesville: University Press of Virginia, 1994.

Gardner, Eric. *Unexpected Places: Relocating Nineteenth-Century African American Literature*. Jackson: University Press of Mississippi, 2009.

Giddings, Paula. *When and Where I Enter: The Impact of Black Women on Race and Sex in America*. New York: Amistad, 2006.

Gooden, Mario. *Dark Space: Architecture, Representation, Black Identity*. New York: Columbia Books on Architecture and the City, 2016.

Giesecke, Annette. *The Mythology of Plants: Botanical Lore from Ancient Greece and Rome*. Los Angeles: J. Paul Getty Museum, 2014.

Govan, Sandra. "The Poetry of Black Experience as Counterpoint to the Poetry of the Black Aesthetic." *Negro American Literature Forum* 8, no. 4 (1974): 288–92.

Graham, Maryemma, ed. *Fields Watered with Blood: Critical Essays on Margaret Walker*. Athens: University of Georgia Press, 2014.

Green, Penelope. "The Life of a Poet Allergic to Endings." *New York Times*, February 6, 2014, D1.

Greene, J. Lee. *Blacks in Eden: The African American Novel's First Century*. Charlottesville: University Press of Virginia, 1996.

Greene, J. Lee. *Time's Unfading Garden: Anne Spencer's Life and Poetry*. Baton Rouge: Louisiana State University Press, 1977.

Gruesser, John Cullen, ed. *The Unruly Voice: Rediscovering Pauline Elizabeth Hopkins*. Urbana: University of Illinois Press, 1996.

Hale, Constance. "There's Parataxis, and Then There's Hypotaxis." *Chronicle of Higher Education*, August 3, 2013.

Hammer, Langdon. *Hart Crane and Allen Tate: Janus-Faced Modernism*. Princeton: Princeton University Press, 1993.

Hardin, Peter. "Documentary Genocide: Families [sic] Surnames on Racial Hit List." *Times Dispatch*, March 5, 2000, A1.

Harris, William J., ed. *The LeRoi Jones / Amiri Baraka Reader*. New York: Thunder's Mouth Press, 1991.

Harrison, Robert Pogue. *Gardens: An Essay on the Human Condition*. Chicago: University of Chicago Press, 2008.

Hayden, Robert, ed. *Kaleidoscope: Poems by American Negro Poets*. New York: Harcourt, Brace and World, 1967.

Hayden, Robert. "A Poet and His Art." In *Collected Prose*, edited by Frederick Glaysher, 129–203. Ann Arbor: University of Michigan Press, 1984.

Hayden, Robert. "A Romantic Realist." In *Collected Prose*, edited by Frederick Glaysher, 115–28. Ann Arbor: University of Michigan Press, 1984.

Heim, Joe. "How a Long-Dead White Supremacist Still Threatens the Future of Virginia's Indian Tribes." *Washington Post*, July 1, 2015.

Hine, Darlene Clark. *Hine Sight: Black Women and the Re-Construction of American History*. Brooklyn, N.Y.: Carlson Publishing, 1994.

Holloway, Karla FC. *BookMarks: Reading in Black and White*. New Brunswick: Rutgers University Press, 2006.

Honey, Maureen. *Aphrodite's Daughters: Three Modernist Poets of the Harlem Renaissance*. New Brunswick: Rutgers University Press, 2016.

Honey, Maureen, ed. *Shadowed Dreams: Women's Poetry of the Harlem Renaissance*. New Brunswick: Rutgers University Press, 1989.

Howard, Jennifer. "Book Lovers Record Traces of 19th-Century Readers." *Chronicle of Higher Education*, May 5, 2014. http://chronicle.com/blogs/wiredcampus/book-lovers-record-traces-of-19th-century-readers.

Hughes, Langston. In *The Collected Poems of Langston Hughes*, edited by Arnold Rampersad New York: Vintage, 1994.

Hughes, Langston, and Arna Bontemps, eds. *The Poetry of the Negro 1746–1970*. New York: Doubleday, 1970.

Hull, Gloria T. *Color, Sex, and Poetry: Three Women Writers of the Harlem Renaissance*. Bloomington: Indiana University Press, 1987.

Hull, Gloria T., ed. *Give Us Each Day: The Diary of Alice Dunbar-Nelson*. New York: Norton, 1984.

Hutchinson, George. *Facing the Abyss: American Literature and Culture in the 1940s*. New York: Columbia University Press, 2018.

Hyest, Jenny. "Anne Spencer's Feminist Modernist Poetics." *Journal of American Literature* 38, no. 3 (2015): 129–47.

Jackson, Lawrence. *The Indignant Generation: A Narrative History of African American Writers and Critics, 1934–1960*. Princeton: Princeton University Press, 2011.

Jackson, Lawrence. "Irredeemable Promise: J. Saunders Redding and New Negro Liberalism." *American Literary History* 19, no. 3 (2007): 712–44.

Jefferson, Thomas. *Writings*. New York: Library of America, 1984.

Johnson, Georgia Douglas. *Bronze: A Book of Verse*. Boston: B. J. Brimmer, 1922.

Johnson, Georgia Douglas. *The Heart of a Woman and Other Poems*. Boston: Cornhill, 1918.

Johnson, Georgia Douglas. *The Selected Works of Georgia Douglas Johnson*. New York: G. K. Hall, 1997.

Johnson, James Weldon, ed. *The Book of American Negro Poetry*. Rev. ed. New York: Harcourt, Brace, 1931.

Johnson, James Weldon. "Double Audience Makes Road Hard for Negro Authors." In *The Selected Writings of James Weldon Johnson*. Vol. 2: *Social, Political, and Literary Essays*, edited by Sondra Kathryn Wilson, 408–12. New York: Oxford University Press, 1995.

Johnson, James Weldon. "Negro Authors and White Publishers." In *The Selected Writings of James Weldon Johnson*. Vol. 2: *Social, Political, and Literary Essays*, edited by Kathryn Wilson, 413–15. New York: Oxford University Press, 1995.

Johnson, Marguerite. "Guide to the Classics: Ovid's Metamorphoses and Reading Rape." *The Conversation*, September 13, 2016. https://theconversation.com/guide-to-the-classics-ovids-metamorphoses-and-reading-rape-65316.

Jordan, June. "For the Sake of a People's Poetry: Walt Whitman and the Rest of Us." In *Passion: New and Collected Poems, 1977–1980*, ix–xxvi. Boston: Beacon Press, 1980.

Kaplan, Carla. *Zora Neale Hurston: A Life in Letters*. New York: Doubleday, 2003.

Karapetkova, Holly. "'Chatterton, Shelley, Keats, and I': Reading Anne Spencer in the White Literary Tradition." *Callaloo* 35, no. 1 (2012): 228–44.

Keller, Lynn. *Forms of Expansion: Recent Long Poems by Women*. Chicago: University of Chicago Press, 1997.

Keller, Lynn. *Thinking Poetry: Readings in Contemporary Women's Exploratory Poetics*. Iowa City: University of Iowa Press, 2010.

Kerlin, Robert T. *Negro Poets and Their Poems*. Washington, D. C.: Associated Publishers, 1923.

Kinney, Arthur F. *Flannery O'Connor's Library: Resources of Being*. Athens: University of Georgia Press, 1985.

Krasner, David. "Dark Tower and the Saturday Nighters: Salons as Themes in African American Drama." *American Studies* 49, nos. 1–2 (2008): 81–95.

Kuenz, Jane. "Modernism, Mass Culture, and the Harlem Renaissance: The Case of Countee Cullen." *Modernism/ Modernity* 14, no. 3 (2007): 507–15.

Lamm, Kimberly. *Addressing the Other Woman: Textual Correspondences in Feminist Art and Writing*. Manchester, U.K.: Manchester University Press, 2018.

Lamothe, Daphne. *Inventing the New Negro: Narrative, Culture, and Ethnography*. Philadelphia: University of Pennsylvania Press, 2008.

Lewis, David Levering, ed. *The Portable Harlem Renaissance Reader*. New York: Penguin, 1995.

Lewis, David Levering. *When the Negro Was in Vogue*. New York: Penguin, 1997.

Manguel, Albert. *The Library at Night*. New Haven: Yale University Press, 2008.

Macaulay, Thomas Babington. *Critical and Historical Essays: Lord Bacon, Sir William Temple, Gladstone on Church and State*. Leipzig: Tauchnitz, 1850.

Macaulay, Thomas Babington. *Lays of Ancient Rome*. Boston: Houghton Mifflin, 1890.

Macaulay, Thomas Babington. *Life and Writings of Addision*. Boston: Houghton Mifflin, 1896.

Martin, Christopher. Introduction to *Ovid in English*, xvi–xxxiv. New York: Penguin, 1998.

McCray, Carrie Allen. *Freedom's Child: The Life of a Confederate General's Black Daughter*. Chapel Hill: Algonquin Books, 1998.

McCray, Carrie Allen. *Ota Benga under My Mother's Roof: Poems*. Columbia: University of South Carolina Press, 2012.

McHenry, Elizabeth. *Forgotten Readers: Recovering the Lost History of African American Literary Societies*. Durham: Duke University Press, 2002.

McHenry, Elizabeth. *To Make Negro Literature: Writing, Literary Practice, and African American Authorship*. Durham: Duke University Press, 2021.

McKibbin, Molly Littlewood. "Southern Patriarchy and the Figure of the White Woman in Gwendolyn Brooks's 'A Bronzeville Mother Loiters in Mississippi. Meanwhile a Mississippi Mother Burns Bacon.'" *African American Review* 44, no. 4 (2011): 667–85.

McWilliams, John P. *The American Epic: Transforming a Genre, 1770–1860*. New York: Cambridge University Press, 1989.

Mencken, *In Defense of Women*. New York: Knopf, 1922.

Milford, Nancy. *Savage Beauty: The Life of Edna St. Vincent Millay*. New York: Random House, 2002.

Miller, R. Baxter. *Black American Poets between Worlds, 1940–1960*. Knoxville: University of Tennessee Press, 1986.

Morrissette, Noelle. *James Weldon Johnson's Modern Soundscapes*. Iowa City: University of Iowa Press, 2013.

Morrison, Toni. Foreword to *The Collected Poems of Lucille Clifton 1965–2010*, edited by Kevin Young and Michael S. Glaser, xxviii–xxxiv. New York: BOA Editions, 2012.

Mumford, Kevin. *Newark: A History of Race, Rights, and Riots in America*. New York: New York University Press, 2007.

Newkirk, Pamela. *Spectacle: The Astonishing Life of Ota Benga*. New York: Amistad, 2015.

Newsome, Effie Lee. *Gladiola Garden*. With illustrations by Lois Mailou Jones. Washington, D.C.: Associated Publishers, 1940.

Nudelman, Franny. *John Brown's Body: Slavery, Violence, and the Culture of War*. Chapel Hill: University of North Carolina Press, 2004.

Ogbar, Jeffrey O. G. *Black Power: Radical Politics and African American Identity*. Baltimore: Johns Hopkins University Press, 2004.

Oram, Richard W., ed., with Joseph Nicholson. *Collecting, Curating, and Researching Writers' Libraries: A Handbook*. Latham, MD: Rowman and Littlefield, 2014.

Ovid. *The Metamorphoses*. Trans. E. J. Kenny. Oxford: Oxford University Press, 1998.

Patterson, Raymond R. "African American Epic Poetry: The Long Foreshadowing." In *The Furious Flowering of African American Poetry*, edited by Joanne V. Gabbin, 209–22. Charlottesville: University Press of Virginia, 1999.

Peterson, Merrill D. "Monticello." In *American Places: Encounters with History*, edited By William E. Leuchtenberg, 269–81. New York: Oxford University Press, 2000.

Phillips, Christopher N. *Epic in American Culture: Settlement to Reconstruction*. Baltimore: Johns Hopkins University Press, 2012.

Poe, Edgar Allan. "The Poetic Principle." In *The Fall of the House of Usher and Other Writings*. edited by David Galloway, 449–63. New York: Penguin, 2003.

Porter, Lavelle. "Life upon These Shores." Poetry Foundation. http://www.poetryfoundation.org/article/251498.

Posmentier, Sonya. *Cultivation and Catastrophe: The Lyric Ecology of Modern Black Literature*. Baltimore: Johns Hopkins University Press, 2017.

Quealy, Gerit. *Botannical Shakespeare: An Illustrated Compendium of All the Flowers, Fruits, Herbs, Trees, Seeds, and Grasses Cited by the World's Greatest Playwright*. New York: HarperCollins, 2017.

"Reading and Writing Long Poems." Poets Forum, Chancellor's Discussions, New

School, New York City, 2013. With Ron Padgett, Anne Waldman, and Toi Derricotte. https://www.youtube.com/watch?v=XqCwHisaTXk.

Redding, J. Saunders. "Black Art, White Audience." In *A Scholar's Conscience: Selected Writings of J. Saunders Redding, 1942–1977*, edited by Faith Berry, 148–50. Lexington: University Press of Kentucky, 1992.

Redding, J. Saunders. *The Lonesome Road: The Story of the Negro's Part in America*. Garden City, N.Y.: Doubleday, 1958.

Redding, J. Saunders. *To Make a Poet Black*. Ithaca: Cornell University Press, 1988.

Redding, J. Saunders. "The Negro Author: His Publisher, His Public, and His Purse." In *A Scholar's Conscience: Selected Writings of J. Saunders Redding, 1942–1977*, edited by Faith Berry, 140–46. Lexington: University Press of Kentucky, 1992.

Redding, J. Saunders. *No Day of Triumph*. 3rd ed. New York: Harper and Brothers, 1942.

Redding, J. Saunders. *On Being a Negro in America*. Indianapolis: Bobbs-Merrill, 1951.

Redding, J. Saunders "The Wonder and the Fear." *American Scholar* 22, no. 2 (1953): 137–39.

Reid-Pharr, Robert. *Once You Go Black: Choice, Desire, and the Black American Intellectual*. New York: New York University Press, 2007.

Reynolds, Margaret. Introduction to *Aurora Leigh*, by Elizabeth Barrett Browning, 1–77. Athens: Ohio University Press, 1992.

Roses, Lorraine Elena, and Ruth Elizabeth Randolph, eds. *Harlem's Glory: Black Women Writing, 1900–1950*. Cambridge, Mass.: Harvard University Press, 1996.

Rybczynski, Witold. *A Clearing in the Distance: Frederick Law Olmstead and America in the 19th Century*. New York: Scribner, 2003.

Reed, Anthony. *Freedom Time: The Poetics and Politics of Black Experimental Writing*. Baltimore: Johns Hopkins University Press, 2014.

Rubin, Louis D., Jr. *A Gallery of Southerners*. Baton Rouge: Louisiana State University Press, 1982.

Ruffin, Kimberly N. *Black on Earth: African American Ecoliterary Traditions*. Athens: University of Georgia Press, 2010.

Saillant, John. *Afro-Virginian History and Culture*. New York: Garland, 1999.

Salmon, Nina V. *Anne Spencer: "Ah, how poets sing and die!"* Lynchburg: Anne Spencer Memorial Foundation, 2001.

Schlereth, Thomas J. *Victorian America: Transformations in Everyday Life, 1876–1915*. New York: HarperCollins, 1991.

Scura, Dorothy M., ed. *Ellen Glasgow: New Perspectives*. Knoxville: University of Tennessee Press, 1995.

Seaton, Beverly. *The Language of Flowers: A History*. Charlottesville: University Press of Virginia, 1995.

Shockley, Evie. *Renegade Poetics: Black Aesthetics and Formal Innovation in African American Poetry*. Iowa City: University of Iowa Press, 2011.

Slocum, Joshua. "Newly Discovered Anne Spencer Poem Unveiled to the Public." February 1, 2002, *News and Advance* (Lynchburg, Va.).

Smith, Kimberly K. *African American Environmental Thought: Foundations*. Lawrence: University Press of Kansas, 2007.

Spencer, Anne. "At Easter, for Jim." In *The Virginia Reader*, edited by Francis Coleman Rosenberger, 520. New York: E. P. Dutton, 1948.

Spencer, Anne. "Creed." In *Caroling Dusk*, edited by Countee Cullen, 51–52. New York: Harper and Brothers, 1927.

Spencer, Anne. "Life-Long, Poor Browning." In *Caroling Dusk*, edited by Countee Cullen, 49–50. New York: Harper and Brothers, 1927.

Spencer, Anne. Review of *An Autumn Love Cycle*, by Georgia Douglas Johnson. *Crisis* 36 (March 1929): 87.

Spencer, Anne. "Sybil Warns Her Sister." In Ebony and Topaz: A Collectanea, *edited by Charles S. Johnson, 94. New York: Opportunity, 1927.*

Spencer, Chauncey E. *Who Is Chauncey Spencer?* Detroit: Broadside Press, 1975.

Spencer-Hester, Shaun. "Annie's Pencil." June 4, 2010, Academy of Fine Arts, Lynchburg, Va.

Stephens, Judith L., ed. *The Plays of Georgia Douglas Johnson: From the New Negro Renaissance to the Civil Rights Movement.* Urbana: University of Illinois Press, 2006.

Stauffer, John. *The Black Hearts of Men: Radical Abolition and the Transformation of Race.* Cambridge, Mass.: Harvard University Press, 2001.

Stauffer, John, and Zoe Trodd, eds. *The Tribunal: Responses to John Brown and the Harpers Ferry Raid.* Cambridge, Mass.: Belknap Press of Harvard University Press, 2012.

Tate, Allen. "Narcissus as Narcissus." In *Essays of Four Decades*, 593–607. Wilmington, Del.: ISI Books, 1999.

Tate, Allen. "Remarks on the Southern Religion. In *I'll Take My Stand: The South and the Agrarian Tradition*, 155–75. New York: Harper and Brothers, 1930.

Tate, Claudia. Introduction To *The Selected Works of Georgia Douglas Johnson* xvii–lxxx. New York: G. K. Hall, 1987.

Taylor, Diana. *The Archive and the Repertoire*. Durham: Duke University Press, 2003.

Taylor, Elizabeth Dowling. *The Original Black Elite: Daniel Murray and the Story of a Forgotten Era.* New York: Amistad, 2017.

Taylor, Ula. *The Veiled Garvey: The Life and Times of Amy Jacques Garvey.* Chapel Hill: University of North Carolina Press, 2002.

Thackeray, William Makepeace. *The Virginians.* Vol. 3. New York: International Book Company, 1859.

Tidwell, John Edgar, and Steven C. Tracy, eds. *After Winter: The Art and Life of Sterling Brown.* New York: Oxford University Press, 2009.

Tocqueville, Alexis de. *Democracy in America.* New York: Colonial Press, 1899.

Tolson, Melvin B. *Caviar and Cabbage: Selected Columns by Melvin B. Tolson from the "Washington Tribune," 1937–1944.* Edited by Robert M. Farnsworth. Columbia: University of Missouri Press, 1982.

Tolson, Melvin B. *"Harlem Gallery" and Other Poems of Melvin B. Tolson.* Edited by Raymond Nelson. Charlottesville: University Press of Virginia, 1999.

Tuan, Yi-Fu. *Space and Place: The Perspective of Experience.* Minneapolis: University of Minnesota Press, 2014.

Tyson, Timothy. *The Blood of Emmett Till.* New York: Simon and Schuster, 2017.

Untermeyer, Louis, ed. *American Poetry since 1900.* New York: Henry Holt, 1923.

Vendler, Helen. "I Heard Voices in My Head." *New York Review of Books*, February 23, 2017, 45–47.

Villard, Oscar Garrison. *John Brown, 1800–1859: A Biography Fifty Years After.* Rev. ed. New York: Knopf, 1943.

Wagner, Jean. *Black Poets of the United States: From Paul Laurence Dunbar to Langston Hughes*. Urbana: University of Illinois Press, 1973.

Walker, Margaret. *How I Wrote "Jubilee" and Other Essays on Life and Literature*. Edited by Maryemma Graham. New York: Feminist Press, 1990.

Walker, Margaret. *Jubilee*. New York: Houghton Mifflin Harcourt, 2016.

Walker, Margaret. *This Is My Century: New and Collected Poems*. Athens: University of Georgia Press, 1989.

Wall, Cheryl. *Women Writers of the Harlem Renaissance*. Bloomington: Indiana University Press, 1995.

Wallace, Anne D. "'Nor in Fading Silks Compose': Sewing, Walking, and Poetic Labor in *Aurora Leigh*." *ELH* 64, no. 1 (1997): 223–56.

Walters, Tracey. *African American Literature and the Classicist Tradition: Black Women Writers from Wheatley to Morrison*. New York: Palgrave Macmillan, 2007.

Warren, Kenneth. *What Was African American Literature?* Cambridge, Mass.: Harvard University Press, 2012.

Wells, Jonathan Daniel. *Women Writers and Journalists in the Nineteenth-Century South*. New York: Cambridge University Press, 2011.

Wells, Jonathan Daniel, and Jennifer R. Green, eds. *The Southern Middle Class in the Long Nineteenth Century*. Baton Rouge: Louisiana State University Press, 2011.

Werner, Marta, and Jen Bervin, eds. *The Gorgeous Nothings*. New York: New Directions, 2013.

Wheeler, Lesley. "Anne Spencer's Epistolary Activism." In *Modernist Women Writers and American Social Engagement*, edited by Jody Cardinal, Deirdre E. Egan-Ryan, and Julia Lisella, 135–52. London: Lexington Books, 2019.

White, Deborah Gray, ed. *Telling Histories: Black Women Historians in the Ivory Tower*. Chapel Hill: University of North Carolina Press, 2008.

White, Jane Baber. *Lessons Learned from a Poet's Garden: The Restoration of the Historic Garden of Harlem Renaissance Poet Anne Spencer*. Lynchburg: Blackwell Press, 2011.

Whitley, Edward. *American Bards: Walt Whitman and Other Unlikely Candidates for National Poet*. Chapel Hill: University of North Carolina Press, 2010.

Whitman, Walt. *Leaves of Grass: The First (1855) Edition*. Edited by Malcolm Cowley. New York: Penguin Books, 1986.

Whittier, John Greenleaf. *The Poetical Works of John Whittier Greenleaf*. Boston: Osgood, 1873.

Williams, Heather Andrea. *Self-Taught: African American Education in Slavery and Freedom*. Chapel Hill: University of North Carolina Press, 2005.

Wilson, Ivy, ed. *At the Dusk of Dawn: Selected Poetry and Prose of Albery Allson Whitman*. Boston: Northeastern University Press, 2009.

Wilson, Ivy. *Specters of Democracy: Blackness and the Aesthetics of Politics in the Antebellum U.S.* New York: Oxford University Press, 2011.

Wilson, Ivy, ed. *Whitman Noir: Black America and the Good Gray Poet*. Iowa City: University of Iowa Press, 2014.

Woodard, Komozi. *A Nation within a Nation: Amiri Baraka and Black Power Politics*. Chapel Hill: University of North Carolina Press, 1999.

Woodson, Jon. *Anthems, Sonnets, and Chants: Recovering the African American Poetry of the 1930s*. Columbus: Ohio State University Press, 2015.

Woodson, Jon. "Consciousness, Myth, and Transcendence: Symbolic Action in Three Poems on the Slave Trade." In *The Furious Flowering of African American Poetry*, edited by Joanne V. Gabbin, 154–68. Charlottesville: University Press of Virginia, 1999.

Woodson, Jon. "Melvin Tolson and the Art of Being Difficult." In *Black American Poets between Worlds, 1940–1960*, edited by R. Baxter Miller. 19–42. Knoxville: University of Tennessee Press, 1986.

Page numbers in italics indicate illustrations.

"Aframerican," 26

"Anne Spencer's Table" (Hughes), 40

"Another April" (Spencer), 123–24

"Any Wife to Any Husband" (Spencer), 64, 106

Apollo 11's moon mission, 114

archives, 159, 199n23; of James Weldon Johnson, 49–50, 176nn74–75; of Spencer, 9–10, 50, 149

"At Easter, For Jim" (Spencer), 52–57

Autobiography of an Ex-Colored Man, The (J. W. Johnson), 82–83

Babb, James T., 57

Baker, Houston, 46

Baraka, Amiri (LeRoi Jones), 8, 41, 127–49; "Black People," 132–33, 195n21; Cobb on, 132; photograph of, *134*; Spencer's nickname for, 127; trial of, 132–34

Barrett Browning, Elizabeth, 6–7, 62, 149, 157, 163nn18–19

Basler, Roy, 117, 157

"Bastion at Newark" (Spencer), 127, 130, 140

Bell, James M., 102

Benét, Stephen Vincent, 102–4, 114

Benga, Ota, 16–18, 166n20

Bennett, Gwendolyn, 42

Black aesthetics, 127, 138, 140; Shockley on, 24, 168n46, 168n50

Black Arts Movement, 51, 128–30, 138, 143–44; Dunbar on, 131–32; Hughes and, 41

"Black Man O' Mine" (Spencer), 138–39, 140

"Black People" (Baraka), 132–33, 195n21

Bland, James, 73

Blight, David, 104

Bontemps, Arna, 28, 40, 54

Book of American Negro Poetry, The (J. W. Johnson), 19, 24, 25, 73, 102

Borglum, Gutzon, 8, 130, *131*, 135, 141

Braithwaite, William Stanley, 173n44

Brooks, Daphne, 12, 50

Brooks, Gwendolyn, 1, 12, 68, 154, 195n4

—works of: *Maude Martha*, 180n9; *A Street in Bronzeville*, 128

Brown, Annie (John Brown's daughter), 188n7

Brown, John (abolitionist), 8, 80, 95–126, 188n5; Benét's poem on, 102–4; centenary of, 41; Harpers Ferry raid of, 41, 95, 104–5, 119, 126; Hovenden's painting of, 8, 96–97, *97*; Till and, 155–56

Brown, Ruth (John Brown's mother), 121–22

Brown, Ruth A. (blues singer), 122

Brown, Sterling, 1, 16, 34–39; career of, 171n14; Cullen on, 38; Federal Writers Project and, 70–72, 76; Redding on, 73; Spencer on, 37–38

—works of: "The Fall of the Year," 34, 36; "Farmer Brown Is Riled at His Boy," 35; "Long Gone," 38; *Negro Poetry and Drama*, 26, 39; "October Idyll," 36; "The Poet Spills His Tea at the Literary Society," 35; *Southern Road*, 21, 29, 36, 71; "Thoughts of Death," 38; "To a Certain Lady, in Her Garden," 34, 36

Brown v. Board of Education (1954), 21, 75

Browning, Elizabeth Barrett. *See* Barrett Browning, Elizabeth

Browning, Robert, 26, 61–63, 106

Bryant, Roy, 154

Buck, Pearl S., 67

Bunche, Ralph, 145

Burr, Aaron, 92

Byrd, Harry F., 60, 87

Cabell, James Branch, 67, 92

Canby, Henry Seidel, 56

Carlyle, Thomas, 65, 83, 95, 117; on democracy, 112–13; Christopher N. Phillips on, 192n69; on Schiller, 109–12; on slavery, 111

Caroling Dusk (Cullen), 1, 14, 25–27

Carroll, Lewis, 152

Chisholm, Shirley, 145

"civilizing mission," 16–17

Clarke, James Freeman, 69, 85, 96, 117

Cloutier, Jean-Christophe, 2, 3, 51; on archives,

In Defense of Women (Mencken), 44
"interimpositionalists," 86
interracial marriage, 84

Jackman, Harold, 49, 176n75
Jackson, Lawrence, 177n89
Jean, George, 33–34
Jefferson, Eva, 145
Jefferson, Margo, 57
Jefferson, Thomas, 79, 80
Jim Crow laws, 9, 16–17; Native Americans and,
    18, 87, 166n27; northern states and, 152;
    Plessy v. Ferguson and, 81; Racial Integrity
    Act and, 17–18, 87. *See also* lynching;
    segregation
"John Brown" (Spencer), 12, 63–64, 95–126, 128,
    134, 140
Johnson, Georgia Douglas. *See* Douglas
    Johnson, Georgia
Johnson, Grace Nail, 51, 55–56, 146
Johnson, James Weldon, 1–2, 16, 146; archives
    of, 49–50, 176nn74–75; on Sterling
    Brown, 73; death of, 180n10; on epic,
    102; journalism of, 76; as NAACP field
    secretary, 18; Spencer's correspondence
    with, 18–19, 47–49; on Spencer's poetry,
    25, 35, 89
—works of: *The Autobiography of an Ex-
    Colored Man*, 82–83; *The Book of American
    Negro Poetry*, 19, 24, 25, 73, 102; *Fifty Years
    and Other Poems*, 19; *God's Trombones*, 19,
    23, 37; *Negro Americans, What Now?*, 25
Johnson, Marguerite, 108
Johnson, Samuel, 79
Jones, LeRoi. *See* Baraka, Amiri
Judaism, 66

Kaleidoscope (Hayden), 25, 27
Kamboureli, Smaro, 191n56
Kant, Immanuel, 91
Keller, Lynn, 102, 107, 189n28, 191n55
Kerlin, Robert T., 25, 26, 169n61
Knollenberg, Bernhard, 177nn76
Koestler, Arthur, 65
Krasner, David, 171n5
Kuenz, Jane, 27, 29, 170n75

Lamothe, Daphne, 33, 46
"Leroi Meets Lincoln" (Spencer), 8, 63, 64,
    127–47
"Letter to Her Sister" (Spencer), 4–8
"Letter to My Sister, A" (Spencer), 1, 3, 4, 7,
    162n16, 167n39
Lewis, David Levering, 23, 27, 30

Lewis, Roscoe E., 69
Lewis, Sinclair, 45, 46, 51
"Life-Long, Poor Browning" (Spencer), 26, 61–
    63, 76, 124
Lincoln, Abraham, 63, 64, 80, 129, 141–44;
    Borglum sculpture of, 8, 130, *131*, 135, 141; Till
    and, 155–56
"Lincoln is Still at Newark" (Spencer), 144
Locke, Alain, 23, 27, 39, 162n14
"Long Gone" (S. Brown), 38
Longfellow, Henry Wadsworth, 80
Loos, Anita, 23, 46
Lorant, Stephan, 197n52
Lowell, Amy, 26–27
Lynchburg, Va., 101, 137–38; Harlem
    Renaissance and, 47; Spencer's literary
    circle of, 15–25, 30–31, 189n20
lynching, 64, 72, 89–90, 140, 144, 164n28; of Till,
    12, 144, 149–56; of Turner, 18, 19

Macaulay, Thomas Babington, 89, 90,
    186n116
marriage, interracial, 84
Maude Martha (G. Brooks), 180n9
McHenry, Elizabeth, 16, 19–20, 50
McKay, Claude, 47
Mencken, H. L., 26, 33–34, 146; on democracy,
    44; on Douglas Johnson, 42; *In Defense of
    Women*, 44; Shaw and, 48; Spencer and,
    43–48
Meredith, Amaza Lee, 4, 162n13
"Middle Passage" (Hayden), 104
"Milam & Till" (Spencer), 141, 150–56
Miller, R. Baxter, 101
modernism, 30, 59, 103, 188n8
Monroe Doctrine, 80
"Mood for Memory, A" (Spencer), 53
"Mortal Sin is Not Unbelief" (Spencer), 113
Moses, William, 71, 72, 182n57
Mott, Lucretia, 80
Murrow, Edward R., 88–89

Narcissus myth, 59
Native Americans, 85; Jim Crow laws and, 18,
    87, 166n27
Negro Americans, What Now? (J. W. Johnson),
    25
Negro in Virginia, The (WPA), 46, 60, 69–73, 76
Negro Poetry and Drama (S. Brown), 26, 39
New Criticism, 190n28
"New Negro," 11, 45, 51; Great Migration and,
    46; Locke on, 27
New Negro Renaissance, 11, 30, 33, 63; Douglas
    Johnson and, 42; lyrical subjectivity and,

New Negro Renaissance (*continued*)
102; universalist perspective of, 68; women
writers of, 149–50
Newark, N.J., riot (1967), 127, 132–33
Newkirk, Pamela, 17
Newsome, Effie Lee, 4, 42, 162n13
"1975" (Spencer), 122
Nudelman, Franny, 118

Oberlin College, 87
"objective poetry," 64
"October Idyll" (S. Brown), 36
Omega Psi Phi fraternity, 71
"On Swahili" (Spencer), 143, 146
Oram, Richard, 167n40, 167n42
Ovid, 58, 108, 117, 162n15, 186n111

Paine, Tom, 79, 92
Petry, Ann, 2, 161n7
Phillips, Christopher N., 111, 125; on Carlyle,
192n69; on epic, 189n24, 190n29; on New
Criticism, 189n28; on Walt Whitman,
191n57, 193n82
Phillips, Wendell, 80
Pilgrims, 69
Pittsburgh Courier, 77–78, 83
Plessy v. Ferguson (1896), 81. *See also* Jim Crow
laws
"Po' Little Lib" (Spencer), 99
"Poet Spills His Tea at the Literary Society,
The" (S. Brown), 35
Poetry of the Negro, The (Hughes), 28, 54
Pope, Alexander, 23, 112
Posmentier, Sonya, 9, 33, 65, 96, 101, 180n22

Racial Integrity Act (1924), 17–18, 87. *See also*
Jim Crow laws
"rational religion," 15, 33
Redding, J. Saunders, 26, 28, 31, 51, 183n66; on
Sterling Brown, 73; at Hampton Institute,
71; on Negro problem, 69; on Wright,
169n73
Reid-Pharr, Robert, 180n23
Reno, Nev., 81
Rivers, Francis E., 59, 115, 132, 144, 195n16
Rubin, Louis, 61
Russell, Richard, 85; as Southern Agrarian, 60;
in "Virginia as Narcissus," 74–75, 90
Russian Revolution, 193n93
"Ruth Brown" (Spencer), 121–22
Rutledge, Archibald, 67

salons, 27, 30, 42, 171n5
Sandburg, Carl, 128, 169n60, 197n52

Scales family, 13
Schiller, Friedrich, 14, 109–12
segregation, 70–71, 149–51; of churches, 84;
of hospitals, 84; of housing, 130–31; of
libraries, 21; Reid-Pharr on, 180n23; in
Reno, Nev., 81; of schools, 22, 83, 84, 87–
89; Southern Agrarians on, 60; "Southern
Manifesto" on, 60, 74–75, 81, 83, 84. *See also*
Jim Crow laws
self-learning, 16
Shakespeare in Harlem (Hughes), 39–40
Shaw, George Bernard, 48
Shockley, Evie, 24, 165n11, 168n46, 168n50
slavery, 69, 80, 121, 142; John Brown and, 95;
Carlyle on, 111; Clarke on, 85
"Some Literary People and the Negro"
(Spencer), 67
Southern Agrarians, 12, 59–60, 103
"Southern Manifesto," 60, 74–75, 81, 83, 84
Southern Road (S. Brown), 21, 29, 36, 71
Spencer, Alroy (daughter), 47, 132
Spencer, Anne, 13–29; archives of, 9–10, 50,
149; Benga and, 17; on democracy, 83, 117;
early years of, 13–16; editorials of, 32, 58,
76, 117, 123; garden of, 24, 25, 33, 40–41, 53–
54, 192n76; on Georgia, 86; later years of,
68, 113, 122–26, 129, 156–57; as Lynchburg
librarian, 16, 21, 22; as New Negro Mencken,
43–48; pen name of, 91; personal library
of, 13, 15, 20–23; photograph of, 75; on
southern traditions, 65–66, 81–84, 92, 151,
153–55; on voting rights, 84
—works of: "Another April," 123–24; "Any
Wife to Any Husband," 64, 106; "At Easter,
For Jim," 52–57; "Bastion at Newark," 127,
130, 140; "Black Man O' Mine," 138–39, 140;
"Commonwealth," 64, 82; "Creed," 14, 106,
109, 120, 152; "A Dream of John Brown," 97–
98, 123; "Dunbar," 21–22; "Earth, I thank
you," 158–59; "For Jim, Easter Eve," 120, 157;
"Generals," 113, 114–16; "God never planted
a garden," 64, 68, 74–76; "Harpers Ferry,"
106–9, 117; "I Have a Friend," 54–55; "John
Brown," 12, 63–64, 95–126, 128, 134, 140;
"Leroi Meets Lincoln," 8, 63, 64, 127–47;
"Letter to Her Sister," 4–8; "A Letter to My
Sister," 1, 3, 4, 7, 162n16, 167n39; "Life-Long,
Poor Browning," 26, 61–63, 76, 124; "Lincoln
is Still at Newark," 144; "Milam & Till," 141,
150–56; "A Mood for Memory," 53; "Mortal
Sin is Not Unbelief," 113; "1975," 122; "On
Swahili," 143, 146; "Po' Little Lib," 99; "Ruth
Brown," 121–22; "Some Literary People and
the Negro," 67; "Substitution," 145, 146–47;

The New Southern Studies

The Nation's Region: Southern Modernism, Segregation, and U.S. Nationalism
    by Leigh Anne Duck

Black Masculinity and the U.S. South: From Uncle Tom to Gangsta
    by Riché Richardson

Grounded Globalism: How the U.S. South Embraces the World
    by James L. Peacock

*Disturbing Calculations: The Economics of Identity in
Postcolonial Southern Literature, 1912–2002*
    by Melanie Benson Taylor

American Cinema and the Southern Imaginary
    edited by Deborah E. Barker and Kathryn McKee

Southern Civil Religions: Imagining the Good Society in the Post-Reconstruction Era
    by Arthur Remillard

Reconstructing the Native South: American Indian Literature and the Lost Cause
    by Melanie Benson Taylor

Apples and Ashes: Literature, Nationalism, and the Confederate States of America
    by Coleman Hutchison

Reading for the Body: The Recalcitrant Materiality of Southern Fiction, 1893–1985
    by Jay Watson

Latining America: Black-Brown Passages and the Coloring of Latino/a Studies
    by Claudia Milian

Finding Purple America: The South and the Future of American Cultural Studies
    by Jon Smith

The Signifying Eye: Seeing Faulkner's Art
    by Candace Waid

*Sacral Grooves, Limbo Gateways: Travels in Deep Southern
Time, Circum-Caribbean Space, Afro-creole Authority*
    by Keith Cartwright

Jim Crow, Literature, and the Legacy of Sutton E. Griggs
    edited by Tess Chakkalakal and Kenneth W. Warren

Sounding the Color Line: Music and Race in the Southern Imagination
    by Erich Nunn

Borges's Poe: The Influence and Reinvention of Edgar Allan Poe in Spanish America
    by Emron Esplin

Eudora Welty's Fiction and Photography: The Body of the Other Woman
    by Harriet Pollack

Keywords for Southern Studies
    edited by Scott Romine and Jennifer Rae Greeson

The Southern Hospitality Myth: Ethics, Politics, Race, and American Memory
    By Anthony Szczesiul

Navigating Souths: Transdisciplinary Explorations of a U.S. Region
    edited by Michele Grigsby Coffey and Jodi Skipper

Where the New World Is: Literature about the U.S. South at Global Scales
    by Martyn Bone

CPSIA information can be obtained
at www.ICGtesting.com
Printed in the USA
LVHW022153190123
737476LV00005B/454